From England to France

From England to France

FELONY AND EXILE
IN THE HIGH MIDDLE AGES

William Chester Jordan

PRINCETON UNIVERSITY PRESS

Princeton and Oxford

Published by Princeton University Press, 41 William Street,
Princeton, New Jersey 08540

In the United Kingdom: Princeton University Press, 6 Oxford Street,
Woodstock, Oxfordshire OX20 1TR

press.princeton.edu

Cover border © daniana/Shutterstock.

Cover design by Marcy Roberts

First paperback printing, 2017
Paperback ISBN 978-0-691-17614-7

Library of Congress Cataloging-in-Publication Data is available

ISBN 978–0–691–16495–3

British Library Cataloging-in-Publication Data is available

This book has been composed in SabonLT

Printed on acid-free paper. ∞

Printed in the United States of America

To
Christine Kenyon Jordan

Contents

Acknowledgments

I wish to thank Martha Carlin, who over a casual lunch at the British Library directed me to an enlightening source on fourteenth-century travel from Dover of which I was unaware. I also wish to express my gratitude to Margaret McGlynn, Shannon McSheffrey, and Karl Shoemaker for making some of their unpublished work on sanctuary available to me. When I was unsure what secondary source to trust on the level of destruction inflicted on manuscript collections in the Pas-de-Calais during the Second World War, I consulted Dr. (and Col.) Paul Miles, whom I wish gratefully to acknowledge. Several of my graduate students, in particular Hagar Barak and Jenna Phillips, listened patiently and graciously to the anecdotes I retold from the felony cases I was reading. Moreover, I shared portions of the manuscript with them at various times for feedback and have shamelessly plagiarized their suggested rephrasings as a testimony of my debt to them. I need also to express my thanks to the members of the Department of History and other friends and colleagues at Princeton who attended my Work-in-Progress report on this project (sponsored by the Shelby Cullom Davis Center) and to the hosts, Professors Scott Bruce and Anne Lester, and audience for a similar presentation, the inaugural James Field Willard Lecture in Medieval History at the University of Colorado, Boulder.

After I had completed a working draft of the book and submitted the manuscript to Princeton University Press, I had the good fortune that my editor, Brigitta van Rheinberg, chose Professor Nicholas Vincent of the University of East Anglia as a referee. His was one of the most thorough and helpful readings any author could possibly receive. My gratitude is immeasurable. My gratitude to my copyeditor and indexer, Katherine Harper, must also be publicly avowed. Last but by no means least I want to mention once again Brigitta van Rheinberg. Her official title at Princeton University Press is Assistant Director and

Editor in Chief. It was to her that I first described this project and kept describing it at different stages over a number of lunches. She always seemed fascinated by it, an impression that was very reassuring. One of the earlier of these lunches, however, was memorable for a wholly different reason. It was accompanied by what turned out to be a ghastly Creamsicle martini, which I ordered, recollecting how much I had delighted in Creamsicles as a child. Brigitta was doubtful from the first, and rightly so. For those who want to give it a try, however—and I have in mind principally two Princeton colleagues, Professors Haldon and Reimitz—a recipe can be found (at least at the time of this writing) at http://cocktails.about.com/od/vodkadrinkrecipes/r/creamsicle.htm. My version was prepared not with vodka but with the distilled spirits of the juniper berry and served in a traditional martini glass, not the Collins glass recommended on the website. I hasten to say that I disclaim all liability for consumption.

From England to France

Introduction

MANY DESIRES AND OBLIGATIONS motivated people living in England to travel to France in the period 1180 to the mid-fourteenth century, a span of years that I shall sometimes call, for variety's sake and as others have, the long thirteenth century.[1] In many cases a Frenchman meeting such a person could not have immediately discerned what brought the visitor to his land. A few came for the sights, for then as now there was the physical attraction of the country. Northern France from May through September enjoys quite pleasant weather, and southern France, much of which came under the political control of Paris in the third decade of the century, had an even more agreeable climate. Although from October and sometimes deep into April most of northern France endures overcast, cold, and damp weather, not unlike England's, certain northerly regions, the Loire Valley being one, often enjoy warm and gentle intervals in the midst of wintertime, thanks to the tempering effect of the great river. Summer heat is also moderated by air currents off the Atlantic. It is not surprising that scholars such as Donald Matthew have documented the penchant of medieval English travelers for spending time in France—and sometimes for expressing the desire not to return at all, although perhaps not solely because of the physical environment.[2]

France also drew people from England in the long thirteenth century for study at the University of Paris, the University of Orléans, and the University of Toulouse and for business—international merchants, government ambassadors and messengers, and clerical dignitaries attending ecclesiastical meetings, such as the Cistercian Order's General Chapters, the annual gatherings of its abbots.[3] The roads—or certain well-trod ones, the pilgrimage routes—were also crowded with penitents of every station.[4] In all these cases there was a lodgings infrastructure, ranging from inns for well-to-do and middling sorts of lay people such as traders; apartments in private establishments, monasteries, and episcopal palaces for traveling clerics; boarding houses for their servants; rooms for masters; hostels for pilgrims and students; and doss- and flop-houses for less fortunate travelers.[5]

At the highest social levels there was no language problem or but a minor one.[6] The post-Conquest English aristocracy and, from the year 1100 or so, most of the kingdom's high churchmen were fluent French-speakers[7]—or they could hire Francophone companions. Less elite travelers—diverse groups of pilgrims, for example, who were visiting France from England—may have counted fewer fluent or passable French speakers among them, but tour leaders were available for leisurely or brisk travel. Indeed, as Margaret Labarge remarked, "[t]he problem of choosing the best itinerary in unfamiliar country was somewhat alleviated by the very common practice of hiring local guides."[8] Italian merchants and bankers with branch offices in England—such as the Bardi, Peruzzi, and Riccardi—had ready access, when they traveled to France, to aides employed at the French bureaus of their companies, men who knew the local *patois*.[9] Of course, many smaller enterprises, in addition to these Italian "super companies," to use Edwin Hunt and James Murray's language, would have had knowledge of and exploited similar, if less extensive, cross-Channel networks.

Finally, wherever they may have been born, high churchmen occupying English offices had the advantage of being able to communicate with more or less ease in Latin with their French counterparts, as well as with clerical visitors from beyond the continental borders of France whom they encountered at general chapter meetings and synods.[10] All university students, many of whom were destined for exalted ecclesiastical offices, were supposed, no matter what their vernacular language, to be able to communicate in Latin. Of course, as Hastings Rashdall long ago drolly pointed out, "invariable is the insistence in the [university] statutes upon speaking in Latin. How far such a regulation was really enforced in early colleges or halls it is difficult to conjecture."[11] His doubt is evident from his very choice of words, but even modest achievement in spoken Latin was helpful in educational and clerical circles.

Many English visitors to France were, by and large, welcome guests. They brought money to innkeepers and to the people who provisioned and worked for them (farmers, vintners, and alewives; cooks and serving men and women; horse and wagon dealers, coachmen, stable keepers, stable boys, and farriers) as they passed through on their travels.[12] They spent their coins at booths procuring badges, votive candles, and other tokens that pilgrims craved and that created a virtual "tourism industry" (again the phrase of Hunt and Murray).[13] Indeed, to some degree pilgrimage routes map nicely onto the geography of economic prosperity.[14] Drunken and riotous students were pests or worse, but students were not perpetually drunk and, in the whole scheme of things, they rarely rioted. Together, masters and students patronized the school-supply shops that sold desks, stools, candles, books, parchment sheets, quills, and ink.[15] Prostitutes and brothel-keepers in the urban centers catered to students, travelers, and sojourners seeking diversion.[16] And great aristocratic caravans traveling through France, like those on their way to crusade in the East, could also produce booms in the local economies through which they passed. True, many estates held by English (Anglo-Norman) aristocrats were lost with the French conquest of Normandy in 1204.[17] There was therefore residual hostility between some Frenchmen and some Englishmen. But long before peace was formally reestablished between the two realms in 1259, English crusaders and their "substantial retinues," with disposable cash, passed through France and were even greeted without crippling enmity by the French king. This was the case, for example, for the crusade expedition of Earl Richard of Cornwall of 1239.[18]

There were four principal categories of less desirable English sojourners in France—less desirable to different degrees—in our period. One constituted the men and women who are at the center of the present study: namely, those sent into exile because of their alleged association with serious criminal activities in England. The other three categories, about which a few words need to be said, were political exiles, demobilized troops, and, as the English regarded them, pariah groups.

Political exiles, typically prelates and nobles, could count on finding temporary shelter with French kinfolk or among French friends and colleagues during periods of personal danger in England, such as the Interdict of 1208–12 and the Baronial Revolt and its immediate aftermath in 1258–68. Their troubles, including the confiscation of their property by a hostile government back home, probably evoked immediate sympathy in their hosts. Moreover, those refugees who managed to get sufficient resources out of England, to use the Baronial Revolt as an illustration, for a time successfully cultivated locals. Nevertheless, the longer the period they were obliged to stay in France and, with this, the spending down of their limited (nonreplenished) fortunes, the more vulnerable and liable to resentment they became.[19]

Unemployed troops were less of a presence and therefore less of a problem in the thirteenth century than before or after, because there was a long period of peace between the two kingdoms. This lasted de facto from 1206 until 1259, with two brief interruptions (1214 and a few years after, and 1242), and de jure with no interruptions thereafter until 1294.[20] The prolonged interval of peace was important because unpaid soldiers, demobilized on the spot, were a major source of both random and terroristic violence in wartime and during short truces, discouraging or compromising commercial expansion.[21] The thirteenth century was fortunate in this regard; its peace was a fillip to prosperity in both realms. Indeed, it was in this thirteenth-century peace that the Italian super-companies found it possible to establish their far-reaching western commercial and banking network,[22] although as we shall see this was not an unmixed blessing for them.

The case of the last category of sojourners, pariah groups, makes this abundantly clear, for Italian bankers in England, such as the Riccardi, were a periodically reviled group. It is true that they played useful and visible roles in certain aspects of royal finance, but this very fact laid them open to blame in even brief periods of fiscal stress. In 1312, King Edward II turned on them, confiscated their wealth, and sent them into exile. They found shelter with the men who ran branches of their banks on the continent, but the latter sometimes also suffered resentment because of their wealth and their association in France with the collection of taxes, making the exiles' sojourn with them all the more worrisome. The woes suffered by the Riccardi have been movingly retold by Richard Kaeuper.[23] Many Italian banker refugees stayed for only a short time in France, preferring to continue their journey homeward to Lombardy and Tuscany, for animosity toward them was also common beyond the borders of England and France.[24]

The other and far larger pariah group consisted of Jews. King Edward I expelled them, up to two thousand in number, from England in 1290. After their arrival in France (at the port of Wissant) they were burdened with discriminatory legislation, but they rapidly succeeded in integrating themselves into communities of their co-religionists, including some from which their ancestors had emigrated to England in the wake of the Norman Conquest of 1066. These communities extended charitable aid, including the payment of settlement fees. But the presence of these exiles would also play a part in helping their enemies stir up resentment against Jews in general in the continental kingdom.[25]

Such, then, is an abbreviated taxonomy of groups of people from England who found themselves sojourning in France at different times in the long thirteenth century. Among them were those who voluntarily chose to spend time on the continent. Others were compelled to emigrate. They included native Englishmen and women as well as people whom natives regarded as aliens. In terms of resources their wealth varied from the riches of a great baron like Earl Richard of Cornwall to the almost minimal possessions of common pilgrims. Some of these sojourners were genuine visitors who stayed for only brief intervals in France before returning to England. Others, like the political exiles, existed in a kind of limbo, not knowing when they might be able to return. Still others (I have the Jews in mind) were commanded by the English crown never to set foot in England again.

The group on which perhaps the least amount of work has been done, but whose history is certainly as compelling as that of any other, is the women and men sent into exile because of their putative association with the commission of felonies in England. They constituted, we shall discover, a substantial population. Some aspects of their lives can be reconstructed in a detail rare for medieval subjects, but other aspects can only be surmised from the fragmentary remains of once-huge archives which have disappeared for unknown causes or were destroyed, to a degree unintentionally, during wars. Despite the difficulties, one can employ the "disciplined imagination" as a tool in configuring the less well-documented aspects of their experience.

What one learns as a result of this exercise is that there is a need to revise existing theories about the operation of England's common law—and by extension the criminal law of other jurisdictions. For exile was a central feature of medieval jurisprudence and judicial practice throughout Europe. It affected unknown but very large numbers of people (technically, felons) who were the subjects of all these juridical regimes. It had a wider impact still by terrorizing through the rituals of banishment those who submitted to the process. Exile impoverished not only those who departed the realm, but also their spouses, children, and other kin. It forever divided families from their criminal kinfolk, at least in the English case. The system demanded and justified horrendous punishments for those who submitted to it if they later illegally tried to thwart it. In projecting exile as an act of mercy and pardon from exile—restoration of law-worthiness—as an even profounder act of mercy, statesmen arrogated to themselves a kind of majesty that, in its implicit claims, was almost sacral in its nature. Finally the endurance of the system of exile for felons raises tough questions about the nature of medieval states and their evident willingness for several centuries to accept within their jurisdictional bounds criminals from adjacent domains. Let us turn our attention first to the factors that justified kings' and administrators' resort to the exile of large numbers of the criminal population.

CHAPTER 1

Abjuring the Realm

E XILE IS AN OLD IMPOSITION on human freedom, older than the text of the Bible, but born, according to that scripture, almost at the moment of creation itself. For the first sin was punished by expulsion from the Garden with no explicit promise of being able to return (Genesis 3:22–24). The second sin, Cain's, was exile of a different sort, but exile nonetheless, and one in which the expellee bore a mark signifying his act of murder and the Lord's monopoly on vengeance (Genesis 4:12–15).[1] Exile was no new thing in the High Middle Ages. Everywhere the hideous representation of Cain, the first murderer, was to be met with in Christian art.[2] But the relationship of the medieval English law of exile to the laws addressing felons and felonies—heinous crimes which in theory deserved severe corporal or capital punishment—is a complicated and, by modern reckoning, an unusual one. This is especially the case because two groups of people suspected of or implicated in felonies in the High Middle Ages regularly avoided the punishments which would have been meted out to them if they had been convicted in a court of law. The evidence will be persuasive, I hope, that scholars have significantly underappreciated exile as a feature of English justice in the Middle Ages. By failing to treat it with the seriousness it deserves, historians, in particular, have misunderstood important aspects of the legal, moral, and social history of the period.

FELONY AND EXILE

Who constituted the two groups of people referred to above? One was composed of men and women who, though not convicted of the crimes of which they were suspected, were in such bad repute that they were obliged to abjure (foreswear) the realm. The other comprised felons who confessed their crimes in sanctuary (on which, more shortly) or in other special circumstances, who also were obliged to abjure.[3] Unlike those few *convicted* criminals who had their punishments mitigated to penitential pilgrimage, within or outside the realm, to forced crusading, or to entrance into a monastery, an abjurer of the realm of England was debarred from living in, or visiting, the kingdom ever again, without the crown's prior permission.[4] The Latin phrase used in this process was *abjurare* (or less often *ejurare* or *extra-jurare*) *regnum*.[5] These exiles were Christians, although English royal officials on rare occasions before 1290 expelled individual Jews and sometimes employed the language of abjuration in doing so.[6] Most of them were also of lower status than the political exiles described in the introduction, and most were poor long before they departed England, unlike political exiles whose property had been confiscated or the Italian bankers, who were suspected of frauds and whose enormous wealth was forfeited at the time of their expulsion.[7]

The abjurers need to be distinguished from simple outlaws (men) and waifs (women), who were, by and large, low-status fugitives from the law and on whom, if apprehended, anyone could in theory execute capital justice, just as anyone could kill a predatory wolf.[8] Outlaws bore the wolf's head, a striking and enduring metaphor.[9] Considerable in number, outlaws and waifs had escaped adjudication and/or punishment by fleeing and sought shelter and safety wherever they could, most often in woodlands. "Desouz le hourail se kevere laroun," one poet wrote: "A thief hides in the forest edge."[10] Indeed, a few notorious exceptions aside,[11] most fugitives were too ill-connected to arrange clandestine travel to distant destinations or abroad unless they lived in the borderlands with Scotland and their destination of choice was the northern kingdom.[12] As to the small minority of outlaws and waifs who did flee abroad, their experiences and the dangers they faced do sometimes help elucidate the abjurers' situation.[13]

Nevertheless, it must be kept in mind that every exile, unlike an outlaw or waif, had undergone *and completed* a form of legal process. This was not—at least in England—conviction at trial. Abjuration was only exceptionally and very rarely made available to judicially convicted individuals.[14] Elsewhere, that is to say, on the continent, exile was employed in the English way as perpetual banishment without conviction at trial in addition to being imposed as a punishment mandated upon conviction for a crime. Like the punishment of mutilation, which varied according to the character or seriousness of the crime, exile in this latter sense was keyed to a term of years appropriate to the nature of the crime and the status of the felon as a principal or accessory.[15] In England and mutatis mutandis on the continent, abjuration into perpetual exile without conviction in a trial typically arose out of two situations: (1) the crown's formal accusation of felony but its failure to convict on the charge, or (2) the registering of a confession of felony with a competent administrative authority without any semblance of a trial. In both situations, to repeat, a solemn promise was exacted from the abjurer never to return to the jurisdiction from which he or she was exiled.

If, following the first scenario, the crown made formal accusations of felony and it failed to convict, by what warrant did it exile exonerated suspects? It was a peculiar set of administrative policies which disadvantaged such people, specifically, those who were acquitted at the unilateral judicial ordeals. Up through the year 1215, the fundamental mode of testing an indicted person's innocence of a felony, in the absence of any *full* proof, such as a confession in open court or the testimony of two eyewitnesses or flight, which was regarded as a sure token of culpability,[16] was the ordeal. It came into play when there was strong presumptive evidence for believing a person to be guilty. Medieval law, in theory and in practice, resisted judgments which condemned a person to death or dismemberment unless there was a full proof of guilt. Circumstantial evidence has often sufficed for conviction for felonies in modern jurisdictions. Evan Mandery, writing of United States federal jurisdiction, notes that "federal practice treats circumstantial evidence identically to direct evidence and permits conviction based solely on such evidence."[17] But circumstantial evidence alone was not generally sufficient for conviction—in theory or in practice—in High Medieval English or continental courts.

Ordeal, the judgment of God, was a full proof, equivalent in probative value to other full proofs.[18] And it was the fallback setting when other full proofs were lacking. In other words, if bad reputation (*mala fama*, as continental and English jurists would say[19]), had led to one's formal indictment for felony, but no full proofs could be produced, the trial court opted to employ ordeal. In the English system the Assizes or ordinances of Clarendon of 1166 and of Northampton of 1176 judicialized the process of identifying—which is to say, indicting *in the king's name*—people suspected of inflicting serious harms on others, employing here the regular presentments of grand juries.[20] These included homicides, thereby providing an alternative to the traditional and, it must be acknowledged, as Paul Hyams' work has shown, tenacious vengeance by feud.[21] The new system also, as intimated, turned the suspects' acts into crimes against the king, in whose name the grand juries indicted suspects, and implicitly into crimes against the community of the realm. Trial by ordeal followed for those who were successfully brought to court. It was thriving in the early thirteenth century in the wake of the increased use of the grand juries.

The most famous types of ordeal were those of hot iron, hot water, and cold water. In preparation the prisoner went through required ablutions, prayers, and blessings. Later a priest blessed the ordeal fire in which a bar of iron of a certain weight was heated white-hot or upon which a cauldron of water containing a stone of a specified weight was brought to a boil. For the ordeal of cold water the water and pit which were to receive the accused were given the appropriate blessing. In the ordeal of hot iron the defendant was restrained and the metal placed in his or her hands for a specified length of time, whereupon it was removed, the hands bandaged, and a three-day wait imposed. At the expiration of the waiting period, the court ordered the removal of the bandages and the examination of the hands in the judges' and suitors' presence. Then the court rendered God's (revealed) judgment. Hands beginning to heal evidenced innocence, while those unclean (bleeding profusely, suppurating, stinking) evidenced guilt, in which case the accused faced sentence of mutilation or execution. The ordeal of hot water followed a similar procedure after the accused retrieved the stone from the cauldron. In the ordeal of cold water, the accused was immersed in the pool. Sinking implied innocence. The holy water received the accused. Floating implied guilt. Presumably, the fear incumbent on a guilty conscience dreading the judgment of God was being revealed in a desperate desire not to drown. In any case, the victim, whether showing signs of calm confidence entering the water or evidencing terror and trying to thrash, was removed from the pit before any serious physical harm could be done. The guilty were liable to mutilation or execution.

Harsh as this process may appear , the whole system was mitigated by the fact that almost 70 percent of prisoners who went to the ordeal were acquitted, a result which has stimulated an extraordinary amount of research and reams of brilliant analysis.[22] Scholars have wondered at the initial origin of the ordeal as a mode of proof and its supposed appropriateness to "primitive" societies. They have puzzled productively over the apparent continued attraction of the ordeal, even when certain sophisticated scholastic thinkers, university men, in the late twelfth century initiated a scathing critique of it.[23]

Perhaps the most curious feature of the place of the ordeal in the justice system seen from a modern vantage point pertains to the immediate consequence of so many defendants' acquittals. It has been argued that the high rate of acquittal by ordeal testifies in part to the strong medieval inclination against imposing dismemberment and, in particular, capital punishment, as often as the law of felony would have required in convictions. Perhaps so. Nevertheless, though success at the ordeal established the accused's innocence, it did so without wiping the slate clean. For those who oversaw the administration of justice, God had not commanded or implied that succeeding at the ordeal should make the judges ignore the circumstances which brought the accused to court in the first place. The accused was compromised by having a reputation so low that he or she was obliged to undergo the ordeal. Since the bad reputation remained, it itself could be censured.[24] Nor was this mere theorizing: as a matter of usual practice those indicted by grand juries and who succeeded at the ordeal were constrained to abjure the realm thereafter.[25] Although in this way abjuration was what we would call punishing the innocent, it served the additional purpose of removing despised persons from the communities where their enemies might take vengeance on them and thereby initiate or perpetuate the feuds that so disturbed medieval life.

To some of the abjurers, this byproduct of abjuration was insufficient to justify it. Indeed, the perplexity felt by some of those exonerated is sometimes palpable. Wille Brun, for example, who succeeded at the ordeal of water in 1212, was dumbfounded when told he had to abjure. He took the oath (*ejuravit*) but protested that he was willing to find a mark—two-thirds of a pound, a huge amount of money at the time—and pledges, men who assured the court that he would pay, for his innocence. No one, he was willing to bet, would accuse him to his face of the murder of which the judgment of God had acquitted him.[26] But of course this was not the point. The end of the process punished his reputation, not his alleged crime. His argument thus availed him nothing.

I have already referred to the fact that there had long been elite academic criticism of the use of ordeals and belief in their efficacy. Although there were powerful counterarguments in favor of their reliability as well, the Fourth Lateran Council of 1215, under the presidency of Pope Innocent III (1198–1216), accepted the superior merits of the academic critique. The fathers of the Council prohibited priests from intoning the formulas necessary to sanctify the ordeal, without which believers could have no confidence that they were witnessing or experiencing God's own judgment. Princes throughout the Catholic world were less than enthusiastic about the Council's pronouncement. With a few strokes of the quill, the fathers, if they had been successful—an important if—would have undermined one of the principal modes of proof in secular law. Most rulers refused to let priests abandon the responsibility of blessing ordeal fires, judgment pits (for the ordeal of cold water), and the like for decades, and it is not clear that priests themselves wanted to abandon it. Those who did wish to were browbeaten—this is the historian Scott Taylor's word—into performing the rituals.[27] Two rulers, however, obeyed with relative expedition: the king of England, Henry III (1216–72), a child under the tutelage of a regency council, which included a papal legate who got his way on the matter, and the king of Denmark, Valdemar II (1202–41), who had on several occasions received papal support in his political struggles and may have been returning the favor.

The English government's willingness to receive the Lateran decree and suspend trials by ordeal led to the filling up of jails with indicted prisoners who could not be tried. This, in turn, led judges and administrators to offer them trial by jury as an alternative. Juries had been used before to gather information, to adjudicate many civil cases, to make the accusations in the form of grand jury presentments (a regular practice since 1166, which led to ordeal for felony), and by private agreement to avoid trial by battle when that was the otherwise appropriate mode of proof.[28] In these other instances juries proffered their verdicts—statements which they alleged were "truly rendered," *vere dicta*, but mostly based on majority votes. The innovation imposed when the jury came to substitute for the ordeal was the rule of unanimity, either in favor of or against innocence. Underlying the innovation and, I would argue, salving the innovators' consciences, was the idea that unanimity guaranteed the active presence of the Holy Spirit in jury deliberations, thus making the verdict an authentic judgment of God as the ordeal had been widely regarded before this time. In papal elections, unanimity was said to be *quasi per inspirationem divinam* (like divine inspiration), but whether Englishmen directly borrowed the idea has, I think, been impossible to establish so far.[29] Unanimity would have been a powerful if not necessarily compelling selling point for judges, jurors, victims' families and friends, and defendants who were being asked to abandon the ordeal, a familiar and accepted mode of proof.

The unanimous verdict of a jury of twelve good men and true, operative even before it came to be formally fixed in law in the fourteenth century,[30] was therefore understood by those who supported it as a full proof of innocence or guilt, just like ordeal. That it did not possess ordeal's respectable patina of ancestral sanctification, however, that it took a while to decide to sever the large indictment jury from the twelve-man petit jury (in the earliest usages the same jury indicted and tried), and that the rule of unanimity became absolute only after some time, were altogether troubling. These factors may account for the fact that trial by jury upon indictment for felony often led to acquittal; conviction rates in some samples are as low as 20 to 25 percent.[31] The average conviction rate in the United States, according to the Bureau of Justice Statistics, is at present 68 percent. In eighteenth-century England it only approached 40 percent, but that was still substantially higher than in the Middle Ages.[32] Comparing justice statistics across time and legal systems is notoriously difficult,[33] but the general point seems well established: namely, that like the ordeal, the mode of proof which replaced it in England exhibited in practice a reluctance to render guilty verdicts and thus to authorize the capital and horrendous corporal punishments which would follow. This reluctance has been shown to have persisted at least down to the late fourteenth century.[34]

In England initial misgivings and disquiet over the reliability of jury trial as a mode of proof also help to explain why the process began as an optional one and, by tradition and practice, remained so for centuries to come. An indicted suspect had to consent to the process. The alternative was to remain in prison—unconvicted and therefore immune from the confiscation of one's property. In no little time frustrations with this possible outcome led authorities to permit extraordinary measures to induce indictees to "voluntarily" accept trial by jury. *Prison forte et dure*, the limitation of prisoners' sustenance to bread and water on alternate days, was employed to weaken the will of resisters. This was subsequently supplemented by *peine forte et dure,* the application of weights, incrementally increased, to the prisoner's chest.[35] A sweeter method of inducement was that authorities, despite perhaps initial hesitation, did not require abjuration after a jury's not guilty verdict, as they did after success at the ordeal. Being found innocent by a jury in court entirely restored one's freedom.

Very frequently, as I wish to show now, abjuration into perpetual exile was not a punishment but in large measure a mitigation of punishment. It was an act of *mercy* available to, for example, the thousands of people who gained sanctuary in medieval England and on the continent.[36] Sanctuary and asylum—or rather, certain important goals of sanctuary and asylum, such as the prevention of socially disruptive blood feuds—were already in place in biblical antiquity and have been well-documented by classical historians and by scholars of religion.[37] The scriptural texts on sanctuary cities as places of refuge and new beginnings (Numbers 35, Deuteronomy 19, Joshua 20–21, etc.) constituted the deep background for High Medieval acceptance of the concept of asylum. There were also Roman precedents.[38] And yet the legal apparatus associated with claims of sanctuary, more or less consistently and routinely applied across Catholic Europe in the High Middle Ages (if not before), was quite distinctive and had little in common with the detailed practices of the biblical system.[39] It was—the word is evoked in T. B. Lambert's article on the historical anthropology of sanctuary—odd, odd as a kiwi bird.[40] Perhaps so. I prefer to think of it as akin to a wayward adolescent, just misunderstood. At base, if a felony suspect managed to flee to a place of asylum, such as a church or churchyard (French administrative records call them *sacra et religiosa loca*[41]), he or she could ask for sanctuary and, if it was granted by the appropriate local magistrate, was allowed to abjure the realm.[42] This is known as general sanctuary and must be differentiated from residential sanctuary in chartered territories, which will be taken up at the end of this book.[43]

The phrase "managed to" in relation to reaching sanctuary is important here. Consider the curious case of John of Hinton.[44] He was a thief who had stolen dies which could be used to coin royal money. He appears to have been observed and followed at a distance by Richard le Guette, a prominent local man. But on his way John still managed to steal a hatchet from a private house. The owner of the house saw him and pursued him. When he caught up with him, the householder overpowered the thief and beat him viciously. The ruckus attracted two other men, who joined in the fun and then helped themselves to John's belongings, including what they did not realize was the loot from his first theft. They left him in a heap, half-dead.

After their departure, Richard le Guette, the original observer of John's theft of the coin dies, found him, but, of course, the latter no longer possessed any of the evidence of his misdeed. Richard simply ordered the battered man to get a move on. Beset by his injuries, John could scarcely do so. Word reached the hapless felon's wife, Cristina, who brought a cart to pick him up. When he told her what he had done, instead of driving him home she took him to the parish church, bringing him into sanctuary on 8 October 1312. Meanwhile, to finish the story, the men who had beaten John searched their take and discovered the dies. Scared witless at the enormity of John's crime and its implications for them if they were discovered with such objects, they decided to hand the dies over to the local coroner, the royal official who oversaw much of the King's justice, with the explanation of how they got them. When the one entrusted with this task reached the coroner, he discovered the royal officer about to take John of Hinton's oath of abjuration. In the end, John abjured, the men who beat him were fined, and all the others involved, including Cristina, were exonerated of any complicity in the original theft.

Getting to sanctuary was hard for John of Hinton just because of a run of bad luck. But it was fraught for all suspected felons because preventing such people from reaching sanctuary was licit and encouraged. Thus, in one incident, reported for 23 February 1293, a porter and a clerk independently observed a prisoner awaiting trial escaping by night from a castle keep. Escape was itself a felony, and if the escapee had succeeded in reaching an asylum, he could claim sanctuary for the escape and for the original felony for which he was awaiting trial. Both the porter and the clerk therefore tried to prevent the escapee from getting to a church. In hot pursuit and in the darkness the clerk got mixed up and thought the porter was the escapee. In the ensuing scuffle, the clerk killed the porter and was himself wounded. Then the authorities arrived and figured out what had happened. By then, the escapee was long gone. The question was what should be done with the clerk. In the end he was forgiven the porter's homicide, for the pursuit of a jail breaker trying to reach sanctuary was praiseworthy. The death was a regrettable mistake in an other-wise laudatory effort.[45]

In another incident, a certain John Alisaundre, suspected as a ha-bitual thief, sought sanctuary in a church, whereupon the local coro-ner was summoned to receive his confession.[46] Locals had no love for John, the perpetrator of multiple larcenies and robberies. Theft in a society where surpluses were low was not a petty crime unless the coveted article or money was trivial in value, and theft, then as now, was often accompanied by serious physical violence. As a felony, therefore, it merited corporal punishment. Habitual thievery, by this logic, deserved the ultimate sanction, death.[47] There was a proof text: in Luke 23:39–43 (AV), one of the thieves—the good thief—crucified at Jesus' side admitted the justness of his and his companion's execu-tion with the words, "we receive the due reward of our deeds."

Yet, there he was, this John Alisaundre, in the parish church, the very center of the congregants' spiritual life, sheltering under the pro-tective cloak of sanctuary. His would-be avengers, doing perhaps their version of God's work on earth, interrupted the coroner on his way to take John's confession, in the avowed belief or pretense that sanctuary began to apply only at the moment the claimant admitted his guilt. If this were true, then they could licitly seize John in church and thereby deny him asylum at any time before the coroner arrived. But it was not true. John's person was supposed to be inviolate as long as he remained in sacred space. There were a few genuine gray areas in the law of sanctuary—not many, but a few. Whether sanctuary applied to nighttime crimes, for instance, was long contested.[48] But a sanctuary seeker's immunity while in church was not a gray area. When this immunity was violated, those who held the rights of sanctuary ex-pected a firm royal response to the transgression.[49] Yet, it was perhaps the vigilantes' awareness in John Alisaundre's case that a few uncer-tainties did exist in the law which encouraged them to advance their claim and act on it and trust to the torpor of bureaucracy to insulate them from serious retribution. They entered the church under cover of darkness, seized the unfortunate man, and beat the also-unfortunate guards, locals like themselves, who had been assigned to protect John from vigilantes. The king's peace and the church's peace were in mul-tiple ways shattered by the perpetrators of these offenses, which took place in 1311.[50]

Sanctuary as a system and properly understood was, despite rare official criticisms,[51] supported by all medieval Catholic princes. However, one can infer from the cases noted thus far that this does not imply popular enthusiasm for it. Indeed, when a suspect managed to reach a place of asylum, pursuers on occasion willfully and in full knowledge and admission of their wrong violated the precincts to exact retribution. Breaking sanctuary almost inevitably put the pursuers at odds with royal justice. An exception in which officials themselves violated sanctuary in the same way as mobs did involved the treatment by Chief Justiciar Hubert Walter of the rebel William Longbeard in 1196. Contemporary apologists were embarrassed by the breach, which included burning William out of hiding, and tried to explain it away. They adduced a reason which was supposed to justify why no one was punished for the breach. William was said to have had carnal relations with his mistress in the church, his semen polluting the holy place, a sacrilege which trumped his claim to asylum.[52] The embarrassment and special pleading here, however, support the general impression of royal repugnance over the violation of sanctuary. Celebrity cases like this, few enough in number (William Longchamp's and Hubert de Burgh's are two other examples), have garnered perhaps more attention than they deserve.[53]

The following cases are more typical.[54] On 20 August 1284, a commission of *oyer and terminer* (a special commission to hear felonies) met to try certain "satellites of Satan," as they were termed by the authorities meting out punishment. On a recent night these satanic men had "entered Saint Mary le Bow (London), violently seized Laurence Duket, who had sought refuge there for some alleged crime, and after various torments hanged him with a rope in the said church." Now the perpetrators would be punished.[55] Another judgment, this one on 4 April 1309, recorded that a group of thieves and other criminals who had escaped the king's prison at Windsor sought sanctuary in the cemetery of Windsor and should by rights have received its protections. But they were dragged from the churchyard by locals, accused later of "slaying and beheading certain of them on the journey back" to prison. The king directed that justice be done on those who committed this offense, for they had broken the king's peace, which included the protection of sanctuary. The names of those slain and those who survived were also to be recorded, pursuant, I presume, to the perpetrators' trials or to facilitate acts of contrition for the outrages on the survivors and the murder of the deceased.[56]

My research suggests that instances of vigilante justice of this kind were rarely successful. Yungwin of Enfield in Middlesex was dragged from sanctuary in 1228, but his guards managed to rescue and restore him. And, so, like most men who got to a place of asylum, he survived long enough to begin the process. The first question was always whether he would agree to stand trial.[57] Declining to do so, as almost every sanctuary seeker did, Yungwin was obliged to confess before abjuring the realm.[58] (This was a separate procedure from religious confession, in which the sanctuary seeker's statements were closed to the coroner.[59]) Thousands of other men did the same from the late twelfth through the mid-fourteenth century.[60] Women did so, too, for they constituted a small but not insignificant proportion of asylum seekers, perhaps as great as one in ten, the proportion of women among accused felons in general.[61]

All sanctuary seekers who sought to abjure had to acknowledge their crimes to local magistrates (in England a task usually although not exclusively confided to coroners). I have remarked already that they could not obtain sanctuary for felonies for which they had already been convicted in court, although a few who perhaps knew no better—such as a judicially condemned man who was hanged poorly, revived before burial, and thereafter escaped to a church—tried unsuccessfully to convince officials that they should be allowed to abjure.[62] They might also knowingly scuttle the process at their own risk by trying to escape. Occasions are known in which compatriots bribed guards to let their friends escape before the abjuration process was complete.[63] If they were captured attempting to flee, they incurred automatic sentence of death and almost invariably execution of the sentence. If their flight was successful, they became outlaws, subject to capital punishment upon capture (on which a great deal more later).[64]

Abjurers were obliged to carry crosses and dress penitentially in acknowledgement of their guilt, and also to announce their protected status on the way into exile. The crosses would have been modest-sized simple wooden objects and the garb of no or little value.[65] Many abjurers, even so accoutered, were frightened of what vigilantes might do to them if they departed sanctuary. Magistrates were torn. They wanted these undesirables to leave at the appropriate time but were loath to pollute a church by using an act of violence to force them out. So, parallel to the aforementioned *prison forte et dure*, they drastically reduced or ceased food deliveries to the sanctuary to induce reluctant abjurers to depart.[66] Starvation was not violence in contemporary terms, but it was not a happy alternative for the abjurers. Also, churchmen did not rejoice to see their asylees wasting away. But, as Henry de Bracton knew, the law was the law.[67] One must be cautious, of course, in depending on Bracton's and other prescriptive texts,[68] which have to be supplemented by documents of practice. Such texts do lend support to Bracton's views. Indeed, even men who expected better treatment, such as the former Chief Justiciar Hubert de Burgh and a disgraced Chief Justice, Thomas Weyland, who achieved sanctuary but did not wish to leave, were subjected to starvation.[69] Whether responding to hunger or not, a number of abjurers, such as John Philpot of Drayton-in-Hales in Shropshire, who was granted sanctuary and abjuration in the monastic church of Saint Andrew of Northampton for homicide and theft, fled rather than set off to foreign lands. In this case the coroner had ordered the bailiffs of Northampton to watch the church to prevent escape until all aspects of the process leading to exile were completed. Presumably they were fined for their laxity.[70]

One problem, of course, was how to identify fugitives who successfully fled sanctuary rather than submit to trial or exile. After all, if they did escape, one would expect them to try to blend in with travelers, perhaps by pretending to be pilgrims if, at the time of escape, they had already been issued their crosses and mourners' garb, which resembled pilgrim attire. Or they could ditch the penitential markers during or following their escape and steal clerical or common lay people's clothes. If, later on, such a one was caught in some other crime or came into custody for brawling, public drunkenness, or lewdness, how would a local beadle or law enforcement officer, let alone an ordinary peasant or townsperson, identify the miscreant? How could he be identified as a one-time abjurer—a man who had forfeited any future claim to mercy by violating his oath to leave the realm?[71] How could one prevent multiple abjurations?

At first it may seem odd that evidence of concern in England over this matter—the possibility of fraudulent multiple abjurations—is quite rare. Records show that a very few abjurers were suspected of or succeeded in obtaining more than one abjuration, but really not many. In a case from the year 1212, one Robert, the son of a certain Geoffrey, abjured at York. He was a parson, presumably a low-level clerk, for abjuration was not supposed to be available to those who enjoyed benefit of clergy.[72] He was also suspected of earlier having abjured at Nottingham. Upon inquiry, however, York officials discovered that the suspicion was groundless.[73] There is a clear case of two abjurations in Somersetshire by a single man, John Hipecok, sometime before 1243. This case involved collusion and was almost unique in type.[74] After John's first abjuration several villagers of Northover managed to rescue him and hide the confessed thief before he could be led away into exile. The collusion was revealed when he again got into trouble for stealing, this time in the Somerset village of Crowcombe. He sought to abjure and succeeded before anyone who knew of his earlier abjuration recognized him. The efficiency of the English administration remains a contested question,[75] but efficient or not, there is no doubt that at best, news traveled slowly and was distorted in the course of the journey, which would help explain John Hipecock's success. Even so, there are almost no other examples of multiple abjurations in England.

To digress briefly, multiple abjurations were a far greater concern on the continent. To prevent them, continental jurisdictions, most of which otherwise had similar systems to the English, branded abjurers.[76] They imposed branding either on a shoulder or a finger with irons purchased for the purpose, usually with the mark of the *fleur-de-lys*.[77] A less-used mark, but one employed in the Champenois commune of Provins in the late thirteenth century, was the sign of the cross.[78] The overall preference for the *fleur-de-lys* over the cross is explained by the fact that penitents on occasion had themselves branded with small versions of the latter.[79] It would be awful to mistake a penitent pilgrim for an abjurer or vice versa.

In ordinary life the *fleur-de-lys*, concealed by clothing, was invisible and a branding mark on the palm side of a finger used to make the ritual sign of the cross was hidden easily enough. Yet, routine examinations of accused criminals' shoulders and fingers while in custody would have revealed the lily-brands of former abjurers to the authorities and resulted in execution. It was thus that in 1273 a woman, who stole some shoes and linen cloths in Saint-Maur-des-Fossés, a southeastern suburb of Paris, was discovered already to have been branded (*que inventa signata*). If customs associated with the execution of women there were followed, she was buried alive under the gallows of the monastery of Saint-Maur, which had capital justice in the village.[80]

An exile branded on the finger could conceal abjuration by amputation of the appropriate digit. Criminals operating on the continent and lacking a finger or two, which they or comrades had severed, were common. Indeed, the *Établissements* of Rouen, the legal customs of the capital of Normandy, which were adopted by a large number of communities, take it for granted that beadles would come upon both branded and finger-severed thieves.[81] However, since fingers were always being lost in industrial, agricultural, and domestic accidents, as well as in brawls,[82] a felon's lack of a digit or two, while raising suspicions, constituted at best an equivocal presumption of earlier banishment.

Branding on the shoulder was just as widely used on the continent, perhaps because effacing a *fleur-de-lys* from a shoulder had less to commend itself in escaping detection by the authorities. However, it is not a question of men and women shying away from the pain of comrades gouging out even a small chunk of shoulder flesh. One could argue in one's mind which was worse, this or the severing of a finger. But unlike a finger, which could be lost in innumerable innocent ways, a deeply scarified shoulder would possibly raise greater suspicions when a prisoner so marked was adjudicated for another crime at the bar of justice or offered a confession in a plea for mercy.

These marks were not meant to shame a person in the manner of Nathaniel Hawthorne's scarlet letter. They were not public signs of infamy in the manner of the severed ear, hand, or foot of a convicted thief or the facial branding of thieves, heretics, blasphemers, even breakers of labor contracts.[83] Such facial markings persisted despite an increasing reluctance in the High Middle Ages, or so it has been suggested, to disfigure the human visage—the image of God.[84] Quite the contrary, they were intended, as Jeremy Bentham long ago observed, to forestall a future claim to abjuration or judicial leniency in general if this ever again became an issue.[85] Exile as mercy or as punishment was ordinarily closed to known recidivists under the terms it was originally offered.[86] Discovery of an attempt to finagle it a second time merited horrific retribution.

This digression on continental practice is justified by the contrast with the contemporary English system, where the branding of abjurers was extremely rare in the long thirteenth century. Yet, the English were familiar from scriptural and classical sources with the interpretative traditions of the mark of Cain and with the long history of human branding (and tattooing, which they may have misunderstood as branding). They were as familiar with this material as were continental Europeans.[87] Authorities on both sides of the Channel were aware that the burning of flesh was used in ancient times for punishment, for initiation into sacred rites or mystic societies, and to signify slaves' owners. Moreover, it appears occasionally as a punishment or judicial warning in England in the High Middle Ages, as the searing of a suspicious vagabond's private parts in Surrey in 1235 attests.[88] In other words, it was not an excess of compassion in England as opposed to the continent which inhibited the branding of abjurers, at least not in a world in which the island's judges from time to time condemned convicted thieves to amputations.[89] That the English did not resort to regularly branding abjurers until much later in the Middle Ages is a subject I shall address and attempt to explain in chapters 5 and 6 in the context of differential rates of illegal return of abjurers to English and continental jurisdictions.[90]

Now let us return to the subject of abjuration as mercy. Mercy was also at work in the abjurations offered to a group of English subjects much smaller in number than that of the sanctuary men and women: a special sort of kidnappers, those who snatched children in order to arrange marriages for them and get their hands on their lucrative inheritances, in cases in which the kidnappers obviously did not have formal feudal rights over the wards. The statute, Westminster II of 1285, which addressed this among many other problems, put the matter this way: "Concerning children, male and female, who have been seized or abducted and whose marriage belongs to another. If the one who carries out the seizure has no right in the marriage, even if he restores the child unmarried or makes satisfaction [that is, pays a sufficient post factum payment] for the marriage, he shall nevertheless be punished by two years of prison. And if he does not restore [the child] or marries the heir after she reaches marriageable age and cannot make satisfaction [for doing so], let him abjure the realm [*abjuret regnum*] or suffer perpetual imprisonment."[91] This provision of the statute has fascinated jurists down the ages.[92] Here we seem to apprehend abjuration as straddling the boundary between mercy, mitigation of punishment (perpetual imprisonment being worse), and pure punishment itself.

The last group of people who benefitted from the royal mercy of abjuration and thus contributed to the exile community was approvers.[93] With this group, mercy and punishment also existed in tension. A member of a criminal gang who knew or believed that the authorities possessed full proofs establishing his culpability could turn crown's evidence, confess his offenses and, playing upon the nearly universal fear of gang terror, agree to identify and accuse (or in technical language, appeal) his fellow criminals.[94] Before the era of jury trials, when an approver's alleged accomplices were apprehended, he was allowed to do judicial battle—to test or *prove* himself, hence the name. Ordinarily women were not permitted to do battle except through champions, an inappropriate option in these circumstances. However, it was possible to adapt approval procedure for them and send the men appealed by women, or women who were appealed by either men or women, to ordeal.

At any rate, male approvers fought each and every one of their opponents, men who they asserted had been their accomplices in criminal gangs, and they did so in single combat, the bilateral form of the ordeal. They fought each of them sequentially to the death or until one or the other party gave up, which was taken as a sign that the loser was not only cowardly (craven) but guilty. Approvers who won every battle avoided execution—remember, they were already confessed felons—and were permitted to abjure. Jury trials subsequently supplanted judicial combat, even though in England battle did continue as a mode of proof in other sorts of cases.[95] The process implicit in the transition to juries also admitted women without having to further modify procedures.[96] Under the jury system, those approvers who were fortunate enough to see all their alleged accomplices convicted at trial were permitted to abjure. The less fortunate—just one acquittal was sufficient to bring on misfortune—were executed as condemned felons.

Approval procedure could give rise to systematic injustices.[97] Some unscrupulous or frustrated law enforcement officials induced criminals to accuse other undesirables, whether or not they suspected the latter were in league with them and sometimes to settle personal scores. Efforts to prevent this were real but not fully effective.[98] The special eyre of Surrey and Kent, generated in the political tensions of the time and over which Hugh Bigod presided, uncovered such instances in 1258 and 1259.[99] There is also something suspicious about the many cases of approvers in Essex in 1291, some of whom claimed as many as a dozen accomplices in their crimes, and about the confessions generated from this process, which the approvers were said to have made "with much joy" (*cum mangno* [sic] *gaudio*).[100]

Few approvers, either in the era of judicial battle or in that of jury trials after 1215, survived the process. A case from 1237, enrolled on the Close Rolls, documents one such instance, in which five successful prosecutions led to the approver's abjuration of the realm.[101] But imagining their more probable fate, approvers must have contemplated breaking jail as they awaited the outcomes of their alleged accomplices' trials. In London in 1325, four approvers came close to translating these thoughts into action. We learn that authorities accused them of abetting the jailbreak of ten other prisoners, assuming, I would suggest, that in the confusion they too might make their escape. Five of the jail breakers managed to get to sanctuary and thereafter abjured the realm, but the other five were captured by guards and nearby residents, an outcome which appears to have persuaded the approvers who saw the capture to stay put. Abetting had to be proved, of course, in a formal trial, which would take time. If it had been, these men would have been led to the gallows. Before this, however, at least one of them, William Broun, an Irishman, died in prison of natural causes.[102]

THE CENTRALITY OF ABJURATION
IN THE ADMINISTRATION OF JUSTICE

Rates of acquittal, to return to an issue raised earlier, have been invoked, whether rightly or wrongly, as evidence of medieval reluctance in certain circumstances to carry out the death penalty and punishments by dismemberment. Although contemporary artists were very attached to depicting corporal punishments and although death and dismemberment vied with fines as the most often *mandated* punishments for felony in England, juries of the early fourteenth century, one scholar has observed, "were notoriously unwilling to convict, as anyone who has studied the eyre rolls of 1329–31 will testify."[103] The recourse to exile, at least in the case of sanctuary men and women, the vast majority of abjurers, constitutes complementary evidence of this reluctance. It is unfortunate that Frederic William Maitland, given his genius, wrote but a few words on abjuration, but he did observe that it "seems to have been very common."[104] In fact, in the period from 1180 to the mid-fourteenth century thousands of people abjured the realm of England.

It would be risky to say how many thousands of men and women abjured in the long thirteenth century, but some risks are worth taking.[105] The largest category of abjurers and that on which the most work has been done comprised sanctuary men and women. Estimates have very occasionally been ventured as to the number of people granted sanctuary in a single county in one year or group of years based on published coroners' rolls and judicial records prepared by the itinerant royal courts. These counts vary according to the population size of the county, the nature of settlement patterns (the proportion of large towns, small towns, villages, hamlets, etc.), and the political, social, and economic conditions which also affected the incidence of criminal activity. Variously extrapolating from these county-level estimates to the entire realm, legal historians have guessed that from two hundred to two thousand persons per year were granted sanctuary in England.[106] The majority of these, as far as one can tell, also abjured. Presuming that the vast majority who abjured went into exile—a contested point, but one which appears likely, based on my own research[107]—a guess can be made as to the overall number of abjured exiles from the later twelfth to the mid-fourteenth century, the period covered in this book.

First, in order to determine a range of possibility, there is no reason to lower the cluster of smaller estimates, around two hundred per year, which have been calculated mainly from sanctuary data drawn from sample sets of published judicial and coroners' rolls of less populous and more rural counties. Nor need we adjust these low estimates downward, even if a few sanctuary abjurers somehow thwarted their exile from such counties and the realm. This is because, as we are aware, there were other categories of abjurers, such as approvers, whose exile, though accounting for only a small number of people, would have compensated for the few successful fugitives who, while in sanctuary, had sworn to depart the realm. Higher annual estimates, such as the two thousand figure mentioned, are skewed upward by extrapolation from inclusion of sources for more populous urban regions. England in the High Middle Ages, however, was a mostly rural society. (One estimate is that in the year 1300, 700,000 of its approximately 4,000,000 population were urbanites.[108]) So, a significant downward adjustment in the upper limit of the annual number of exiles is reasonable in this instance. Let me therefore err on the side of caution and be drastic in my reduction, reckoning, say, five hundred men and women foreswearing the realm in a typical year.

On average, this would come to little more than a dozen abjurers per year per English county, the mean population of which was approximately 100,000–150,000. I offer a range because average county population depends on the estimate of the size of the general population of the country. Four million was the suggestion cited above, but five and a quarter million is also commonly estimated by demographers.[109] Whatever the case, the median number of abjurers per county would be much lower because of the distorting effect of London and a few other areas. So, most counties would have been abjuring into exile fewer than a dozen persons a year. Finally, since the system of exile was well in place by the turn of the twelfth/thirteenth century[110] and (as will be demonstrated) was functioning routinely through the mid-fourteenth, we are talking about 150 or so years of continuous operation. Even with the restrained estimates I have made, this would mean that approximately 75,000 men and women were sent into perpetual exile through abjuration in the period under consideration—and I feel certain this is a significant undercount.

It is lamentable that conventions of text editing dull the perception of the scale of the enterprise and inhibit more precise calculations than are possible here. Abjurations were so routine and often so formulaic that more than one editor of judicial and administrative rolls has chosen not to print them at all or not in full. The editor of one set of inquisitions, for example, mentions a case from Bedfordshire, that of John Tibbe of Saint Albans, while remarking in passing that the roll with this record contained many other abjurations that he decided neither to print nor enumerate.[111] Another editor, a bit more helpful, at least noted the precise number of abjurations he saw fit *not* to print.[112] A third published a few "interesting" abjurations while noting inconsistently how many other less interesting ones were on the roll.[113] Despite these editorial practices, which have served habitually and substantially to undervalue the significance of abjuration, exile, as I expressly averred at the beginning of this chapter, was close to the very heart of the treatment and control of criminals and people of bad repute in England during the High Middle Ages.

Moreover, just about every European polity appears to have had structures and procedures in place which were similar or parallel to those which in England led to abjuration, or even went far beyond them to employ abjuration and exile as a punishment of the first instance. The High Middle Ages constituted, in the words of Henri Bresc, a "world of exiles."[114] These structures and procedures, varying by region and over time,[115] also began to coalesce, as in England, into a tight system in the late twelfth and thirteenth centuries, although, also as in England, they drew on far earlier and disparate practices which anthropologists have associated with weaker political formations than the High Medieval state.[116] In Ghent, to give one example, the infliction of exile was so common that its municipal clerks kept a special register, the Book of Exiles (*ballincboek*). The thousands of entries are a staggering number for a town of Ghent's population: say, forty thousand at any one time.[117] Contemporary allusions to and examples of similar registers in contemporary France, Flanders, and Central European polities and jurisdictions such as Krakow document thousands upon thousands more.[118] In a word, exile—both as punishment and as mercy—was among the core principles and practices of European jurisprudence in the High Middle Ages and, for many jurisdictions, well into the early modern period.[119] The language of banishment permeated the legal discourse of the entire age.[120]

A FEW WORDS ON MERCY

Exile as a form of mercy in England and elsewhere fits comfortably with an ideology which came to articulate good rulership as a balance between rigor and *clementia*.[121] But this does not mean that the system of justice employing it was "soft" or that mitigation of punishment was necessarily motivated by compassion. I believe I have shown this. So, I am not trying to paint a picture of a gentler and kinder Middle Ages. As a form of mercy, abjuration into exile was harsh, and mercy itself, in various other forms, was sometimes problematic, both in theory and practice.[122] Like plea bargaining in those modern liberal polities which retain the death penalty, the offer of abjuration to approvers, for example, though formally an act of mercy, had its principal legal aim in obtaining convictions, not in showing compassion. This is, in part, why there have been attempts to curtail plea bargaining in the United States. As a kind of coercion (bargain or die!) it has more than a light whiff of forced self-incrimination in violation of the Fifth Amendment to the Constitution, a point beautifully argued in Joseph Hoffmann, Marcy Kahn, and Steven Fisher's classic article, "Plea Bargaining in the Shadow of Death."[123]

So when Karl Shoemaker wrote, rather touchingly, that "poor and friendless [felons] could still turn 'approver' and save their necks by defeating those they accused in judicial battles,"[124] he went too far. The old law commentaries deem the king's response to successful approval, his "pardon . . . as to life."[125] It was technically a bestowal of mercy, in other words, but every aspect of the process leading to this act of grace smacked of brutality. Nor, despite Shoemaker's phrase "poor and friendless," is there any compelling contemporary evidence, as far as I know, that the justification for approval was concern for the poor or the friendless felon. Approval was designed, after all, to find more people to kill because criminal gangs so affrighted society or, again in the words of an old standard law commentary, to "discover . . . accomplices." There is not a word about compassion.[126] Letting one felon go free into exile in order to get at and punish the rest of the gang of which he was a part seemed worth the price. And, in the end, the approver almost always failed to achieve freedom; few managed to "save their necks." One unsuccessful judicial combat or one failure in the jury prosecution of an alleged accomplice meant the approver's own death, soon after his loss to his opponent, in the earlier instantiation of the system, or at the order of the court in the later.[127] Did any law-abiding subject believe that there was anything so bad about an outcome of this sort for a terrorizing felon like an approver, a member of a gang? Not so far as I have been able to discover from contemporary sources.[128]

Other expressions of mercy were almost as harsh as approval, with its infinitesimal hope of a successful outcome. The case of a woman who, out of fear, harbored a gang of thieves and murderers for a short time and concealed their booty for them illuminates the matter. In the course of an investigation, the authorities interrogated the woman. Frightened at the possibility of reprisals from gang members, she lied to her questioners. But they managed to run down the criminals despite her lies, and after doing so obtained convincing information about her role, *including her coercion into it*. The lies were what galled the authorities, lies to shield a gang of murderers and thieves who had terrorized law-abiding folk in the community. If a man had told such lies out of fear, it would have been chalked up to cowardice and requited with death. But what was the proper judicial response to this woman's fear? The authorities noted that "she has deserved death, but by favour [*per dispensacionem*] let her eyes be torn out." Such was the mercy meted out at Shrewsbury in 1203.[129]

At Hilary Term a few years before, in the winter of 1200, a horse thief was brought to justice. Opinions differed as to the nature of his culpability. Many thought he was a horse thief pure and simple and nothing else, but a few people were convinced that he genuinely believed he had stolen the horse at the instance or for the sake of God. They did not share his belief, but the judges decided that, guilty as he was of the crime, his motivation, however weird, was pure. So, though they acknowledged that he might deserve severer retribution, meaning death, they limited his punishment to the amputation of a foot.[130] This, then, was another—albeit another draconian—act of mercy. Even dragons, of course, have degrees of ferocity. The mercy meted out to the God-inspired horse thief, harsh as it was, was less severe than that inflicted on a different convicted felon at the Trinity Term in the spring of the same year—the loss of a foot along with an arm—but it was mercy in the same key.[131]

How should one characterize the various severe forms of mercy which we have seen at work? As one now speaks of "tough love" to indicate the strong and strong-arm discipline embraced by some boot camp enthusiasts in dealing with self-destructive and violent adolescents, one might also speak of medieval "tough mercy." At first blush, it seems appropriate. The creators and administrators of the system were themselves tough and tough-minded men. The difference is that tough love has rehabilitation and repatriation from boot camp to home and everyday society as its twin goals. The mercy of exile, the mercy of primary interest in the present study, held out very little promise of future repatriation, but rather a chance for rehabilitation *outside the realm*.[132]

If tough mercy is not quite the right phrase because of the conceptual baggage associated with its counterpart, tough love, one might invoke a different phrase adapting Christopher MacEvitt's notion of "rough tolerance," which he has used to describe Latin domination of non-Chalcedonian Christians in the first few decades of the existence of the Crusader States. One could speak of the system and experiences described in this book as "rough justice" or "rough mercy." "Rough" suggests a painful motif in the system and in the intended and expected experience, which is accurate enough. It is suggestive in this regard that early editors of the Curia Regis Rolls, the rolls of the chief court, indexed "abjuration" purely as a subcategory of "punishments," without the least nod to its character in far more instances as a formal act of mercy. The adjective "rough," however, also and unfortunately suggests a certain crudeness, an unofficial or *ad hoc* quality to the set of structures and practices which were in the process of being regularized. (An analogy is worth making with the use of the adjective in the phrase "rough music" for vigilante violence.[133]) This does not reflect the true nature of the sophisticated and routinized system of exile which was in place in the thirteenth and early fourteenth century.

So, the phrase I have chosen is "fearsome mercy." The adjective lays stress on the retribution which threatened those who contravened the system and the consuming uncertainties of the exile experience itself for those who were unable to avoid it. It also suggests the ambivalence which those granting mercy must have felt about their reluctance to *exterminate* malefactors who might yet commit terrible crimes. As Claude Gauvard put it so well, "Le banni fait peur et il a peur": "the exile generates fear and is himself afraid."[134]

CONCLUSION

The fully articulated system of abjuration into perpetual exile emerged in England at a time when criminal prosecution began increasingly, thanks to the invention of the grand jury, to lie with the king, and when the crime was held to offend what might be called the community of the realm (as opposed to merely the victim's family or his lord). Elsewhere—that is, on the continent—it arose when, not to put too fine a point on it, there was no medieval state to speak of, diplomacy was local, and peace among localities was precarious at best. There was little or no sense in either case that the exiling authority had to take into consideration the sentiments of all other jurisdictions to which its exiles might travel. By the time such a laissez-faire attitude was, circumstantially speaking, less justifiable, practices were already firmly in place, indeed had achieved the status of immemorial custom, and changes in them would have smacked of undermining ancient traditions, never a very attractive sensibility among medieval jurists and administrators. One need only think back to reactions to attempts to suppress ordeals, which, despite the English and Danish examples, remained ultimately unsuccessful for decades and in some cases for centuries in over 90 percent of Catholic Europe.

But there was a further consideration which complicated attitudes in the specific case of English abjuration. The exile system was easier to accept in regions where multiple capital jurisdictions abutted one another, as they did on the continent, and where no one jurisdiction was receiving the whole mass of another jurisdiction's exiles. I have no illusions as to the character of abjurers from England. A few, as I shall demonstrate in chapter 2, were caught up in circumstances and were perhaps harmless enough, but many were hardened criminals and opportunists, and all were so down on their luck upon their exile that they were susceptible to engaging in antisocial behavior of the most heinous sort. Moreover, the central problem in the English-French example, as I shall discuss in chapters 3 and 4, is that almost every English abjurer *went to France*. Even if, as I later estimate, there were no more than two, three, or four such people on average daily leaving the country as exiles in the 150 days of the high shipping season from Dover, the principal port of embarkation, the steady arrival of such people at one Franco-Flemish Channel village, Wissant—which is where they all debarked—could not help but strike some observers as both a morally questionable and potentially dangerous immigration. The long and special relationship between the English crown and the county of Boulogne, within which Wissant lay, may help explain the absence of voluble local resistance.[135] In any case, Englishmen did not have to worry about the dumping of French felons into their country as an act of "retaliation," which otherwise would have been a motive to curb their practice. For most French exiles who abjured the realm were absorbed into the vast array of bordering continental territories along its more than 2,500-km land borders. Those exiled from towns and other jurisdictions with capital justice within France merely went elsewhere in the kingdom. In the event, almost no exiled French felons took ship to England.[136]

French anxieties did rise significantly by the mid-fourteenth century under circumstances in which the negative effect of the asymmetry was brought home. But before I treat this issue in the epilogue,

I shall address in chapter 5 those English exiles, a distinctly tiny minority of my "sample" of over two thousand, who, in one way or another, returned to their homeland during the long thirteenth century.[137]

CHAPTER 2

The Abjurers, Their Crimes, and Their Property

S EVERAL SORTS OF EVIDENCE identify and provide a wealth of additional information on England's abjurers. Coroners' rolls register abjurers; judicial rolls and royal letters refer to those who abjured from sanctuary, became approvers, or succeeded at the ordeal and then faced exile.[1] Petitions for pardons describe the putative conditions of life for exiles, including the invariably sad and often allegedly unjust circumstances leading to their abjurations.[2] High and late medieval legal commentators invoked and dissected specific cases involving abjurers to make points about aspects of the judicial system.[3] Bishops' registers are of some value for finding evidence of mistaken abjurations.[4] The Patent and Close Rolls are vast repositories of information.[5] Abjurers also show up in huge and still uncounted numbers in the Inquisitions Miscellaneous, investigations of the holdings of people, including confessed felons (which sanctuary men and women were), whose property was to come either for a term of years or forevermore into the king's hand. These investigations were archived with Inquisitions *post mortem*, which addressed the passing of property by inheritance (some scholars, indeed, have made no distinction among the records[6]) and Inquisitions *ad quod damnum*, which were meant to precede royal grants in order "to ascertain whether the king's interests would be damaged in any way should the grant[s] be allowed."[7] All of these documents reveal details on abjurers, among many other matters, and have already been used by scholars for purposes far beyond those for which the investigators conducted them.[8]

THE ABJURERS' STATUS AND WEALTH

Anger, greed, paranoia, lust, desperation, insanity, hunger, ambition, the thrill of mischief—the emotional underpinnings of the crimes that had brought abjurers to forsake their homeland—were distributed among all classes. But the evidence convinces that abjurers tended to be of low or middling social and economic status. Many, indeed, were mired in poverty. This is not to say that every inventory of landed property appearing to undergird statements like the foregoing is accurate. Without assiduous analysis, documents often have the potential to distort and obscure scholars' discernment of poverty and wealth.[9] The investigative process that accompanied abjuration from sanctuary, for example, has to be understood as an imperfect technique and one, moreover, which unfolded over time. Initial inquests might identify a tiny holding or two in one county, while subsequent inquiries revealed an abjurer's holdings in other counties. Also, although estimates of chattels in the possession of abjurers at the time of exile were not arbitrary, they could be flawed and, in any case, were inconsistent among investigators and for various reasons might be falsified.[10]

Accurate assessments of the wealth or status of abjurers who were not native to a district, who misled their questioners about their place of residence, or who had lived as transients were particularly difficult to make. Morkin of Enfield abjured from London around 1252–53 after confessing to the crime of sheltering a known thief. At first nothing could be found out about Morkin's background or whether he had any possessions. This means that the shelter he provided the thief, which got him into such trouble, was metaphorical or, if material, did not belong to him. In all probability Morkin shared some dark corner with the fugitive, some place where they could sleep and stay out of the elements until the owner, or a servant or a beadle, discovered them and they fled in panic to sanctuary. The investigators could have left the matter at this and declared Morkin a pauper. Yet, due diligence led them to trace the career of the unfortunate abjurer back to Middlesex, where his suspected poverty was confirmed. There he was well-known as a penniless tramp.[11] Despite this evidence of thorough investigation, of course, some misjudgments as to status and wealth were inevitable. Nevertheless, the information as a whole seems reliable and is consistent for the thirteenth and first half of the fourteenth century on the main points.

A very large proportion of abjurers who came from rural areas were peasants. In making this statement, I am employing Jan Titow's characterization of an English peasant as a holder with ten acres or less.[12] Many examples of abjurers who were small landholders of this level are identifiable.[13] It is probable that a significant number of abjurers recorded either as possessing no holdings except their dwellings (messuages) or as holding no more than ten acres besides their messuages fell into the same category.[14] A great deal, however, depends on the nature of the acreage. When William of Asby in Westmorland abjured the realm, the inquest, whose findings were recorded on 4 May 1295, detailed his holdings as six and one-half acres (arable, one presumes) but with an additional one acre of meadow, a pretty valuable property, and rents that he was collecting of 2s. 2d.[15] He was not a rich man by any means, but he was closer to middling rank than the tramp Morkin of Enfield.

A significant presence of low-status and poverty-ridden abjurers is also suggested by the references to many of them as strangers or vagabonds.[16] Although I have not classified individuals who failed to enroll in a local surety group (frankpledge/tithing) as vagabonds, many such people in major towns, such as Alan Bereman and Roger Byndedevel, turn out to have been destitute and may have been vagabonds as well. Sometime before 1287 these two men abjured Bristol, where they were found not to have been in a tithing and also to have been penniless.[17] On occasion a scribe will be more colorful if not more precise about the shadowy underclass among those facing exile. The abjurer might be a stranger *and* a vagabond (*extraneus transiens*).[18] He could be unknown (*ignotus*) because a coroner could not remember his name when it came time to enroll it.[19] One can imagine a disgusted official eyeing with contempt an otherwise unknown wastrel who he believed had no property worth his or the crown's time to search out and inventory. Such an official might not expect to be called to account for the administrative lapse of failing to record a vagrant's name. Another abjurer was described as a wandering scoundrel (*quidam ribaldus itinerans*), which registers this kind of official contempt.[20] Other vagabonds had behaved badly (*stulte gesserunt*).[21] Perhaps worse—to the English at least—some people who ended up abjuring had wandered deep into the English countryside or entered its towns from Ireland and Wales.[22] Men *and women* these various abjurers were, now otherwise unknown to memory, among them

Alice of Ireland, thief; Cicely of Winchelsea, thief; two nameless fool-
ish girls, thieves; Agnes, Robert's wife, accompanied by her husband,
thieves; Agnes, vagabond from Oxfordshire, abjurer from London,
thief; Sibilla of Ashbourne, Henry of Boyleston's wife, abjurers both,
thieves.[23]

Notwithstanding the caveat that not every assertion of poverty
may be accurate in detail, I am confident that the clerks could tell the
difference between haves and have-nots. Chattels were often valued
at trivial amounts, a few pennies.[24] Richard Mandeville, who abjured
in Northamptonshire in 1301 after confessing to thievery, owned but
a flail, a cap, and a coat that were worth valuing. The flail was estimated at a halfpenny and the cap and coat at one penny each.[25] As
one might expect, such chattels as impoverished abjurers possessed
were often limited to clothes, including purses, that had a small resale
value, and/or weapons—knives, staves, old swords. Four other abjurers from proceedings in Northamptonshire, Walter Alway, William
of Grendon, John Bird of Barnwell, and Richard Lubbe, exemplify
this. Walter Alway abjured for homicide. The inquest of 22 March
1318 found that he possessed two silver pennies and a farthing, a
coat worth three pennies, and a workman's apron he wore about
his waist and a purse worth, together, another penny.[26] William of
Grendon and John Bird of Barnwell were confessed murderers who
abjured on 10 March 1324; the inquest on their property noted that
between them they had one knife and two staves worth one penny.[27]
The same day, the thief Richard Lubbe gave up his six silver pennies,
a work apron, a purse, and three knives, altogether worth 2d.[28] One
could go on.[29]

The most deafening refrain is "no chattels," for it occurs everywhere in the sources.[30] It cannot be taken as definitive evidence of
abject poverty in every case. For example, when John of *Gildhousdale*
abjured from Yorkshire in 1361, the clerks wrote that he had neither
chattels nor lands, but they also noted that his wife Margaret had a
homestead (toft) valued at 4d. and several other bits of property.[31]
Taken together it did not amount to very much, but assuming that
John at least at some time in his life enjoyed harmonious relations
with his wife and was able to draw on her resources, it would be hard
to conclude that he suffered under persistent unrelieved poverty. It
is possible that his life of crime (he abjured for theft) alienated his
spouse and reduced him to living on his own and that this explains

the clerks' use of the phrase "no chattels." Or perhaps she threw him out and then he turned to crime to eke out his living. One cannot be sure either way at this distance in time. Nevertheless, it seems reasonable to suppose that abjurers said to have no chattels were, more often than not, closer to abject poverty, even if brought there by recent developments.

The other large group of abjurers comprised men and women of middling status and wealth. Even without other information, I have chosen to regard a rustic with a holding greater in extent than ten acres as middling, as in the case of John Brito, who abjured from Norfolk in 1249, thereby giving up his twelve acres.[32] These still small acreages are often broken down according to type, which, in turn, often confirms the middling status of the possessors. For some of the descriptions (meadow and pasture are instances) refer to property that was more valuable on average than ordinary arable. The Staffordshire inquest of 1294 describing Stephen of Bagnall's abjuration listed his property, fourteen acres, as twelve (arable?) along with two more which were meadow.[33] The Essex abjurer James Martel's fourteen acres of land in 1299 consisted of five arable, one more in meadow, and eight others of pasture.[34]

On occasion the acreage attributed to an abjurer's holdings is, by itself, sufficient reason to argue for his or her middling status. This is not to say that any individual abjurer was exploiting properties in ways that conduced to maintain the outward trappings of middling status. Just as celebrities now, even with gigantesque incomes, can fall into bankruptcy, abjurers' mere possession of good-sized agricultural holdings on the eve of their exile is no guarantee that they themselves or those holdings were flourishing. Indeed, something like crop failure, fire, or some other disaster could have been a factor in the crimes that led to abjuration. It does suggest, however, what might be called the holders' reasonable expectations or hopes about their quality of life. Thomas son of Goce represents the type: he had half a virgate (fifteen to twenty acres) at the time of his abjuration around 1224.[35] John of *Aundeville*, who abjured from Essex in 1236, left behind real property exceeding thirty-six acres in extent.[36] Henry le Petit also represents the type; he had a virgate (thirty to forty acres) along with four and one-half additional acres in Kent according to the assessors' inquest of his lands recorded on 13 May 1276.[37] There are any number of other examples.[38]

Those abjurers who possessed (or through a spouse had use of) a messuage as well as acreage apart from it, or rents from other properties, were also of middling status or expected, in comparison with peasants who lacked even ten acres, to live more comfortable lives. John of Bourne abjured in Lincolnshire; the inventory of his lands of 1289 made reference to his former holdings, a messuage and additional land.[39] William Sauvage was noted as having a messuage and seventeen acres in the *inquisitio* of his property completed in Essex on 10 November 1307.[40] The year 1311 saw the abjurer John Beche's property in Yorkshire reported as a messuage, five acres of arable, an additional acre of meadow, and a bovate (about fourteen additional acres) of cultivable fields. He paid a rent of 2s. 6d. for the five acres and an additional 5s. for the bovate.[41] Thomas Chaundelan of Gloucestershire and John Cobbe of Herefordshire each had a messuage and a virgate at the time their estates were inventoried (1293, 1308) for their abjurations.[42] Peter of Eling lived with his wife Joan in Hampshire on her messuage and from the issues of a virgate of land, which, the inquest of July 1285 discovered, was also hers by right.[43]

Based on the inventory of their landed property, the upper reaches of middling prosperity had been achieved, perhaps through inheritance, by Geoffrey, the son of William and the grandson of Henry of Conington; by Geoffrey of Knuston, who was a resident of Abingdon (then in Berkshire, now Oxfordshire); and by John Crok(e), to give just three examples. Abjuration obliged them to yield the lands. Geoffrey (William's son and Henry's grandson; the genealogical description may imply a lineage with local prestige) left behind two messuages, one with an acre appurtenant, the other with a half virgate appurtenant to it, all in Huntingdonshire, according to the inquest of October 1294.[44] The inventory record, dated 4 February 1331, for Geoffrey of Knuston, who the year before had killed his wife on a Saturday and abjured in Northamptonshire on the following Thursday, attested that by his exile he lost his two messuages and the half virgate and one acre attached to them.[45] John Croke abjured in Warwickshire. There he had property consisting of a messuage and three virgates. The inquest establishing this is dated 13 May 1294. A second inquest, enrolled on 28 April 1295, documented additional holdings that he was obliged to forfeit elsewhere in Warwickshire including a messuage and dispersed agricultural land varying in extent—four acres, sixteen acres, twenty-two acres, and two virgates.[46]

That abjurers had lands did not mean that assessors were indifferent to other forms of property—or that we can be. Those who held land could and often did possess noteworthy chattels and hold leases (chattels real) in the form of rents—all of which can be used to infer status.[47] An example of the first is the case of John, the son of Robert of Rothwell, who at the time of his abjuration had a homestead in Lincolnshire plus ninety acres of arable and one acre of pasture; he also had rents in the village of Ireby amounting to 8s. 6d. per annum. The inquest providing this information is dated 22 August 1313.[48] Townsfolk were perhaps more apt to have rents than both rents and lands, as in the case of Peter of Dalton, who abjured from York in 1236–37, ceding his possession of 16s. in rents.[49] Marsilia Sperlenge abjured at London in 1244, thereby forsaking rents that she had been collecting amounting to two marks.[50]

A few more examples: Staffordshire abjurer Robert, the son of Roger of Madeley, had six acres of land according to the assessment of 1228, but his chattels, which *might* have been worth several shillings, would bring him above the line dividing the poor and middling rustic. I use "might" because his chattels were valued together with those of another abjurer, his confessed partner in homicide, William son of Nobus, but the value attributed to the goods was considerable: 9s.[51] A certain Roger Germeyn had half a hide or homestead and a messuage in addition to chattels amounting to £8 17s. 6d. when he abjured in 1240–41.[52] Richard the son of Geoffrey Boleng of Thirsk, who abjured at London, was said in 1251–52 to have possessed two bovates (about twenty-eight acres) of land in Thirsk and chattels—sheep—worth 24s.[53] Enjoying a similar level of wealth was William of Postlip. He abjured from Gloucestershire on the Tuesday after Ascension in May 1297. The initial inquest revealed that he had goods and chattels worth 5s. and 2½d., but it also noted that his mother, Juliana, had a messuage. Evidence must have reached the assessors that this information was incomplete. A subsequent inquest completed in November of 1299 showed that he had a right in a virgate.[54] When John Parkwell of Northwell in Nottinghamshire abjured, to give a final example, he had to abandon his messuage and the curtilage or attached grounds worth 12d. per year. Twenty acres more were valued at the low rate of 3d. per acre per year, but it was noted that these were not in cultivation. He had also possessed two acres of meadow, which at 2d. per acre could not have been very good grass producers. Yet, he had sufficient waste (scrub for various uses, such as the pasture of pigs) to be worth 20s. per annum. Those of his chattels mentioned by name were a trough valued at 4d. and a table-top estimated at twice that.[55]

For several reasons it is easier to assess status from land holdings and chattels that are described in specifics (a trough, a table-top) than from a mere estimate of the value of the chattels, unless the last is very high, like the 55s. valuation for the belongings of Robert of Baldock, who abjured Staffordshire in 1252.[56] Among the reasons for caution is, first, that some estimates of second-hand goods were little more than guesswork. Second, one may suppose that assessments were often designed to undervalue the goods, permitting those who assessed and/or capitalized them either to rake off otherwise unacknowledged profits or, contrariwise, to avoid having to answer for shortfalls for overvaluing goods that fetched less than expected when sold. A third reason for the relative complexity of drawing conclusions from the estimates is that they were affected by inflation. The same chattels estimated at 2s. in 1200 might be valued at several times that amount one hundred years later. Or, put the other way around, an estimate of 2s. in 1320 cannot be taken as anything other than an indicator of very modest possessions; the conclusion for an estimate of this size in 1200 would be quite the reverse, given the general pattern of inflation. Of course, even the *general* inflation rate may provide an insufficient corrective in that it masks the variable rates of inflation for different kinds of land, commodities, and services.

The final and central challenge in inferring status from chattels is the problem of theft. One ought not to assume that strangers to a region, in particular confessed thieves, owned rather than plundered the chattels confiscated from them. This is explicit in the case of Robert le Blund. When Robert abjured for homicide in 1248, it was discovered that he possessed 40s. in chattels. But this sum was shown to have been stolen from the murder victim, a Scottish clerk named Gilbert. A certain Roger, the late Bishop of Carlisle's cook, the present bishop attested, had discharged the old prelate's debt by delivering 40s. of his own money to Gilbert. The present bishop asked for the money to be restored to Roger.[57] Restoration of money and chattels to those who had lost them was procedurally correct.[58]

The same doubt as to the ease of inferring status from chattels attaches to cases involving strangers. William of Langford, a native of Oxfordshire, abjured not from Oxfordshire but from London as a thief in about 1256; his chattels were valued at 2s.[59] We do not know whether any additional chattels were sought or uncovered in Oxfordshire. It was similar with John, son of Robert of Iver, another stranger to London, where he confessed to being a thief around 1266; he had in his possession chattels to the amount of 14d.[60] Who can say whether there were more back home? Or, again, consider the case of a Hampshire man, John, son of William le Muleward, who abjured in London for robbery in 1323: he had in his possession a gown and a green hood, together worth 18d. One could hazard that the expensive clothes confiscated from John were loot.[61] Even so, he may have had unknown chattels back home.

The case of Juliana of *Kyngton*, though involving a confessed day-thief, might or might not provoke similar suspicions. When she abjured in 1293, her chattels were valued at 2s. It is possible that they included stolen objects. Although she is not identified as a stranger or vagabond in Staffordshire, the identity of the King(s)ton which may account for her name is uncertain. Moreover, strangers who abjured from sanctuary were usually shown little leniency beyond the fearsome mercy of exile itself. Juliana, on the contrary, evoked the coroner's tender consideration. He commanded her to depart into exile, but he also allowed her to take along some of her own surplus clothing and shoes. Either he was attracted by her and yielded to the impulse, or his sentiment represented the reluctance of the community, of which he and she were a part, to demean her. Had she once enjoyed respect? If so, community sentiment got its comeuppance in the fine imposed on the village for failing to apprehend her before she made sanctuary—and the coroner's leniency placed him under a cloud.[62]

Evidence from abjurations for homicide is often inconclusive in determining status, too, because even if it was not mentioned directly, theft was often the occasion of the killing. Nicholas of Canterbury abjured, along with Richard of Canterbury, from Somersetshire, in or before 1243, for homicide. We know that his chattels were valued at 2s., which in theory might point to middling status at the time. Richard's were estimated at 6d.[63] However, if both men, though not identified as strangers, did hail from Canterbury in Kent and were vagabonds in Somersetshire, the argument in favor of Nicholas's middling status fails. The same is true for John Wyne of Cleeve, whose chattels were assessed at 18d. around the same time in Somersetshire.[64] One

William King might have been a Somersetshire man whence he abjured, but it is an argument from silence. The confessed homicide's chattels were valued at 2s.[65] One would not want to make an argument about status on such flimsy evidence.[66]

Would our findings be more satisfying if we set the bar for considering an abjurer to be of middling status higher, in multiple shillings if not quite as high as the estimate of Robert of Baldock's goods at 55s.? William *le petit* and his wife Margery abjured in 1243 or thereabouts from the county of Somerset for homicide, which, to recall, does not mean that theft did not figure in their crime. Their chattels were valued at 3s., which, if theft were not involved, would suggest a middling household. That William *le petit* was also identified as a miller lends credence to the inference.[67] Other cases present greater challenges. The chattels possessed by the Somersetshire abjurer John Osmund amounted to 4s. in value, but one guesses they included the sheep he had stolen.[68] Similar statements can be made for Clement the son of William of St. Botolph, who abjured from London in 1240–41, and for Henry of Ockendon, who abjured from the metropolis in 1258–59. Clement's chattels amounted to 5s., including two heifers he had stolen; Henry's also amounted to 5s., including two oxen he had tried to make away with.[69] Two London abjurers for homicide, Robert of St. Osyth (1236) and John the son of Richard of Baldersham (1260–61), as well as another Somersetshire abjurer, Richard Pinel (ca. 1243), each had chattels assessed at 4s. The first and third had confessed to homicide, the second to theft. It is unwise to infer these men's status and general well-being on the eve of their crimes or the status and general well-being of any number of other cases of abjuration for homicide and/or theft, with chattels assessed up to perhaps as high as 10s.[70]

Even forfeiting chattels assessed at 10s. or above is no guarantee that the abjurers in better times were of middling status.[71] As thieves they could have specialized in lucrative crimes such as horse theft or rustling in general, and been caught with the goods or money collected from intermediaries, women and men we know as fences.[72] Nevertheless, it is clear that high assessments do sometimes reflect the existence of comfortable households. Abjurers of this level of wealth were guilty of crimes of passion or other outbursts; they were not poor people driven to crime or professionals who made a life of theft and intimidation. Consider the case of William Aguillon, with chattels valued at one mark. Subsequent investigation revealed that a Yorkshireman might have owed him a debt of 35 marks, which points to William as a substantial member of his community before the unfortunate events that led to his abjuration from Lincolnshire in the mid-1220s.[73] More interesting is the case of John of Malton in 1324. He had established a household with his lover (concubine). Their somewhat irregular arrangement was nonetheless materially comfortable, judging from the value of their possessions, 32s. But John abjured from London for killing the man with whom he caught his lover having sex.[74]

The firmest evidence of status is explicit mentions of it, which, by a stroke of fortune, are not rare. Abjurers included haywards, millers (like William *le petit* above), shopkeepers, bakers, taverners,[75] and at the upper end a taverner turned mayor and even a physician,[76] just to mention a few. Several of these cases will reappear in future contexts. Men in minor orders, otherwise classified as clerks or chaplains, also appear.[77] In theory, those in major orders were ineligible for abjuration, having already the benefit of clergy.[78] (Other jurisdictions, Normandy for instance, did permit abjuration after degradation from the priesthood.[79]) But incidents involving clerks and chaplains were not always straightforward. Consider, for example, the case of William of Bugbrooke, identified as a chaplain. William was fornicating with another man's wife, when—so the story goes—he became wary and thought that he might be caught *in flagrante*. He leapt out of his lover's embrace and hid himself in a large storage chest, until it seemed safe to steal away. Fearing that he might have been seen leaving, he fled to a nearby church. It was the year 1270.

When the coroner came, he demanded that William confess his crime before being granted sanctuary. It was in the course of this conversation that the chaplain discovered that he had not been observed, that no accusation had been laid against him, and that fornication was not an abjurable offense. To his misfortune, what he had now confessed openly would become common knowledge, and, no surprise, he desired to escape his lover's husband's wrath. Nonetheless, the coroner followed the letter of the law. He would not confirm William's sanctuary unless he agreed to go to trial for a felony or admitted committing one.[80] (Not all such coroners were so scrupulous, though they ran the risk of being fined if their actions were found out.[81]) So William confessed to having stolen 8d. from the storage chest in which he had hidden. This was a just-sufficient amount to be considered a felony.[82] He was then permitted to abjure the realm. Either because William's status was queried after the fact (was he in minor orders?) or because no one claimed a loss by theft from the chest or because someone challenged the status of an 8d. theft as a felony, a further investigation was ordered into the case, but William spent twelve years in exile before it was resolved.[83]

One of the most prominent people to abjure was Thomas Weyland or, as the family, though of humble, even peasant, origins, came to prefer, *de* Weyland, the preposition being intended to imply gentle birth. It has been supposed that Thomas rose under the patronage of a magnate to become a royal justice in 1272 and to Chief Justice of the realm in 1278.[84] His income, from his salary, but, more so, from lands he had acquired before and during his time as Chief Justice, positioned him in wealth among what Paul Brand calls the "upper gentry."[85] Why he chose to abjure is a subject that can serve as the transition to a catalog and discussion of the crimes and suspicion of crimes which sent men and women into exile.

THE CRIMES SUSPECTED OF THE ABJURERS

Those who abjured did so after coming under suspicion of committing felonies, but the substance and number of offenses of which they were suspected or which they acknowledged differed from instance to instance. Thomas Weyland was slurred by contemporaries and therefore seen by early historians, who credited the testimony, as the very incarnation of judicial corruption. Paul Brand has shown that the best evidence does not support this characterization of Thomas. Nonetheless, he does accept that there is strong suspicion of serious misconduct on the justice's part, including tampering with the plea rolls.[86] It was not this misconduct that brought about Thomas's fall, but if suspicions of it reached Edward I, they may have prepared the way by weakening royal confidence in him. Whatever confidence was left eroded when an even more serious allegation arose: to wit, that without justification Thomas was insulating his servitors from prosecution after they committed a series of felonies. He knew of their acts, for which they would later be hanged, but he also did nothing to bring them to trial and, as Brand notes, may have harbored them until they were apprehended.[87]

When these suspicions were aroused, the Chief Justice was arrested. As a high officer of state, he was treated with some indulgence in the first instance and permitted to spend the initial night of his arrest in custody at his home in the village of Witnesham (Suffolk) in anticipation of being arraigned the next day at Ipswich, about six kilometers distant.[88] Seizing the opportunity, Thomas managed to escape and found asylum in the Franciscan priory at Babwell near Bury St Edmunds, more than thirty kilometers to the northwest. Further trying to thwart royal justice, he assumed the Franciscan habit there and was tonsured.[89] Officials did not violate the friary, but it "was blockaded on royal orders, and after two months, during which the friars were allowed to leave, Weyland was starved out and taken to the Tower. When parliament met, he was given the choice of standing trial, permanent imprisonment, or exile."[90] He chose to abjure the realm.

This was an extraordinary use of abjuration, for, though Parliament was a court, indeed the King's High Court, abjurations were most often local matters managed by coroners or other inferior officials. This instance comes quite close to political exile. Indeed, whenever one finds the direct intervention of the king in the initial phase of an abjuration (on the whole a rare thing), the process is likely to deviate from normal practice.[91] Notwithstanding the procedural distinctiveness evidenced in the case of Thomas Weyland, his actual crimes—harboring suspected felons, fugitives, or outlaws and escape from custody to avoid prosecution, each abjurable in itself—were common among those attributed to abjurers.[92] It is easy to find examples. Receiving criminals and their associates was the crime confessed by John le Stiward on the occasion of his abjuration in 1204.[93] Harboring a thief was the pauper Morkin of Enfield's crime, leading to his abjuration from London in the mid-thirteenth century.[94] And a case contemporary with Morkin's witnessed William le Pape abjure as a result of confessing to the same crime.[95] Those who harbored felons but were not saved by sanctuary, successful approval, or some other process leading to abjuration were executed. In a sensational case, Juliana of Elm Bridge sheltered her adult son Walter, a felon. Both were taken into custody. Both were hanged in 1284, she for harboring him.[96]

Escape from custody to avoid prosecution for another felony was taken as proof of guilt of the original crime, as people still often assume, and in the medieval period it was treated as a second felony requiring confession before abjuration.[97] Abetting a felon's escape was also a felony. A woman who abjured Somersetshire sometime before the end of 1243 was believed to be a she-thief (*latrona*), the female member of a gang that had been rounded up and incarcerated awaiting trial, but she had not been arrested as a thief herself. Rather, she was discovered trying to get food to sustain her comrades along their escape route. When she learned that she had been found out, she fled to sanctuary, after which she abjured for aiding the escapees. The events were notorious and led to the prosecution of the jailers for the escape.[98]

Of course, jailers ordinarily tried to thwart escapes, unless circumstances compromised them. In Bristol around 1287 three prisoners, two men and a woman, broke jail. One of the men and the woman made it to sanctuary and abjured. The other man was apprehended and hanged for the killing of the guard who had tried to stop them. Two other prisoners, a married couple, had abetted the escape, therefore enabling the killing, though they had not themselves managed to escape. Faced with the certainty of execution, they then tried to break jail again. The husband was caught and thereafter hanged as he was supposed to be, but his wife reached a church, from which she abjured.[99] If the jailers were fortunate and survived the desperate escapees, the possibility of prosecution stared them or the corporate authorities that employed them in the face.[100] It helped if the escapees were caught by others who joined the pursuit and executed justice on them by, say, beheading them. Then the jailer might receive a pardon.[101] Even before such possible turns of fate jailers sought preemptive pardons in order to overcome suspicion of and possible prosecution for complicity in escapes.[102] The English situation did not differ from the continental. In late medieval Valenciennes a jailer, under whose watch a prisoner escaped, himself fled to sanctuary until his friends could procure a pardon for his lapse.[103] Of course, on occasion suspicion of complicity, whether for venal reasons or from sympathy, was well-founded.[104]

I would not be surprised if an abominable reputation, a long history of bitter relations with neighbors, or strange behavior, combined with strong suspicion of criminal activity, led to a few cases of abjuration even without a formal indictment or a confession in sanctuary. This appears to have been the situation with Roger Carpicat in 1232–33. There was an unconfirmed suspicion of homicide based on circumstantial evidence, but he would not put himself on the country, which is to say, have a jury trial. The weight of the circumstantial evidence was sufficiently strong to get Roger arrested, but not strong enough to move the authorities to use measures to induce him to accept trial by jury. They hoped instead that someone would come forward and accuse him. At the period when this case was pending, an appeal of this sort would have led either to trial by battle or, if the parties agreed, to a jury trial. Roger's options were limited. Battle, being an ancient mode of proof, could not be declined without incurring automatic conviction. But to yield to the substitute, trial by jury, was the very thing Roger was trying to avoid. Of course, Roger, if he chose to fight, might best his accuser, and to be bested meant the conviction of his accuser for a false appeal of felony, itself a felony. So, the authorities were worried that no one would come forward. They stipulated that if no one did, Roger should be released, but that he still had to abjure and to pay ten marks up front for the privilege of doing so.[105]

Nevertheless, most of the evidence that might support the notion of genuinely wide flexibility in the offering of abjuration turns out to be misleading or inconclusive, since it comes from non-criminal records. Criminal records are very specific about the felonies of which abjurers after successful ordeals had been accused or to which those in sanctuary had confessed. If non-criminal records, such as those involving the disposition of real property, make mention of the circumstances of earlier abjurations, however, they tend to do so in general terms. So a certain William, the son of Alice, is said to have abjured for his badness (*nequitia*).[106] An abjurer named John of *Aundeville* foreswore the kingdom, it was noted in a different record, for his ill-repute.[107] I feel certain that the badness imputed to Alice's son was specific when he confessed in sanctuary, but it was unnecessary to specify his misdeeds in detail in a property dispute that recalled his abjuration. *Nequitia* was sufficient. And John of *Aundeville*'s ill-repute rested in a concrete abjurable act or acts, whose specificity again did not have to be inscribed in the Fine Roll that recorded a later payment touching the property of which he was once the tenant.

Without dismissing the possibility of flexible impositions of exile, it seems safe to say that specific crimes, felonies such as theft or arson or counterfeiting, stood behind almost all claims for or resort to abjuration.[108] Theft, indeed, was among the abjurers' most often alleged felonies.[109] It was a felony, whether the take was as slight as a bread box or two nice fish (in this case, hake).[110] Many of the abjurers from sanctuary confessed to far more extensive thefts. In rural areas but also in London, with its active markets, objects of choice included livestock: sheep, oxen, and cows.[111] Horse thieves operated in both country and towns.[112] Cutpurses, though town-based,[113] were attracted to rural fairs, too. Churches anywhere, but perhaps London's more so, were targeted by those who wanted to get possession of elegant ecclesiastical books or ornate reliquaries whose elements they could resell for profit.[114]

There were any number of female thieves who perpetrated such acts. It is possible that Agnes Daythef (the term means one who steals during the daylight hours) was so-called because she refused to steal at night, the contemporary definition that set burglary apart from other types of theft.[115] Whether or not Daythef was an epithet or (as elsewhere attested) a surname,[116] she was a vagrant who confessed in sanctuary to being a thief and abjured the realm from Oxfordshire in 1253–54.[117] In the mid-thirteenth century one also encounters in the records Emelota Latronissa (She-Thief), a Cornish woman, who abjured from Devon. Emelota She-Thief, no surprise, was a thief.[118]

Discovery of theft, whether the perpetrator was a man or a woman, was sometimes convoluted. A noteworthy case involved Richard Mandeville, who was playing a game with his brother in which each threw stones at a stationary object to see who could come closer, a variant of horseshoes or of the ring-toss game known as quoits. On one throw Richard accidentally struck his brother. The impact was hard, but was it lethal? Richard's brother later died; yet, the coroner's inquest did not link his demise to the accident. Why, then, had Richard fled the scene and sought sanctuary? We are informed that he did so out of fear. But why should he be afraid, except that he was regarded as a reprobate or that there had once been bad blood between him and his brother? When the coroner would not construe the death of his brother as a felony, Richard decided to come clean and confess that he was a thief. A possible scenario and my best guess are that he perceived the hostility of his community, surmised that some of his criminal activities might be uncovered or suspected as a result of the investigation into his relations with his brother, and decided to avoid the consequences by acknowledging his career as a felon and foreswearing. He abjured Northamptonshire in the spring of 1301.[119]

Homicide was apparently almost as common as theft as the background for abjuration.[120] On occasion, as we have seen, they were expressly linked.[121] There is nothing surprising in this, but a notorious instance occurred in 1252 when a burglary led to the (unintended?) murder of a child. The crime of child murder was as close to an unforgivable offense in the medieval popular reckoning as any. The law in this case nonetheless protected the confessed felon, who had fled to sanctuary, and permitted him to abjure.[122] It did so also in another troubling case of child murder involving Matilda Curteys. She abjured from thirteenth-century Devon after going on a rampage and hanging one Mariota la Prinress and after that a young girl named Matilda. The girl Matilda did not die straightaway. Hers was a lingering suffering before she expired. Matilda the murderess got to a church and was granted sanctuary and permitted to abjure.[123]

As one might expect from modern experience, domestic and family violence led to a fair number of homicides and thus abjurations in our records. Such was the case of one William who was the bastard brother of another William. The bastard fled to sanctuary after murdering his sister-in-law and abjured the realm in 1222. It was revealed in the process around the abjuration that the crime took place in the house of the half-brothers' father, where the woman was staying, and was abetted by a local squire (*armiger*) named Walter. On the one hand, Walter's connivance may suggest that the object of the home invasion had more to do with a dispute between the father and his bastard son and the latter's friend than with the unfortunate woman. On the other, it was she who had chosen to move in with her father-in-law while her husband went on pilgrimage or crusade to Jerusalem; it is possible that she did so in what turned out to be the vain hope of protection from the man who would later kill her.[124]

Cases of domestic violence can be multiplied. In mid–thirteenth century Exeter, two married women, one named Alice, the other Margaret, conspired to kill Alice's husband, Richard le Blunt. They were apprehended and convicted of the death. Margaret was burned, the penalty for abetting her co-conspirator's petty treason, but Alice was rescued on the way to the place of execution by a mixed group of more than ten men and women, including two chaplains. She managed to reach sanctuary and abjured, although a judicially convicted felon had no right to do so. She must have been a victim of terrible domestic abuse to merit a rescue of such daring and connivance by so many respectable people, including of course those who permitted her to abjure.[125] Though not describing a case of domestic abuse, this rare but expansive use of sanctuary is illustrated in a case from Devon in 1232 in which a deaf-and-dumb man achieved asylum after killing John Baldwin. (Baldwin, I believe, tormented him once too often. Someone must have helped the man to sanctuary.) How could he confess and abjure? No one in authority was comfortable about abjuring such a person into the bleak future of exile. So he was simply allowed to remain in sanctuary—for eight and one-half years. The gesture was generally accepted. At long last, however, word reached the king, and he intervened, whereupon the deaf-mute was allowed to depart sanctuary not for exile, but to occupy a room at the Abbey of Sherborne.[126] According to the letter of the law, he would have been arrested when he exited the sanctuary, having stayed there far beyond the prescribed forty-day limit.[127] But the authority of the king prevented this.

To return, however, to family violence, acts of abuse took many forms. The wife of Peter Crossbowman cut their son William's throat and threw his body in a cesspit. She abjured from Bristol ca. 1287.[128] Ernebald, a traveling thief from the Welsh Marches, was not married to the woman who was accompanying him, but however enduring or transitory their relationship, it came to a deadly end at a good spot for the killer, right in front of a church in London, which he ran into for sanctuary and whence he abjured in 1239–40.[129] William of *Yhade-fenn* of Wiltshire appears to have fled to Somersetshire after killing his wife; he abjured from the latter county sometime before the close of the year 1243.[130] John le Mazon's wife, Emma, abjured London after killing him in 1257 or 1258.[131] And Geoffrey of Knuston of Abingdon abjured Northamptonshire where he fled five days after he killed his wife in 1330. Her name was Felicia.[132]

Domestic violence of course included that done to servants. A homicide that accompanied arson is illustrative. The arsonist in this case was Roger le Sauser, who claimed that his act was meant to avenge a victim of abuse. He had intended to defend (*ad defendendam*) the honor of a servant girl by killing the man who had defiled her. After accomplishing his purpose Roger reached sanctuary and abjured the realm in 1240–41, but in his deposition before the coroner he also let slip that Inga, the servant girl, had instigated him. If she tried to flee, she failed. What is known for certain is that she was taken into custody, convicted, and executed by burning.[133]

To the great good fortune of the victims, not every attempt at murder was successful, although living with the consequences of being seriously wounded was sometimes an unpleasant prospect in the Middle Ages. In any case, mayhem in itself was an abjurable felony. An ugly case arose in 1238. John Lichefot and Richard of *Mistsel* had their bows with them and noticed two Jews—a man and a woman—walking along. Perhaps they had no intention of harming the couple, desiring rather the thrill of scaring them when they shot off their arrows. The Jews were wounded but did not die. John managed to escape to sanctuary and abjured the realm. Richard was less lucky. He was incarcerated after being apprehended in a violent struggle that left him wounded. He did not live long enough to go to trial.[134]

John Scrogaine of Bristol was another abjurer whose crime was violent, but not lethal. He stabbed his victim in the stomach with a knife and abjured from Somersetshire around 1243.[135] In 1260 a clerk who broke his victim's finger and inflicted other enormities also succeeded in being permitted to abjure the realm.[136] The dismemberment of a hand in 1267 and confession to it earned a perpetrator who got sanctuary the mercy of abjuration.[137]

Mistakes could be made. Was the clerk mentioned in the previous paragraph eligible for abjuration? An inquiry was ordered.[138] Was the private house of the Hospitallers in Bristol from which the thief Robert Fromund abjured a sanctuary? The answer upon investigation was no, and the borough was fined, put in mercy, for accepting it as such.[139] Milo Webley and Matilda of Dunhurst were convicted thieves. Milo was executed by hanging, but the municipal authorities in Bristol let Matilda abjure, simply because she was a woman. The whole thing was absurd and contrary to custom, the authorities claimed. The too-tenderhearted borough judges should have executed her: therefore, to justice on them.[140]

One could go on. Did William Godinogh commit an act that could be deemed a felony? He thought that he had done so when he struck Adam Coffin with a knife. Convinced that Adam was dying, he took no chances and fled to a church for sanctuary, was granted it, and abjured around 1225. But Adam did not die. In truth, he was only scratched, although the blood may have made the wound seem more serious. He recovered. In hindsight the authorities wondered whether they had made an error in judgment in considering William's act a felony rather than a trespass.[141] This kind of error and the remorse over it is even clearer from evidence brought together in an inquest in 1267 on the abjuration of one John, the son of Roger of Fincham. First, it was acknowledged that the coroner had erred in classifying the crime for which John abjured as a felony; it was a mere trespass. Worse, the inquest discovered that John was under age at the time of his abjuration and "out of simplicity and fear" had not raised any objections to what was happening to him.[142]

It was dangerous, as Roger's son found out, to look older than one's age. Boys could be malicious and dangerous, but they were still boys. Simon, the son of a certain Robert, had fallen in with the wrong kind of friends, a gang of thieves. Gangs, we know, could and did terrorize communities often enough. Moreover, when the authorities seemed to be close to striking, gang members sometimes decided to forestall capture by seeking sanctuary and abjuring en masse.[143] When Simon and his companions were confronted in 1214, they were not taken in the act, though plenty of other evidence raised suspicions against certain of them who were known thieves. Simon protested his innocence. Having the wrong kind of friends, after all, is no crime, albeit it contributed to the air of mistrust. He was sent to the ordeal of hot water, and like so many others he succeeded, whereupon he abjured the realm. None of this should have transpired. Perhaps Simon did not want to shame himself before his friends and went to the ordeal like a man. But later, perhaps through the agency of his family, it was discovered that he was under age (*infra etatem*), which is to say under the age of twelve.[144] Neither ordeal nor abjuration should have been inflicted on him.

The circumstances were different in the case of Walter Colier, but the outcome was also unjust. Walter ran over Maud, Clement of Woodstock's daughter, with his cart and killed her in 1251. (Referred to this way, as the daughter of Clement, Maud was presumably young and unmarried.) Walter took no chances because of factors that either raised suspicions that his deed was intentional or persuaded Walter that his neighbors would think it was. So, in fear he fled to a church, confessed to homicide, was granted sanctuary, and abjured from Wiltshire. Upon subsequent investigation, it was ruled that the death was accidental, but Walter's exile was by then a simple and perhaps tragic fact of his life.[145]

Fear—of many kinds—is a recurrent theme in abjuration cases. A new father whose daughter was but six weeks old took her for a horseback ride. It was a stupid thing to do and in this case almost unimaginable in its consequences. In restraining the baby so she would not bounce around and hurt herself, he accidentally cut off her air supply. Before long she was dead of suffocation. The man was frightened by what he had done and of whatever reaction he imagined there would be to it from neighbors and family. He fled to the church and confessed. Whatever he said in his deposition, including perhaps a self-imputation of gross irresponsibility, led the coroner to regard the death as felonious, not a "mere" misadventure. The grief-stricken father abjured the realm in 1242, leaving his wife to mourn her infant and face life bereft.[146]

THE FATE OF THE ABJURERS' PROPERTY

In the simplest scenario as well as the most common, any real property held by abjurers would go to the crown for a year and a day before being ceded to their lords; chattels would be retained or capitalized to the crown's profit. The principle was stated in law books, by judges in cases, and by clerks making records. Practice mirrored principle.[147] On occasion clerks employed phrasing—a year and waste—that emphasized the older principle that the king's receipt of the revenues was a vestige of his right to devastate, that is, to expropriate all the productive resources of a felon's property over the course of a year.[148]

Of course, either by design, law, accident, or fraud, not everything to which the crown had a legitimate claim came into its hands or did so with dispatch. Sometimes the rendering of accounts was slow and provoked a royal reminder to speed it up.[149] Or the king might agree to look into a counterclaim that he or one of his predecessors had granted away the crown's year-and-a-day rights by conferring a franchise on a religious house.[150] Looking into a counterclaim was no guarantee that the case would go the petitioner's way, as the abbot of Waltham learned in 1219. He had sent three men to the ordeal of hot water. They succeeded at the ordeal, but, supported by the jurors of four townships, he compelled them to abjure the realm. Royal officials then stepped in and challenged the legitimacy of the abbot's claim to exercise ordeal and abjuration proceedings in the case. They found that his actions were contrary to custom. The abjurers were therefore allowed to return and to have their property restored, if they could find sureties for a proper follow-up adjudication of the matter that had brought them to the abbot's illicit ordeal and abjuration in the first place.[151]

A little later, around 1228, London civic officials allowed a penniless murderer, Henry of *Buke* (Bukenham or Bukent), to abjure from the church of Saint Ethelburga in Southwark. Though confiscation of his property seemed at first to be a non-issue, the crown was suspicious and noted an error in the process. Southwark, though by and large *in* London, was not *of* London. It was in the county of Surrey, beyond the legal boundaries of London. That the municipality had acted anyway raised the possibility that its officials had an ulterior motive, for they must have known the limits of their jurisdiction. Crown officials launched an investigation to see if any property had been overlooked, but discovering that the abjurer was not in frankpledge, it became clear to them that there was no London real estate to be confiscated. They contented themselves with amercing the city's officials instead.[152] This case demonstrates the crown's perspicacity, at least in the environs of the capital, when there was even a hint of a suspicion that property belonging to it was being withheld.

Sometimes the king decided he would settle confiscated real property for the year and a day on a third party to whom he owed a favor, who was needy, or whose support he wanted to curry. These rationales were not distinct. Giving to a penurious religious house that succored the needy was a double act of charity and a means of sustaining or creating a political and spiritual alliance. Paying off a long-overdue debt was good for the soul, might help a needy creditor, and could reignite positive political relations. Cases such as these are frequent.[153]

Out of compassion the king might decline to accept a forfeited property because of the negative impact either on the party from whom the felon held it or on the felon's innocent wife and children. (As far as I know, the husbands of female felons never evoked such clement regard.) In doing so, the king's officers also had occasion to reaffirm the royal *right* to the property and the exceptional nature of the concession.[154] In 1240 a concession in King Henry III's name was made to the wife of an abjurer in Derbyshire of some of the movables that he had forfeited—cloth, utensils, two cow hides, and two joints of beef.[155] The king's men could have required recompense, as his agents had demanded in Bedfordshire in 1224 from the wife of the abjurer Philip Stettel, payment equal to the assessed value of the chattels, or in 1240–41 from Henry Germeyn, a kinsman of the abjurer Roger Germeyn, for his messuage and half a hide.[156] But the case in Derbyshire turned on the abjurer's wife's poverty. Probably motivated by the same circumstance, Queen Eleanor, acting on her husband's behalf while he was in France in 1262, ceded the chattels of one Kettel, an abjurer, to his wife Felicia of Deddington *gratis*.[157] The king duplicated his consort's act of grace the next year when he bestowed the chattels of the abjurer Robert of Balderstone on his wife, Cecilia.[158] In 1327 Edward II permitted Ellen, the wife of the abjurer John Sandre of Dover, to retain a messuage in the town, which should have reverted to the crown for her lifetime, but in return asserted the privilege of granting it to whomever he wished after her death.[159]

The king's men were also responsive to demands for redress when property that should not have been confiscated or forfeited did appear to have come by accident into royal hands, as, for example, when a possessor had no real right in a piece of land. At least they were willing to investigate the claim.[160] Often the property at stake had something to do with abjurers' wives being deprived of lands that were their own, not their husbands', as of right. Thus we read notes such as the following in descriptions and exclusions of property from confiscation in a number of inquests: Walter Colier, who abjured from Wiltshire in 1251, had no right in the messuage and land his wife Edith had inherited.[161] The crown acknowledged in a case from 1285 that it should not confiscate a messuage and virgate belonging to Joan, the wife of Peter of Eling, a Hampshire man who had abjured, because the property was hers by right and inheritance.[162]

Still, disputes—claims and counterclaims—over the disposition of property involving women (and men as well) were complex and recurrent.[163] Disputes over chattels were rarer than those over real property, but they arose. Ordinarily if the chattels of an abjuring thief could be identified as stolen and the owner located and verified, the authorities would return them to the victim.[164] But what if a lord, say, an abbey, possessed a privilege from the king to the goods of felons and fugitives apprehended in its bailiwick? Was the felon's loot part of his goods? It might be, depending on when the abbey made its claim: that is, whether it was when the thief was still in transit to abjuration or after he or she had foresworn the realm. Or perhaps it would be better to say that franchise-holders' lawyers were willing to argue the point with the crown.[165]

Additional disputes tended to crop up during and after the proverbial year and a day. For the crown could convey forfeited lands at any time rather than retain them for the interval.[166] It could cede the abjurers' lands to their overlords after the elapsed period and thereby harm other interested parties. In 1222, a poor woman named Felicia tried to get one-third part of nine bovates of land which she learned that the abbot of Rufford held. She contended that it was her dower and not part of her inheritance. She could not understand why the abbot of Rufford was holding her land and not paying her any rent. Her wretched husband, as far as she knew, had deserted her, but that was no reason that she should be denied her marriage portion. The truth was that her husband had abjured for homicide: she had never been informed, or no one had cared to tell her. Thus, in complaining against the overlord, she was making a false claim. The court acquitted the abbot of any wrongdoing and levied a fine on Felicia but, noting that she was a pauper, pardoned her.[167] Much the same happened with a certain Maisenta, who made a "false" claim against the prior of Bushmead in 1225 for one-third of three parts of one virgate in Bedfordshire as her dower, without realizing that she had been deprived of it through her husband's abjuration. There is no evidence that the fine imposed on her was forgiven.[168]

This harshness in the law, the dispossession of an innocent wife from her dower lands because of the abjuration of her husband, was corrected late in the century, in 1291 to be exact, and dower was walled off from confiscation.[169] No more would there be incidents such as that of Matillis, the wife of Andrew Pig. Matillis was angry over having been deprived of her dower, one-third part of one-half virgate in Buckinghamshire, after Andrew abjured the realm on a charge of theft. Like these other women, she protested and made what was in turn a false claim that the dower should be restored to her by right. The facts and the law were all against her in 1225, and she incurred a fine, but her poverty being recognized, she was pardoned.[170] As far as Matillis was concerned the judgment (if not the pardon) was unjust, and it did not stop her from bringing her opponent to court again the next year before a different panel of judges. The defendant cited the earlier decision and was acquitted. This time Matillis was incarcerated as her punishment, since she was still a pauper, too poor to pay the fine for a false claim.[171]

No doubt many abjurers wondered what was happening back home and lamented the difficulties they had caused their families and friends. Many a Felicia, Maisenta, Matillis, and unnamed daughter and son troubled the abjurers' thoughts and haunted their dreams. I doubt that, however grateful for their lives, they "abjured the realm, and merrily sailed away," as an erudite but quaint old history put it.[172] Yet, even if the adjective "merry" could describe a very few of them, they were in for a shock. They would face considerable difficulties from the moment they set foot in the lands of exile. But before telling this part of the story, let us get our abjurers to their ports of embarkation.

CHAPTER 3

The Journey Begins

ABJURATIONS OF THE REALM occurred throughout the kingdom, and residents of some populous localities, such as London or Bristol, could expect to see them and to hear of them far more often than elsewhere. But in most towns, even county seats, and in any and every village, to witness an abjuration was unusual; it was an event. A disreputable stranger was evading well-deserved punishment, saved by an unfathomable act of grace or even a double act—success at the ordeal and, by exile, avoidance of the people's justice. Or, a neighbor was leaving who might never return, perhaps amid tears from loved ones, disdain from authorities, relief from clergy wishing to rid their churches of a confessed felon, and curses from those he or she had harmed. In the shadow of the church doors,[1] the abjurer was to declaim, "Hear this, O ye coroners, that I will go forth from the realm of England and hither I will not return save by leave of the lord king or his heirs, so help me God."[2] Abjurers from other jurisdictions, such as Normandy, also had to offer such public vows.[3]

We may be misled by the early modern law book renderings or quaint translations of these oaths provided by recent authors who even now are influenced by such renderings. The truth is that the oaths, though formulaic, more likely came out of the mouths of un-lettered men and women speaking crudely in the manifold dialects of medieval England. Might this not explain why there are variant versions of the oath in texts produced within the same jurisdiction?[4] Perhaps something like the following invented dialog brings us nearer to the grittiness of reality. Eyes downcast or defiant, the voice weak or strident, the manner submissive or mulish, the abjurer stands at the authority's side:

"Now, take the oath, repeat it!"
"You heard me, I promise I'll leave the kingdom."
"Say it louder and say the kingdom of England and the coroners."
"I promise you coroners I'll leave England, the kingdom of England."
"And you'll never return again."
"And I won't ever come back unless the king forgives me."
"Say 'the king or his heirs,' future kings, if the king dies."
"The king or his heirs. I promise."
"So help you God! Say it!"
"So help me God."

Thereupon the abjurer received a public shaming, a civil anathema. At the rarest times this rite even included the torching of an abjurer's home, if the crimes committed were enormities, disgusting or perverse beyond "run-of-the-mill" felonies, which were terrible enough, and if the dwelling was situated in a place where a fire could be contained. Where it could not be effectively contained, simple destruction of the house might ensue. The publicity value of such acts could, of course, advantage the crown by showcasing its moral indignation at the most malevolent criminal behavior, but in general property was too precious to be destroyed. Confiscation alone, properly managed, had considerable positive publicity value and would benefit the king materially, as well. Authorities typically therefore loudly cried out their decision to confiscate an abjurer's property. And they might add, for effect and to endear the king to the community, that there was a chance their lord and master would donate as alms the proceeds realized from the confiscation.[5] The sequence of these acts—humiliation in the sight of the community, forced public oaths, confiscations, and, in extreme cases, acts of punitive destruction—had the intention of fixing in popular memory the baleful consequences of crime, even in the absence of punishment by mutilation and death. The scenes played out were to be an example and terror for generations to come (*ut nequicie eorum memoria futuris exemplum pariat et terrorem*).[6]

Banishment everywhere, it is safe to say, was made audible and visible—in striking, disturbing, fearsome, memorable ways.[7]

Such memorable events served a more prosaic but important ancillary administrative function in providing information to answer future questions vital to the fair and efficient regulation of social relations. For example, when a local landholder's heir came of age and should be entrusted with control of his landed property turned on the date of his birth, but neither parish nor civil registers of births or baptisms were being kept in a regular manner in our period. So witnesses were sworn and asked to recall the heir's birth with reference to a contemporaneous event or events whose time of occurrence could be checked against dated government records. There were other reasons as well, too many to detail, to search memories in this manner. The answers were by and large straightforward, and what struck local people as worth recalling is revealing: a juror said in one case that he remembered something because it happened *the same year that John Hardy abjured the realm from the church of Essendine in Rutland,* which had occurred, as cross-checking confirmed, in 1336.[8] I know quite well, said a juror asked about a date in another unrelated case, that the events at issue transpired *the year William Norman abjured the realm from the parish church of Desborough in Northamptonshire.* This was verified as having taken place in 1337.[9]

POINTS OF EMBARKATION

Abjurers quit the site of abjuration—in memorable ceremonies—but where did they go in order to depart the realm and how was the determination made? The evidence is ambivalent on whether abjurers chose their place of departure, had it imposed on them by crown authorities (considered an abuse by the author of the *Mirror of Justice*), or were, either by choice or assignment, encouraged to accept the port.[10] Documents of practice speak in some cases of the abjurers' choices, in others of their assignments; so far as I have been able to determine, there is no evident trend one way or another over the course of the long thirteenth century.[11] Options were limited, or there would not have been prosecutions on occasion for sending abjurers to the wrong ports. Should the coroner have given Lyme as the port for the abjurer William Flambord? The authorities who looked into it did not see a sufficient reason: therefore, the coroner was to be tried for malfeasance.[12] Was Portsmouth appropriate for William Barbe? The answer was no: to justice on the coroner.[13]

The documents, however, are not ambivalent on the favored port, whether chosen or assigned. This was Dover.[14] The king, in particular Henry II, may not have favored Dover for other purposes quite so much as his successors.[15] But for a multitude of reasons, in particular its proximity to the continent, it was a common embarkation site in the thirteenth century. Efforts in 1226 and as late as 1389 to compel travelers to the continent to embark on ships at Dover or a small set of seacoast towns that included Dover may have had more to do with being able to protect pilgrims efficiently in troublous times than with the economic centrality of the port.[16] But it was the long and vigorous tradition of travel out of Dover which made the government's choice of the town in 1226 and 1389 predictable.

Other ports chosen by or assigned to abjurers departing for Ireland or the European mainland included Bristol, Portsmouth, Southampton, Harwich, Bawdsey and so forth.[17] (Abjuration to Scotland was overland or, typically but not exclusively, via northern English ports until complications arose in the later Middle Ages.[18]) Usually these secondary ports—secondary with respect to the transport of abjurers—were enlisted when there were simultaneous multiple abjurations from a single location.[19] So one abjurer chose or would be given Dover while the other(s) had to use a different embarkation point.[20] In this way, many dreaded gangs and smaller criminal partnerships were broken up and hindered from reconstituting themselves later on. The practice was too common to reflect merely the idiosyncratic imposition of a few creative coroners *pace* J. Charles Cox. [21] But this gets us a little ahead of the story. We need to establish the literal and mental cartography of abjuration, the roads that abjurers followed and the fortunes and misfortunes they experienced on the way to port.

Depending in part on distance, abjurers were told how long they could take to get to the chosen port, and they were instructed as well as to how far they had to travel each day.[22] (The English system was not unique in this.[23]) Walter the son of Beatrice Gomme abjured from London and was allotted four days to travel to Southampton. At the end of the first day he was to have reached Cobham, at the end of the second, Farnham, and at the end of the third, Winchester. He

finished his journey to Southampton the following day. In the mean-
time his accomplice in crime, William le Soutere the son of William
le Lede of York, who also abjured, was assigned Dover. It was somewhat unusual for the authorities to give William three days instead of
four to reach the port, the interim destinations being Singlewell and
Ospringe.[24] Adam Nouneman and John of Great (or Little) Bedwyn
each received four days to reach Dover and Southampton when they
abjured from London.[25] William le Toliere of Manby in Lincolnshire
abjured London in the early summer of 1325 for Dover and parts
overseas. His partner in crime (homicide), Roger le Leche, the son of
Roger le Walshe of Wellington-under-Wrekin in the Shropshire-Wales
borderlands, abjured from the metropolis on the same day, but he was
allotted three days to travel to the port of Harwich (Essex).[26]

Quite out of the ordinary, one John of Wheatley, a homicide who
abjured in London in 1324, was permitted to choose Bristol. But the
authorities offered him a mere five days to travel there.[27] Each leg
of his journey was therefore almost forty kilometers. Had he chosen
Dover, it would have been closer to thirty kilometers per day. This
mattered when traveling barefoot, as abjurers did. Royal messengers,
who of course wore shoes, made about thirty miles per day when
traveling on foot.[28] So, thirty kilometers (18.6 miles) was a genuine
concession to the abjurer's difficult circumstances. For John to choose
instead to do forty kilometers (24.9 miles) a day—and he had to have
had some general sense of what he was letting himself in for—he must
have been motivated by a strong attachment to Ireland. Or perhaps
the sanctuary historian Cox is right that an element of vindictiveness
moved some coroners to mandate travel to very distant ports.[29]

Although the custom was to give those who abjured from London four days or at least three to reach Dover, the person's physical
condition or other circumstances could lead to a prescribed slacken-
ing of the pace. Thomas Weyland, the disgraced Chief Justice, was
allowed nine days from London to Dover in short stages of about
fourteen and a half kilometers per day, because his health had become fragile from being starved out of sanctuary.[30] How merciful this
was is a legitimate matter of dispute. The ailing Thomas made his
nine-day barefoot journey in the beastly month of February.[31] John de
Malton and his concubine Juliana Aunsel both abjured from London
and both were allowed to choose Dover. Yet, the authorities found
an alternative way to sunder the pair, by specifying notably different

timetables rather than separate ports. John got the usual four days to reach Dover going along the road to Dartford, then Newington, and on from there to Canterbury and then the port. Juliana had five days; she was with John until Dartford, at which point she followed a different timetable requiring her to stop at Rochester, Sittingbourne, and Canterbury before reaching Dover.[32]

By and large those who abjured elsewhere than London also traveled the sometimes long distance to Dover, although a few abjurers, for reasons not always clear now, obtained leave to depart from ports nearer to where they took their oaths. Thus, when Richard the son of Picot of Norton abjured in Oxfordshire in 1230, he obtained leave to take ship from far more convenient Portsmouth. That he was given eight days to reach the port instead of the customary four suggests that he, like Thomas Weyland, was in a bad physical state.[33] The system and the men who ran it intended a confessed felon like Richard to suffer a good bit on his last journey in England, but they had little or no desire that he die, a consequence that would oblige them to see to his obsequies and burial. The next year, William of Bray, who also abjured in Oxfordshire, received the same favor, a Portsmouth embarkation.[34] In 1356 the authorities assigned John Somer of Kent, who abjured from Suffolk, to the port of Bawdsey, within the same county.[35]

THE CIRCUMSTANCES OF THE JOURNEY

It has long been assumed that the abjurers, almost penniless, barefoot, bareheaded, and carrying their simple wooden crosses (much later these seem to have been colored white[36]) set out *on their own,* under the solemn and intimidating admonition not to leave the king's highway until they reached their destinations. The eccentric commentator who wrote the late thirteenth-century *Mirror of Justice* thought some of these provisions to be abusive, which is to say inhumane.[37] But his opinion on these matters carried little weight. Abjurers were garbed as penitents, their garments sometimes crudely marked with the sign of the cross.[38] They set out with a minuscule portion of their chattels, if they possessed any, or alms that were made over to them for the purchase of food for the journey.[39] Their counterparts banned from jurisdictions in France were treated in similar fashion: one set of instructions directed that they be granted nothing beyond a loaf, a pint of wine, and a bundle of sticks to make a small fire as they commenced their lives as exiles.[40] The English were also warned in express terms that if they deviated from the highway, they would incur the status of outlaw and be liable to immediate execution by anyone upon their capture—"quasi-legal lynching," in T. B. Lambert's words.[41] This last rule was mitigated solely by the necessities of nature. One could take a brief rest off-road to urinate and defecate in relative privacy or to shelter from a storm as long as one remained visible at least in part from the thoroughfare.[42] But the regulations in general were strict. Even when abjurers reached the interim stops on the way to their port of embarkation, they could not shelter themselves in inns or houses and could not have an extended rest, unless they were suffering dire debilitation.[43] Once again, continental practice was similar. The Custom of Normandy forbad any abjurer from remaining more than one night in any stopping place unless he or she was in a grievous state ([n]isi gravi et evidente infirmitate teneatur).[44]

What is untrue is that abjurers set out *by themselves*. In fact, low-level police-type officials accompanied them and kept them under surveillance.[45] This is implicit, first, in the provision under which abjurers might answer the calls of nature: to be visible from the highway was to be visible by someone in particular, not by a random traveler but by an overseer. It is explicit in a record pertaining to the thief and jail breaker Roger le Cornur, who abjured from Surrey in 1220 and was taken (*ductus*) to his embarkation point, Shoreham, in Sussex *per conductum quatuor hominum*, that is, with a four-man escort.[46] A few years later Henry *de Capella*, a royal sergeant, and two of his aides received 20s. for their expenses in accompanying the abjurer William Aguillon to Dover, another explicit proof.[47] To say that this evidence points to the exceptional rather than the regular use of transit guards is arbitrary.[48] What is exceptional is the crown paying for it—and thus notice of it surviving in royal records. It also fails to consider the routine and thus suggestive evidence of such practices in continental jurisdictions.[49] To say that the occurrence of escapes along the route supports the traditional scholarly opinion is insufficient. We have no idea of the proportion of successful escapees.

Yes, there were escapes. The four transit guards who led Roger le Cornur to port and the three who led William Aguillon must have had a large number of abjurers under their oversight, not just the two

individuals mentioned. For consider the fact that a great many crimes
were committed at times of the year when it was out of season for
maritime travel to the continent.[50] A man might commit a crime in
winter and stay the maximum of forty days in sanctuary but still be
kept in custody after his abjuration, the intent being to hold him until
the spring or summer when regular shipping between Dover and the
continent picked up in frequency. Such was the case with John Philpot
in the mid-fourteenth century. He managed to escape the town guards
of Northampton assigned by the coroner to guard him in the monastic church of Saint Andrew following his forty days of sanctuary. The
royal official's intent was to keep him in custody much longer.[51] A
native of Canterbury, John atte Loke the son of Richard atte Crouche,
committed an act of homicide at Christmastime 1321 for which he
abjured at London, but he did not begin his assigned four-day journey to Dover until 20 July 1322.[52] The most plausible explanation is
that John was held with other abjurers until Channel crossings were
frequent and a sufficient number of abjurers could be gathered for the
journey—not too large to be considered unmanageable by two, three,
or four transit guards, but neither so small as to result in an inefficient
use of these men, who were otherwise ordinary local beadles. (That
ex–Chief Justice Thomas Weyland's journey was not delayed in order
to fulfill either of these conditions is another indication of how "political" his abjuration was, and how inflamed Edward I was against
him.)

Did the authorities' best-laid plans sometimes fail? No doubt, but
it was not always because the number of transit guards necessary to
prevent escapes was being underestimated. John of Bradford, for example, abjured for homicide in Nottinghamshire in 1284, but the men
of Robert de Brus, the lord of Annandale, either prevented him from
beginning his journey or managed to get hold of him once he set out.
In their lord's name they laid claim to him for another felony, that of
severing the hand of one of Robert's yeomen, committed in the Brus
liberty of Annandale. Lord Robert thought or pretended that he had
a right to have justice done on John, despite his abjuration, but the
crown was not pleased by the nobleman's reluctance to release the
abjurer from prison so he could make his way into exile.[53]

In a way this John was lucky. At least Robert de Brus did not take
summary vengeance. Not so lucky was another John, John Dobyn,
who abjured the realm in Reading for homicide in 1241. Soon after

he set out, relatives of the victim frightened him by raising the hue and cry and pursuing him as he fled. Whoever was guarding him either chose not to try to rescue him for fear of the overwhelming force or was constrained by the need to control other abjurers in the party. When John was caught by the victim's kinfolk, he was taken to Charlton, not back to Reading, and there accused of homicide. The local authorities entertained the charge, having no evidence that he had earlier abjured for the crime. The local bailiff and representatives of Charlton and the surrounding townships decided to try John as if the hue and cry had been in pursuit of a criminal caught in the act.[54] As Frederick Pollock and Frederic William Maitland wrote, a man caught in the hue and cry "will be brought before some court (like enough it is a court hurriedly summoned for the purpose), and without being allowed to say one word in self-defence, he will be promptly hanged, beheaded or precipitated from a cliff."[55]

Although frightened, threatened, and abused, John Dobyn must have struggled to protest that these men could not do justice on him, because he had already abjured. The local authorities did not take him at his word and hanged him anyway. When royal officials got wind of the story (perhaps from the transit guards) and followed up, they were incensed. They may have been impressed by the audacity of the claim the locals made to them, but they were not persuaded by it. It was, the locals said, the custom in the fee of the abbot of Reading, where the church from which John abjured was located, to limit the protection of abjuration. The inviolability of abjurers' bodies lasted as long as they traveled within the abbot's franchise. Once they passed its bounds, they were fair game for vigilantism. It comes as no surprise that those who claimed this absurd defense of their actions were amerced.[56]

A Huntingdonshire abjurer whose name is now unknown and who is said to have opted to leave the kingdom from Dover in 1267 did not even have the summary trial of John Dobyn. Not far from Sudbury in Suffolk, his enemies, who had been following at a distance, saw their chance and made their move, inflicting terrible punishment on him for his crimes. They "assaulted him with swords and wounded him in the heart, so that he fell at once. Afterwards in the king's highway outside of Sudbury, they decapitated him with an axe." Leaving his dismembered body on the royal thoroughfare where he was supposed to be safe during his journey was a ritual affront to the mercy of abjuration and thus to the royal majesty. And it provoked the expected response.

The crown issued an order to track down the pursuers and bring them to justice.[57] I do not know whether in this difficult period of post–civil war guerrilla disruptions in England anything much came of the supposed royal wrath.

Around 1342 an abjurer by the name of Philip Hodynet, who was assigned Dover, was said to have been caught off the royal highway. The bailiff referred to in the case, his transit guard, had laid a plot in which he induced Philip under some pretext to deviate from the highway. He was preparing an excuse for exercising his own summary justice on Philip. Fortunately, he did not have the full opportunity to pull it off. An observer's suspicions were aroused and the plot was interrupted. Thereafter Philip was allowed to put himself before a jury where he pleaded coercion to leave the highway on the part of the bailiff. There turned out to be enough supporting evidence to suggest that Philip was telling the truth, and he was saved from court-ordered capital punishment for the alleged attempt at escape. The victory before the jury also saved Philip from the summary fate the bailiff had intended for him. This was all very well and all very good, though it must be added that it had no effect on Philip's abjuration per se. The sheriff of Staffordshire saw to his restoration to the royal highway for the resumption of his journey to Dover.[58]

Genuine attempts at escape that succeeded were abetted on occasion by abjurers' friends and neighbors, who rescued them, hid them, and gave them sustenance. (French officials faced the same sort of problems with their *bannis*.[59]) Whenever the English crown concluded that local authorities were complicit, either by not delivering the escapees or by failing to inform on them, there was the devil to pay, with the emphasis on pay. Several townships are known to have suffered the punishment of royal amercement for these offenses.[60] Understandably, unsuccessful escapes had severer consequences for abjurers. In the spring of 1276 a hayward named John, the son of William of Westfield, abjured for theft from the village of Houghton in Bedfordshire. The transit guards were natives of Houghton, including one William, who took his surname from the place. On his way to Dover the hayward tried to make his getaway, but the men of Houghton led by William pursued him, raising the hue and cry for additional aid. They caught him. They beheaded him.[61]

John the Franklin committed homicide in Cirencester in the county of Gloucester in 1287. He fled and was outlawed, but for whatever reason he risked his security further by returning—further, I say, because being an outlaw was already a precarious status. Matters did not go well. He found it expedient to seek sanctuary in a Cirencester church, where he confessed to the homicide and flight. Officials then permitted him to abjure. But the truth was that he did not wish to leave England or even his local *patria*. He risked his life again by fleeing the route that was assigned him; yet, he did not choose the life of an outlaw this time either. He once more sneaked home. Spotted, he was pursued by a posse from nearby Erlingham. They apprehended him, and, as in the previous case described, they beheaded him.[62]

This was all quite legal, as was the treatment meted out to the confessed robber John of Ditchford. On the day that he abjured from the parish church of Wooton in Northamptonshire, the first day of spring in 1322, he tried to make his escape. He threw down his penitent's cross as he fled from the royal highway, but the pursuing guards were dogged and in time overcame him "until he was beheaded while still fleeing." They left him where they had caught him and went back to report on their work. The coroner directed them to retrieve John's severed head for a special purpose: to wit, for transport by representatives of the neighboring four townships to the royal castle at Northampton as proof of justice well done.[63] It was, to repeat, all quite legal, and all quite memorable, too.[64]

This is not to say that the exercise of capital justice on captured escapees was encouraged heedless of all other circumstances. This is a bit tricky. For the men whom I have called transit guards, it was an obligation to enforce the king's peace and exercise justice on would-be escapees. But what if the runaways eluded the guards and the news spread? Any tramp, though innocent, might arouse suspicions, leading to vigilante justice and in its wake the crown's retribution. The colorful and unchanging rhetoric of bearing the wolf's head masked practices that became less esteemed with every instance in which it turned out that an innocent person had been targeted. Better to let a magistrate decide and follow the prescribed procedures. In the special commissions to deal with rampant crime, known as the London Trailbaston trials of 1305–06, there is a case which evokes this set of considerations. Word had spread that an abjurer had escaped his initial pursuers after abandoning the route to Dover. A furtive-looking wanderer was espied and suspected of being that man, but restraint was exercised. Spared immediate beheading, the suspect was taken and delivered to the authorities for considered judgment. This fortunate reprieve, if one wishes to call it that, did not save him in the longer term, however, for in the course of the inquest, his judges did determine that he was the escapee and in consequence handed him over to the hangman.[65]

A happier ending awaited one Walter Haket, who abjured from Worcestershire in the summer of 1233. It appeared that Walter was reconciled to obeying the command not to break away from the king's highway as he headed off to port. Then, all of a sudden, he made a dash toward the woods. Later he proffered an explanation: something had struck him as suspicious, something requiring instant action. So, not taking time to explain himself, he pursued a man whom he recognized as a notorious criminal. Barefoot though he was, Walter caught up with the man and in the course of the confrontation killed him. These facts, having been reported to those who had been in pursuit, were reported to the king, whose initial response was ambivalent. No abjurer was to flee the king's highway without permission; yet, Walter's action could be construed as justifiable in the circumstances, for the man whom Walter pursued was in truth an infamous felon. The abjurer's family and friends pleaded; they offered ten marks to buy a pardon for Walter. The crown agreed, bestowed the pardon, forgiving his flight and setting aside his abjuration, and as an additional act of grace restored some of Walter's chattels.[66]

Notwithstanding the happy outcome for Walter Haket and the relatively few instances where successful escapes can be documented in the whole universe of tens of thousands of abjurations, there is every reason to believe that the presence and charge of transit guards, together with the fear of consequences from victims' kin and friends, were sufficient to discourage most abjurers from making last-ditch en-route efforts to avoid deportation. One other piece of evidence strengthens this inference. It should be recalled that branding of abjurers was virtually nonexistent in thirteenth-century England but common on the continent, for across the Channel the abiding fear was that exiles would easily make their way back along myriad roads to the jurisdictions that expelled them. When this happened the authorities needed to be able to identify them as recidivists. But the absence of branding in England suggests that there was not much apprehension that the poor human dross they intended to deposit in France would escape en route to the port of embarkation or ever have the means to return over sea to the island kingdom once they left it.

Branding was perhaps an option but it was not considered a necessity in English sensibilities of the time.

AT THE PORT

The brunt of the evidence therefore suggests that most abjurers arrived at their ports of embarkation without adventures, albeit with fear never far from their minds and rather the worse for wear given the circumstances of their journeys. And most, as we know, arrived at one port in particular, Dover, where they had to stay until taking ship to France. Where were they "housed" in the interval? (I do not believe that they treated "the beach" as their "resting place," the claim of one otherwise perceptive scholar.)[67] I shall argue later that Dover Castle, the imposing emblem of royal authority in the port town, served this function, much as the Tower of London, another imposing medieval edifice—or rather, set of edifices—was enlisted to hold more than one thousand exiled Jews who were awaiting transport to Normandy in 1290.[68]

Upon being immured temporarily, the abjurers, I believe, relinquished their crosses to the transit guards who had accompanied them to the port. The latter would have returned home with them (as blessed objects) and given them back to the churches where the abjurers had obtained sanctuary, so that they could be stored in the sacristies or in a cabinet until needed again. It is not likely that such simple artifacts, despite the important role they played in protecting the abjurers' lives, have left much of a trace in medieval church inventories, which tend to enumerate precious, elaborately crafted objects—sacramental vessels (chalices, monstrances [ostensories], cruets, and patens), altar cloths, reliquaries, ornamental and processional crosses, and the like.[69] On occasion, however, I have come across continental inventories which make reference to small lots of undescribed crosses which might have been used and reused by abjurers there, although it almost goes without saying that portable crosses served multiple needs (Holy Cross Sunday and Palm Sunday processions being two).[70] These inventories, like one from Millau dated 1271, otherwise specify the decorative aspects of the artifacts surveyed, including ornamental crosses.[71] So, it might be worthwhile to do a systematic search of English ecclesiastical inventories. An alternative theory is that abjurers from England kept the crosses until reaching their port of entry across the Channel. It has been presumed that possessing such an object, given their quasi-penitential garb, would have aided the exiles in soliciting alms.[72]

For most abjurers this would have been the first—and last—time they ever saw Dover, its castle, and the chalky cliffs that give the location such a distinctive mien. The castle's imposing presence was still a somewhat new sight in the early thirteenth century, for the structure had been enhanced in a building campaign completed late in the reign of Henry II (1154–89).[73] As Charles Coulson has observed, "[d]onjon towers preceded and long outlasted the twelfth century. Henry II's 'keep' at Dover (1179–88) is of them all the grandest."[74] It has been deemed in another scholarly analysis, "preeminent."[75] Yet, maintaining its greatness and preeminence was no easy task. The castle needed frequent repair, as voluminous records for the allocation of funds for labor and materials such as iron, lead, steel, and timber indicate.[76]

A constable governed the castle.[77] Contingents of royal guards protected it and performed other related tasks such as keeping tabs on the building repair materials that were delivered to maintain the castle works (*opus*).[78] These guards were provided in part through direct employment and payment by the king.[79] The town of Faversham, or rather the abbot of Faversham and those living in the town who held property of the king, also provided guards—sometimes in a begrudging manner but as an obligation of their tenure.[80] Indeed castle guard service at Dover was owed by many entities in the region and beyond.[81] In times of war or credible threats of war or invasion, as in 1204–5, mercenary troops supplemented the regular guards. Their wages appear in the instance referred to on the Pipe Rolls.[82] These rolls also provide abundant evidence of large purchases of food, fodder, and military equipment.[83]

Dover Castle also had containment areas, secure facilities sufficient in size to hold prisoners of war during the French invasion under Prince Louis in 1217.[84] These are the same facilities referred to as the "king's prison at Dover" (*prisona regis apud Dovor'*) in some sources and were used for the incarceration of both common criminals and political enemies.[85] Available holding areas were so extensive that they could double as muster sites for whole companies of armed men during wartime—civil or foreign.[86] All of this leads to the conclusion that there were ample facilities in the castle to accommodate any number of abjurers as they awaited transportation—and plenty of security.

I am aware that this opinion, granted the special dignity accorded Dover Castle, will not meet acceptance from every scholar, but I am not persuaded that there is a better one.[87] True, the obvious alternative to the Castle was another substantial building, specifically a church. But is it likely that churchmen would have desired or could have been coerced to shelter the whole range of felons in the abjuring population who passed through Dover, including murderers and thieves? Were clerics prepared, even with their vocation as caretakers of the poor and vulnerable, to feed and nurse these criminals, many of whom after their harsh journey to the port were suffering physically? If worship services continued during the interval of their presence, how could the church deny entrance to friends and kin who had followed the abjurers to the port? What sort and level of security were required to prevent the former, if they got in, from rescuing the latter or, alternatively, to prevent the abjurers' enemies from seizing them? Surely, the imprecations of the authorities would have been insufficient. After a few threats, the most conscientious priest or sacristan might stand aside to save himself and simply curse the intruders under his breath. Finally, even in the absence of friends, kinfolk, or enemies to compromise the situation, was there sufficient security to prevent escapes, and would not any number of potential escapees, many of whom were thieves and all of whom were desperate, have tried to help themselves to church plate or other treasures that could be fenced later on? (Many of them had abjured for the crime of robbing churches.) These questions and observations raise, to my mind, insurmountable doubts about churches as holding pens in Dover.

The town and port of Dover had their own institutions and facilities, separate from those of the castle, which to a considerable extent were relevant to the experience of the soon-to-be exiles, relevant because of the temporary presence of some of their kinfolk and friends at the place.[88] The town was mid-sized for a medieval settlement, with a population estimated at 3,000.[89] It had an intimate political relationship with the crown as one of the Cinque Ports (on which, more later), but it nonetheless had its own sophisticated and independent-minded municipal government.[90] It was a government administered by the "barons of the port," men who were jealous of the town's liberties and dignity and of their own, and were willing to contest and even defy royal claims they thought to be excessive, inappropriate, or unjustified.[91]

The provision of welfare was an important aspect of urban life in Dover. There were two hospitals.[92] One, Saint Bartholomew's, a daughter house of Dover Priory, had come over time to concentrate on ameliorating the lives of lepers; the other, the Maison Dieu, served a more diverse clientele.[93] There was also the so-called "almonry gate of Dover Priory," a site where servants of the priory offered victuals for the poor and for pilgrims heading abroad or recently arrived in England to visit its shrines or return home. Both Saint Bartholomew's and the Maison Dieu engaged in similar kinds of almsgiving.[94] The latter complained in the year 1315 that another obligation the crown was imposing on it, the housing and sustenance of government pensioners, was undercutting its ability to give traditional charity. The clerk who received and endorsed the Maison's petition characterized the complaint as an excuse, while acknowledging as was typical that the matter was for the king to decide.[95]

It is altogether reasonable to suppose—and indeed it has long been accepted in the literature—that the poorest of the men and women who chose to follow their abjured kinfolk and friends into exile appealed for alms and succor from the institutions listed, money that would be useful later on when, having debarked on the continent, they could at last freely communicate with the abjurers.[96] It could also be expected that prosperous travelers would, before they took ship, distribute alms to the poor, including the abjurers' followers, as a gesture that might please God and garner His protection for their own voyages. When Edward III's sister Eleanor departed the port on 5 May 1332 en route to her wedding at Nijmegen, she responded by offering one penny each to twenty-four poor folk who sought alms from her (*pauperibus petentibus elemosinam*).[97]

Dover, like all ports, was notorious rather as a cesspit of sin than as a philanthropic center of poor relief or a locus of religiosity, though the description "port of dogs" may evoke the abjurers frequently passing through rather than the permanent residents.[98] Stereotypes aside, there was another side to its reputation. A female recluse, Emma of Sheppey, resided immured in the castle church of Saint Mary for decades in the thirteenth century.[99] In a practice not unlike that followed in France, royal alms of one and one-half pennies per day were supposed to be allotted to her each quarter. (The contemporary continental rate of six French pence per day for holy hermits, to judge from royal payments to Saint Yves of Brittany, was identical in value.[100]) Emma's alms from the king were often in arrears, once for 450 days, another time for 320, the equivalent of more than 56s. and 40s. respectively.[101] The delays in payment had more to do with Henry III's political and financial troubles than with indifference; and locals would not have let her go hungry. The support of anchoresses bestowed a patina of virtue on donors, who were rewarded with highly valued intercessions, and their presence imparted a modicum of holiness to the places where they made their abode, a fact that may help explain the diffuse practice of naming places with reference to the *quondam* residence of a recluse.[102] The self-sacrifice of women such as Emma of Sheppey was in general a living critique of the greed and chicanery that were believed to accompany commercial life.[103] Some time after Emma passed away another hermit came to dwell on the outskirts of the port and filled the void created by her demise. Embarking for the continent, the aforementioned Princess Eleanor favored this recluse with a gift of 6s. 8d. (half a mark) on the day of her sailing.[104]

During the time sojourners were at the port, there were also the formal institutions of the Catholic faith to help sustain them.[105] The four parish churches were dedicated to Saint Peter, Saint James, Saint Mary, and Saint Martin, the last of which, known as Saint Martin-le-Grand, served three parishes. They addressed both the inhabitants' and the transients' spiritual needs, including the provision of significant alms in the form of food to those in need. (Saint Mary's did so on seven special days in the year, including the Feast of the Nativity of the Blessed Virgin, 8 September.)[106] Another church of Saint Mary existed in the castle, and the priory church was dedicated to Saint Martin. Ordinary travelers would not have been given access to these two, apart from the alms at the gate of the latter. But the lesser clergy of the castle church, perhaps in concert with parish clergy,[107] could have attended to the immured abjurers' most serious spiritual and, to some extent, material needs. Moreover, this sacred space would have provided the continued penumbra of sanctuary, which may be what is meant when prescriptive texts speak of a return to sanctuary in port while awaiting departure. Many scholars note this without explaining it.[108]

For travelers who had a little extra money, such as some of the ab-jurers' friends, there were also inns and taverns.[109] The owners of four taverns are known by name (John Giles, Henry Blank, John Monin, and John Atte Halle) from the mid–fourteenth century Dover Chamberlains' Accounts, but there were many more drinking houses in the town, not counting hostelries.[110] At these establishments troubled travelers could drown their sorrows, at least for a while, and even indulge in amusements that helped pass the time.

Perhaps more important, people in need of information could seek it both from parishioners in and about the churches and from local patrons of the taverns, information that might be valuable later on when they reunited with their exiled loved ones after the journey to the continent—or, if feasible, illegally even before. There were important things to learn. Where in Dover could travelers exchange coins to get the kind of money that was used in France? Where was the best place, after they reached France, to make contacts with people who could facilitate finding shelter and work for them and for their kinsmen or friends who had abjured? Had anyone heard any stories about what life was like for an exiled Englishwoman in France? They might pose a guarded question to people thought to have contacts with or be members of the "criminal underworld," which Henry Summerson describes as "a milieu inhabited by professional criminals with their own operating methods, meeting places and skills":[111] Might there be ship captains who could be persuaded, by whatever means, to smuggle their kinfolk back into England or employ them in the piracy for which many Dover shipmen were noted?[112]

One may doubt whether the modern saying, "Dover, a Den of Thieves," which lays stress on at least one aspect of the underside of life in the port, has its remote ancestor in the pirates and the unscrupulous men and women who peddled information to distressed travelers for more than it was worth.[113] But many Dover shipmen in the Middle Ages did exploit unfortunates by charging exorbitant fares. The practice is well attested because wealthier travelers who had the means and time to protest it did so.[114] Con men got their hands on good English pennies from travelers in exchange for what the former said were sound French coins but which in reality turned out upon arrival in France to be worthless tokens and counterfeits. This was a longstanding problem. On 20 May 1299 Edward I tried to address it by licensing trustworthy "merchants of Lucca to keep a table at

Dover for changing money of persons coming into the realm or going out."[115] The context—it comes as no surprise—was the concern over false money.[116] Never ceasing were efforts like Edward I's to regularize currency exchange.[117]

But the crown addressed a myriad of other problems at Dover and throughout the Cinque Ports, the cluster of Channel settlements and their limbs (smaller, dependent settlements) which girded the southeastern coast.[118] To serve as constable of Dover Castle or as warden of the Cinque Ports was to enjoy prestige but also to incur burdensome responsibilities. Scholars have sometimes written about the latter as if they were limited to the wartime services of the ports. This in turn has given rise to the common belief that the Channel ports played a crucial, perhaps the most crucial, role in England's medieval naval warfare, a contested opinion in the specialized scholarship.[119] What is true and what at first sight may seem to support this assertion is that wartime naval obligations were recorded in meticulous detail, as, for example, in a charter of Edward III of 1342, and that the material, financial, and labor obligations owed the crown, given the size of the settlements, were heavy.[120] Whether or not the Cinque Ports were the backbone of naval defense in wartime, however, remains uncertain. In the period of the thirteenth-century peace with France, it is also irrelevant. In this interval their ships' primary use was to ferry nonmilitary travelers (including high-born men and women) and trade goods to and from the continent. It was a bustling industry and had scores upon scores of ships and barges at its disposal. Something like a fleet was assembled from the local carriage alone for the transport of Eleanor, Edward III's sister, and her entourage across the sea for her marriage to the count of Guelders in 1332.[121] It was this industry far more often than war service that demanded the most attention from royal and municipal administrators.

Part of this industry serviced abjurers. After they arrived at Dover, the abjurers were supposed to wade into the sea and plead for transport. Accounts and evidence differ as to the height the water was to reach—to the knees or neck. They differ too on how long the abjurers should cry out. One treatise alleges that they should continue to do so until a ship picked them up.[122] These apparent discrepancies reflect, I think, changes over time, rather than simultaneous practices and, thus, confusion. In any case, entering the sea was read as confirming the confessed felons' willingness to adhere to their promise to leave the kingdom. It was as if they were checking the shore and searching the horizon for ships that would bear them away into a new life.[123] To analogize it with baptism and its hope of salvation is suggestive. More so, as it is worth thinking about the symbolism and perception of this obviously liminal rite in the broader penitential character of the journey from abjuration into exile.[124]

I have some doubt, however, that these ritual prescriptions were expected, let alone followed every day at Dover, even though they were perceived by authorities to have value in humiliating the abjurers in the sight of kinfolk and friends who had followed them and could observe the spectacle at a safe distance. "[A]bjurers," it has been remarked with justice, "were well guarded" in Dover.[125] But organizing the transfer of groups of them from the castle, even smallish groups over the short distance to the shore, and monitoring their wading would require close supervision and the occasional rescue of the old, weak, and sick. (Think of how lifeguards need to be alert.) Allowing the "prisoners" to spend time outside the castle walls was also an invitation to the strongest or most desperate of them to make one last attempt at escape. (There would have been less danger of this at the alternative ports, which handled one or only a few abjurers at any one time and that seldom.) This is not to say that movements back and forth between Dover Castle and the shore were never undertaken, but the occasions for them were also limited. In general, abjurers arrived in spring and summer. Outfitted ships were everywhere, and the ships *meant for them* were always or soon at the ready.

To be sure, problems on occasion compromised travel. Gales, heavy rains, and thick fogs slowed or even prevented passage to the continent or the return of passenger ships from it. Bracton seems to have had Dover in mind when he acknowledged that storms and contrary winds caused delays for which there was no alternative but endurance.[126] A great storm in 1287 wreaked havoc on all the Channel ports, and "Dover was forced to rebuild its harbour."[127] Sometimes political and economic disputes interrupted the flow of seaborne traffic. The *Annales Paulini* record that during the spring and early summer of 1324 a dispute came to a head "between mariners of Dover and of the French port of Wissant, so that ships did not ply the sea route between them or provide passage for a long time."[128] This was important to the abjurers' story because Wissant was the principal

destination of ships from Dover to the continent in the long thirteenth century, indeed until England's seizure of Calais in 1347 during
the Hundred Years' War.[129] Yet, when the weather calmed or disputes
were settled, regular shipping recommenced.

It was the authorities' expectation that the time spent awaiting embarkation would be short. Record evidence makes clear that
no abjurer was supposed to stay in Dover—or in any other port of
embarkation—beyond the coming of the first favorable tide.[130] Twice
a day tides come in and go out, but whether a tide is favorable is a
more complicated question, for conditions beyond the cyclic gravita-
tional pull of the moon (and its alignment with the sun) can affect the
height of tides. Surges in the Atlantic may accentuate a high tide in
the Channel by as much as a meter, and strong winds can prevent the
full recession of an ebb tide.[131] Still, every competent sailor and fisher-
man had a sensible knowledge of the tides in the main shipping season and expected them to be favorable unless affected by out-of-the-
ordinary meteorological or oceanic conditions. When those abjurers,
the unmarried lovers John of Malton and Juliana Aunsel, departed
London for Dover in June of 1324, the first having been given four
days to the port, the latter, five, a reasonable person would expect that
John would take ship before Juliana arrived.[132] Little did the abjurers know—little did even London coroners know—that a shipping
embargo, the result of a commercial dispute, had just been imposed
on passage between Dover and Wissant that would last all summer.[133]

THE SHIPS AND THE CONDITIONS OF TRAVEL

Sooner or later abjurers boarded the ships designated for them. A few
scholars have assumed that they had free choice in booking passage,
but this assumption raises insurmountable problems, well evidenced
in the following quotation. "It seems difficult to believe," one scholar
has written, "that any but an exceptional few [abjurers] could find
means of transport [in a free-choice system]. They had no money, and
could not buy a passage. They could not all work their passage across;
and least of all the women. What became of them?" Faced with the
conundrum the author of these words, William Bolland, came up
with an explanation even more difficult to accept: that the authorities
were indifferent. Having rendered the abjurers penniless, miserable,

and vulnerable, they had forced them to migrate to Dover and hang around in the port with no means of passage available to them. This, he speculated, was considered punishment enough—sufficient atonement, in his phrase—whereupon the abjurers were allowed with a blind eye from the authorities to drift back into English society! "It seems as though something of this kind *must* have happened" (my emphasis).[134] Of course, this is nonsense.

A different scenario is equally farfetched, namely that the abjurers could compel shipmen to ferry them to the continent.[135] Dover shipmen were many things, but they were not likely to be compelled by the mere sight of a ragtag abjurer or two to offer a ride to France free or in return for unskilled labor, as R. F. Wright supposed.[136] Yet there is a nugget of truth in the use of the word "compel," if one identifies a different and far more plausible compeller. Like many ports (Sandwich is an example), Dover owed annual ship services to the king, twenty vessels in number (known as *passagers*), each with twenty-one men, for fifteen days per year.[137] This was three hundred ship-days. If two ships operated each day, with one going out of Dover to Wissant and one returning, then the season would last for some hundred and fifty days. This maps well onto the period from late spring, the end of May, to very early autumn, the beginning of September, the height of the shipping season. The crews were of sufficient size for a few men to double as guards, oversee the exiles (given my earlier calculations perhaps never more than a half dozen or so on any one voyage), and prevent them from seizing the ship during the hoped-for short journey to the mainland, which was about forty kilometers and took a few hours under ideal conditions. Persistent contrary winds and even brief squalls could delay departure or after embarkation blow the ships far off course and lengthen the distance and the time considerably. Contrary winds delayed Anselm, the archbishop of Canterbury, for two weeks from taking ship at Dover for Wissant—and he had every inspiration to depart in haste, considering that agents of his enemy, King William II Rufus, were trying to (and did) overtake him.[138]

Any of the abjurers' friends and family members who were determined to link up with them on the continent would have made their own arrangements for cheap passage in other ships. What was in it for the captains and crews of these other ships? So far as I can tell there was no sharp distinction between cargo ships such as *La Nicholas*, which transported grain, and the many other kinds of Channel craft.[139] At least, the carriers were comfortable with ferrying both goods and people. Captains and crews craved profits and went to dangerous lengths to obtain them.[140] One way to boost profits was by the crowding of low-paying passengers into cargo ships and the overcrowding of passenger ships. Entrepreneurship was a notable quality of shipmen.[141] This did not always express itself in reputable activities. It would be wonderful to know more about the culture and practices of shipmasters and crews.[142]

Many ferrymen were honest and forthright or at least commanded respect. Cok Bretun was a crewman in the 1260s and once had the prestige job of transporting a cardinal-legate and his entourage on the sea lane from Wissant to Dover. Cok rose to become a baron of the port of Dover by 1278 and proved himself to be a stalwart defender of the town's privileges, while also being well-esteemed by the king.[143] Other ferrymen, on the contrary, including those who dealt with poor passengers needing to get to Wissant, such as the abjurers' friends and kin, were unsparing. The crown sought to regulate the ferrymen's fares and prevent the intimidation they sometimes practiced on susceptible travelers as well as bring an end to the overcrowding of people, animals (horses), and goods, which put the ships at risk, but which also promised the handsomer profits I have hypothesized to the mariners upon successful journeys.

The rolls of complaint are long and grim. One observer noted in the summer of 1315 that the shippers "load more horses into the ship through greed, so that at times some of the horses are crushed to death, and others maimed and killed: for whereas a sufficient load would be a ship containing 24 horses, or 26, they put 40 and at times 50 horses in a ship."[144] One wonders what the cramped human passengers remarked among themselves as they suffered similar conditions aboard ships christened with such reassuring yet misleading names as *La Charité*, *La Gracedieu*, and *La Trinité*, *La Welyfare*, *La Bien Venu*, and *De la Swan*, *La Jolivette*, *La Lightefote*, and *La Blithe*.[145] Surely the bitter irony struck home to someone. Surely. Yet no one could afford to linger much on ironies. A new and unpredictable world awaited everyone in Wissant and beyond.

CHAPTER 4

Life among Strangers

WISSANT IN THE LATE NINETEENTH and early twentieth century was the home of a small artists' colony. The painters employed an Impressionist-like style in their sea- and dune-scapes and as a group have come to be regarded as a distinctive *École de Wissant*. Today the village of about one thousand inhabitants also bills itself as the surfing capital of France. Exploitation of the sand and gravel deposits in its vicinity in the early twentieth century created artificial pools and lakes that have by now morphed into refuges for wild waterfowl and favored destinations for ecologists, birders, and nature buffs. The dunes and dune grasses, the pretty cottages with the gorgeous seasonal blooms in their flower boxes, and the colorful and beautifully maintained fishing boats, whose crews take their catch according to so-called authentic traditional practices, give the village a quaint appearance to tourists. Cafés and restaurants offer hospitality to transients. The Chunnel train reaches France very near the village, which makes it all the more accessible to summertime daytrippers from Britain and the French interior.[1]

The Wissant of the High Medieval past is invisible in the modern tourist village.[2] Yet, until the mid-fourteenth century, the settlement (referred to occasionally as *britannicus portus*) was a critical link in maintaining regular contact between England and the continent.[3] It was an emporium, with ties to cloth towns such as Ypres.[4] It was also a staging point for troops needing naval transport.[5] And in times of peace and war it was the regular site of embarkation and disembarkation for diplomats.[6] The village, because of its importance, was home to an English agent and his staff who represented and tried to protect their countrymen's interests there.[7]

Clerical and lay elites, including religio-political exiles such as Thomas Becket and members and would-be members of the English royal family, passed through the village in their travels to and from the continent.[8] In 1243, two of the latter were Sanchia of Provence, the bride of Earl Richard of Cornwall, Henry III's brother, and Sanchia's mother, the dowager countess.[9] On 7 December 1265 the English queen, Eleanor of Provence, Sanchia's sister, used the same sea lane when she came to England after one of her visits to the continent.[10] A very big present from the king of France to the king of England, an elephant, was also dispatched from Wissant to Dover in 1255.[11] Even when parties from Dover traveled to other continental ports—as when the entourage of Princess Eleanor (Edward III's sister) for political reasons disembarked at Sluys for her wedding trip to Nijmegen in 1332—they could choose to ship their baggage via the shorter and cheaper route to Wissant and to return via Wissant whenever they had occasion to visit to England.[12]

Well-off medieval travelers, like their present-day counterparts, would have found a layover of a few hours or even a day or two in the village quite tolerable, whether they were waiting for companions to arrive or sitting out a period of contrary winds, as the constable of France had to do on his way to a mission in England around 1330. He ran out of money in the interim but sent a two-man delegation to Saint-Omer to borrow a hefty sum (400 l.p. [French pounds]) to carry out his mission.[13] As there are a few tolerable inns now, there were acceptable ones then in which he could have stayed and eaten and drunk his pleasure. (There were bad ones, too; the variety of inn and tavern cultures in medieval France was staggering.[14])

Singers of the time sang French songs of adventure in the better venues to entertain guests and to earn money from travel-weary clerics and diplomats resting up in these establishments. Aristocratic English crusaders, many of whom knew French and were in transit to and from the Holy Land, had perhaps a special fondness for these songs. In time their own tales of derring-do found their way into a few of them. Wissant itself figured at least in passing in the songs.[15] It also was mentioned in a number of epic tales, including the *Chanson de Roland* and the *Commedia*. In the *Chanson* Roland's doomed last battle is said to have been accompanied by the earth's groaning and shaking throughout Charlemagne's realm, from Mont-Saint-Michel to Sens and from Besançon to Wissant.[16] In Dante's poem the reference is to the dikes that crisscrossed the landscape from Wissant to Bruges and had their analog in the pilgrims' hell-scape in the opening to Book XV of the *Inferno*.[17] It has been suggested that the Italian polymath Brunetto Latini, who knew the region, described it to the Italian poet and inspired his usage, although Gladstone argued rather cleverly that Dante actually visited the region on his way to England.[18]

Diversions for the lower-class exiles who disembarked at Wissant did not extend to the posher entertainments or the respectable establishments of the medieval village. In general, indeed, the newly arrived Anglophone abjurers and whoever among their friends and family had followed them into exile could not understand songs, stories, or much of anything else expressed in sophisticated chanted or spoken French, and they comprehended nothing of the *patois*, a variety of Dutch, which was the language in general use among natives in the village and the region. So, to the English exiles beginning life anew on the continent Wissant was a disorienting, dispiriting, and altogether wretched hole. If they did stay long enough to pick up a few words of Dutch, they might have learned that the village took its name from the ubiquity of the "white sand."[19] They might also have learned that the name was a homophone of the local word for the stinking polecat (*wissantz*) which must have been a wonderful stimulus for rank punning among natives.[20]

To the archeologist Louis Cousin, who carried on excavations in the 1850s, and to most other post-medieval observers down through the end of the nineteenth century, Wissant was almost as depressing as it was to England's medieval exiles, but for different reasons.[21] The bustle of the High Medieval site was long past by the time these observers took the measure of the shrunken village. The port had always needed regular and costly maintenance (good surf made and makes a bad harbor), but locals failed to undertake it in the later Middle Ages, in large part because of the fiscal and military crises of the Hundred Years' War (1337–1453).[22] Moreover, the year 1346 saw Edward III, in the full pride of his victory at Crécy during the war, destroy Wissant's port facilities for military and commercial reasons.

Wissant, a burgher of Valenciennes wrote a little later, "was completely destroyed by fire" along with a vast hinterland (*fut Wissant toute brûlée et tout le pays environ à VI lieues en tous sens*).[23] The historian of the Hundred Years' War Jonathan Sumption, drawing on such reports, describes Edward III's work as one of obliteration; the nineteenth-century local historian Pagart d'Hermansart concluded that the English troops wrought a consummate work of destructive dismantlement of the harbor facilities.[24] Daniel Haigneré, writing in the late nineteenth century, would have thought these conclusions hyperbolic and the contemporary reports themselves perhaps exaggerated, since there is evidence that Wissant somewhat bounced back and was once again operating as a significant port ten or fifteen years after Edward III's attack.[25] Nonetheless, the destruction was severe. Thousands of charred beams were soon covered by blowing sand and lay hardening into faux ebony for centuries, periodically harvested for use in building repairs.[26] Thousands of parchments, long lamented by local historians, perished in the sacking of the village and the other settlements in its vicinity: "Où sont les archives de la ville de Desvres, celles de la ville d'Étaples, de la ville d'Ambleteuse, de la ville de Wissant?" Haigneré asked himself rhetorically.[27] Far more records were destroyed, one might add, than were available for that fate during the Allied raid that recaptured the then-fortified village in World War II, its defensive armaments serving as part of the German occupiers' Atlantic Wall.[28]

Soon after Edward III's successful attack on the vulnerable unwalled village had "left Wissant to solitude and sand," the walled town and port of Calais also fell to him in 1347, these after a long siege.[29] Calais had already emerged as Wissant's competitor in the late twelfth century, but it gained a privileged place in English commercial and military calculations after its capitulation, the exile of its French citizens, and their replacement by Englishmen.[30] In any event, Wissant's position as the principal embarkation point for seaborne travel to England and the usual disembarkation point for travelers from Dover never recovered.[31] In hindsight, citizens came to imagine that this inexorable deterioration had actually had no human cause. Rather it was explained that the choked and ruined harbor of "old Wissant was buried by the moving sands in a single night," or so this popular story was reported in the *Westminster Review* of 1862.[32]

The village, whether before 1346 or in its truncated state thereafter, was inhospitable and depressing in wintertime (when ex–Chief Justice Thomas Weyland arrived) and remained so until well into the twentieth century. Despite some natural geographic shelter,[33] it suffered from the frequent winds and driving rains and sleet off the Channel that blew the abundant eponymous white sand and choked the streets with it. In order to compensate for their lost income after the 1347 rise of Calais, unemployed and underemployed ferry crewmen switched to fishing in order to supply inland settlements, but in the end this resulted in the overexploitation of the once-thriving herring stocks. (The species was wistfully recalled in Wissant as the Holy Herring). This aggravated the village's decline.[34] The squat one-story houses with thatched roofs and impoverished occupants possessed no charms for Louis Cousin, *archéologue et savant*, in 1850. And the fishing boats, in the absence of the tourist trade of today, were tired-looking work vessels in various states of decrepitude when he saw them, dragged up from the seashore to the dunes and anchored to prevent their being battered and washed out to sea pending preparation for future use.[35]

THE ENGLISH OFFICIAL PRESENCE IN WISSANT

In peacetime in the period of our principal interest, that is, before the middle decades of the fourteenth century had passed, Wissant, together with the other Franco-Flemish Channel ports, was a center for the export of cloth to England from Picardy, Artois, and Brabant and, when there was also peace between the French and the Flemings, from Flanders, of which the Wissant region was a linguistic extension.[36] It was preferred because the crossing was so short there, and merchants wanted to avoid the danger of the longer sea journeys from the more northerly French and Netherlandish ports.[37] When war between France and Flanders undermined this path of exchange, the English were predisposed to sell raw wool and purchase cloth at Antwerp and Mechelen (Malines), which were east-northeast of the French coast, or to use Brabantine merchants or other intermediaries to do so.[38] Such practices, sometimes crossing the line into smuggling, piracy, and embargo breaching, provoked Frenchmen's retaliation, which also skirted legality. Although less common during the thirteenth century, these actions and reprisals became an important and growing bone of contention in foreign relations throughout the fourteenth.

Time and again English merchants called upon their government in petitions to Parliament to intervene and speak and act in behalf of their interests.[39]

So, a great variety and quantity of business relating to official travel and commercial interests came under the purview of the appointed English liaisons (somewhat analogous to modern-day consuls, but by contemporary rank, royal sergeants) in Wissant. The chief liaison in the mid-thirteenth century, to concentrate on one example, was Eustace Bricun.[40] He, his predecessors, and his successors needed to be attuned to local mercantile and maritime politics in and around Wissant, and to that end the English crown provided him with the means to get around the region on horseback, as is implied by the payment of ten marks from the royal treasury on 16 November 1257 for a mount of his that died in the king's service.[41] He also had to be attentive to French royal policies and activities that might affect commercial relations and to politics back home in England, all of which could compromise his ability to do his job.

Eustace, we know, also acted in more sensitive situations for the king during Henry III's troubles with his barons, between 1258 and 1265, when the latter dominated the country or at least contested Henry's rule. An entry on the rolls for 12 February 1264 shows him, for instance, standing surety for Henry's promise to repay 100 marks borrowed from Saint Mary's of Boulogne during one of the monarch's trips to France during the crisis. It was stipulated that if the loan were not repaid by mid-Lent, Saint Mary's or its proctors were not to harm Eustace himself, a provision that prohibited them from detaining his physical person, although his goods were liable to distraint and potential forfeiture.[42]

Despite his good work of this sort on the king's behalf, Eustace was susceptible, like so many of Henry's supporters during the years of troubles, to interruptions in the wages to which he was entitled and to a general insufficiency of pay. On 5 May 1262 the crown directed that he receive ten marks per year drawn on the Exchequer at the Michaelmas term, 29 September, for his maintenance, but it was noted on the roll that this payment was low and that the king wished to augment it in the future.[43] Moreover, less than two weeks later (18 May 1262) Henry acknowledged that these ten marks, if my understanding of the record is correct, were more like a gift to cover part of the arrears of the royal sergeant's pay than the regular wage itself.[44]

Still, when generosity was possible, the king was inclined to show it, this itself being another, if indirect, indication of Eustace's loyalty and good service. On 18 June 1261, an order was issued to buyers for the king's wardrobe to provide a robe as the king's gift to the royal sergeant.[45] On 18 January the next year an order was given to deliver another ten marks to him, as the king's gift, for a trip Eustace had to make back to England.[46]

POLITICAL AND JURISDICTIONAL AUTHORITY IN WISSANT

The activities of the English royal sergeant of Wissant were constrained by indigenous authorities who exercised paramount, if divided, control. The village was in the county of Boulogne. The count exercised his jurisdiction and his economic rights in the port per se through a *prévôt* and *vicomte* (viscount) who answered to the count's regional administrator, the *bailli* of Boulogne.[47] These officials had much to do, including dealing with English interests in the county. For example, Canterbury Cathedral priory enjoyed a long and beneficial relationship with the comital lineage. Over the years the priory had been granted immunity from tolls at Wissant and other privileges bestowing freedom of travel on its monks, message bearers, and other servants.[48] These costs could otherwise be considerable for aristocratic and ecclesiastical entourages, and their collection fattened the Count of Boulogne's purse.[49] The organizational structure or hierarchy (*bailli-prévôt* and *bailli-vicomte*) of the officials who oversaw all these matters paralleled that of the French royal administration in Normandy and elsewhere in the north.[50] Also, just as the great lords often shared jurisdiction with lesser lords or had limited jurisdiction in many of their towns and villages, so too the count of Boulogne shared power with the mayors and aldermen of the "commune" of Wissant. The very word "commune," used in contemporary records, together with the village's possession of a corporate seal implies a substantial level of self-government and judicial authority exercised by the permanent residents of Wissant.[51]

This was instantiated in the size of the old village hall, far larger than structures similar in function elsewhere in the rural settlements of the region, because, as scholars have supposed, the business of a major port (indeed *the* major Franco-Flemish port for entering from and returning to England for at least a century and a half) made it necessary. The antiquarian Jules Lecat considered the edifice, which was later razed, an imposing relic of the medieval period. Based on his reading of an early modern deed involving its conveyancing and the still-current local lore of the mid-nineteenth century, he concluded that as long as the building existed it evoked the "past"—and, one might add, long lamented—"grandeur of the old village." Ernest Deseille, the historian who communicated Lecat's notice to the *Société académique* of Boulogne-sur-Mer, concurred.[52]

To guarantee that one's requests or demands had a chance of receiving a positive response in our period from both the authorities who operated from this building and others who were headquartered elsewhere meant soliciting all parties. One sees the truth of this inference from a criminal proceeding in 1266, which has the added benefit of a focus on an Englishman. In that year an English barber by the name of Richard of Rochester (*quidam Anglicus, qui vocabatur Richardus de Roucestre, barbitonsor*), who had been a boarder in a house in Paris in the bailiwick of the abbey of Sainte-Geneviève, fled to Wissant after being accused of murder, intending to take ship to England, perhaps by appealing to his countryman Eustace Bricun to help him secure passage. But he was apprehended and surrendered to local beadles before he could depart. He would have been better off to abjure France and be repatriated to his native land. The abbey of Sainte-Geneviève abjured (*fourjura* in the original) similar miscreants the same way.[53] This time, however, the abbey could and did claim the right to adjudicate the fugitive for the homicide, because it had high justice in its bailiwick in Paris.[54] In transmitting this claim to the authorities in Wissant, the abbey officials took no chances and addressed their letter to multiple recipients, including the *bailli* of Boulogne and his *prévôt* in the village, as well as to the mayor and aldermen of the commune.[55] The request was received with favor, but rather than insist on Richard of Rochester's extradition, the abbey as a matter of convenience allowed the authorities in Wissant to execute sentence on the English fugitive, who in remorse (*super periculum anime sue*) and voluntarily, it was alleged, had confessed to the crime (*spontaneus, non coactus, recognoverat quod dictum murtrum perpetraverat*). He was drawn on a hurdle to the village gallows and there hanged. (The abbey of Saint-Geneviève of Paris exonerated the owners of the boarding house in the capital, who had at one time been suspected of the murder, and also by right the abbey took possession of the movables the executed Englishman had left behind.)[56]

Besides providing information on the nature and possession of judicial authority in Wissant, this case reveals the existence of a gallows in the port for the execution of capital justice, a significant privilege in the High Middle Ages and another instantiation, like the village hall, the seal, and communal status, of the importance of the port. One could deduce from the same case the existence of a prison or holding pen, where Richard of Rochester was kept while negotiations were going on between the abbey of Sainte-Geneviève and the various authorities in Wissant. Explicit evidence of prison capacity in fact exists already from a somewhat earlier period. There were facilities available or made over to hold English captives of war around the time of the failed French invasion of England under Prince Louis in 1217.[57] Nothing is known now of the nature of this structure or structures, whether they were imposing or ramshackle, but they were extensive since they could have served as a prisoner of war camp. It would not have been difficult for the exiles from England to learn from English-speaking captains and ferry crews the location of the holding pens that awaited them if they ran afoul of local beadles.

One other building besides the village hall which would have impressed the newcomers was the church of Our Lady, also known as the church of Saint Nicholas because one of its major chapels was dedicated to him.[58] Already an imposing edifice in the thirteenth century, it was refurbished and enlarged in the course of the fourteenth. The extant church still has a remnant of the fourteenth-century building at its core along with a fifteenth- or sixteenth-century choir, despite the reconstructive impulses of the post-medieval period, including the rebuilding of the nave in 1835.[59] The sanctuary was "considerée comme le secours de sombres," an asylum for those fallen into deep depression and despondency and needing religious refreshment.[60] This reputation may have originated from mere association with Wissant's tiny contiguous hamlet of Sombres, in which the church was actually situated.[61] But it was appropriate at the least to the presumed state of mind of the transient population of abjurers and hangers-on. It was at and from this church that the needy exiles and those who followed them would have appealed for alms and advice—which estate managers were hiring? would they be recruiting at the portico of the church?—as a few later ones would do from the religious institutions at Calais.[62]

Nicholas, with the Virgin Mary the co-patron of the church at Wissant, was venerated in part as the protector of sailors and in part as the benefactor of children in general and girls in need of money to marry in particular. He was also noted for his succor of prisoners.[63] This cluster or elements from this cluster of associations, and the expectations that went with them, may have solaced a few of the more prayerful among the abjurers, as they did pious people in general, such as the pilgrims in transit at the port.[64] The priest of St. Nicholas's altar was indeed overworked by the care these folk requested. Men and women competed for his comfort and support. In 1273, the native seamen of Wissant, who felt a particular fondness for the saint and his altar and resented sharing the priest's attention with other worshippers, tried to secure a second celebrant to minister to their needs exclusively.[65]

From the early twelfth century Wissant's social welfare landscape also included a hospital (Saint-Inglevert) with brethren who had received lands near Luton in Bedfordshire and Brill in Buckinghamshire from Henry II early in his reign, as is attested in sources of both English and French origin.[66] The king, it has been suggested, may have provided the endowment in gratitude for the hospitality furnished to him during one of his trips to the continent or, perhaps more likely, as part of the arrangements accompanying the reestablishment of peace after the long period of unrest in England and on the continent during the Civil War (1135–53).[67] The modest English hospice that took root on the endowment remained dependent on Saint-Inglevert until the fifteenth century. During this long period the Buckinghamshire house was reckoned an alien priory, existing as a daughter house of the continental establishment under the same regulations as a great many other local English ecclesiastical establishments which men in the retinue of William the Conqueror had offered as gifts to their families' continental abbeys after their victory in 1066.[68] One could imagine the inmates of Saint-Inglevert, in gratitude for their English endowments, giving alms to needy English folk, such as the exiles and their companions, although I have no found no explicit evidence of this.

The close economic relationships between governmental authorities in Boulogne and England and among institutions on both sides of the Channel make the idea of cooperation in the matter of accepting English exiles plausible. Through his spouse, King Stephen in the times of trouble in the first half of the twelfth century clearly cultivated interests in Boulogne, and his penchant for exiling his enemies is well-attested.[69] Other kings of England were less intensely committed to nurture relations with Boulogne,[70] but undoubtedly as a residual effect of Stephen's good will, local comital and communal authorities on the continent tolerated, as we have seen, a registered English government agent and his staff in Wissant. And other kings of England at least continued to cultivate institutions like the hospital of Saint-Inglevert by endowing it and then enforcing over the long term its dependency on a hospice and lands in the heartland of their realm. Even when English influence in the county waned and French influence increased in the 1230s,[71] traditional trade and other economic relations between the island kingdom and Boulogne persisted. At times, as for example when King Edward I through his wife exercised the countship of Ponthieu from the 1280s, English interest in the region was reinvigorated.[72] True, no agreement has been found about the exiles, but it is not unreasonable to suppose—and I borrow this idea from Nicholas Vincent—that among the many understandings governing relations between Dover and Wissant was one between an English king, probably Stephen, and a count of Boulogne to accept English exiles transported from the one port to the other whence they would speedily fan out as best they could after their disembarkation.

THE EXILES

What were the exiles to do, having arrived in Wissant and before making their way inland? Are we doomed to take refuge in J. Charles Cox's puzzled wonder?[73] There is evidence for several plausible scenarios.[74] They could have learned a little something of the village from the English-speaking shipmen who transported them. After all, the latter frequented the inns and hostelries and other specialized shops—such as the *charcouteries* for sausages[75]—during their layovers. Those abjurers whose friends and kin had followed them had access to additional information garnered in Dover's taverns and churches, which could now be passed on to the exiles. A central element of this information was the names of taverns to patronize in Wissant, for there was a good deal to be learned—and plotted out—in establishments known to be sites of contact for the English exiles.

Taverns were exploited as information centers for marginal people throughout France.[76] Indeed, this was the case throughout Europe. And wherever foreigners congregated over any length of time or at regular intervals there would always arise an establishment or two catering to them, places where the languages of the foreigners were spoken.

Many newcomers, a remarkable proportion, chose to open or work in inns and taverns for this very reason: in a number of towns from 30 to 95 percent of hostellers and staff were foreigners.[77] Native English taverners in France could exploit a niche market that was loyal to them, made up of patrons who did not frequent establishments where, for instance, Breton, Dutch, or French monopolized communication. Many upscale and midlevel establishments, although somewhat more cosmopolitan than their cheaper counterparts, functioned in the same way. The English boys and young men of the "English Nation" at the University of Paris, consisting of English, Germanic, and Slavic students, congregated together at their favorite taverns, which offered something like protected environments where they could lapse from Latin into their native tongues and meet women and other countrymen, students or not, who haunted the same establishments.[78] Whether this flocking together of people of the same origin occurred "naturally" or not, it is quite understandable.[79]

In establishments that catered to English travelers in Wissant, exiles and their followers formed a small proportion of customers. Perhaps two, three, or four exiles a day disembarked in the shipping season and on some days even fewer friends and family members. (How many of them would or could afford to leave their jobs behind even briefly?) At the taverns the exiles encountered men and women who could, for a drink or a few small coins obtained from kith and kin or begged at Saint-Nicholas church, put them in touch with bosses and recruiters of work gangs who performed seasonal labor as they moved through the countryside. Some women would have made their first contacts with other women who could help them find jobs as scullery maids or other servants in local households or eating and drinking establishments or, either by preference or in desperation, as prostitutes. Of course, crime was a possibility. I shall return to and address all of these options later. The point that needs to be made now is that the "luckiest" among the exiles should have been able to exploit the various initial contacts they made and thereby begin the process of constituting new networks of economic support and friendship.

To speak of the luckiest, with the word ornamented by quotation marks as in the last paragraph, is to intimate how inauspicious were the prospects of even the most fortunate of the exiles and their companions.[80] For matters could be much worse, and for many they were. This is brought home from a grim discovery made in the nineteenth century. It was in order to test the theory that Wissant was an ancient port known to Julius Caesar and used in his conquest of Britain that Louis Cousin undertook the excavations in the 1850s referred to earlier. Though local patriots have never given it up, Cousin came to believe that there was little if anything to commend this theory.[81] Wissant was a medieval village with no antique past of consequence. But he did notice one thing that was astonishing. The medieval cemetery, which provided little or no material evidence for him of ancient burials or inurnments, was nonetheless, his excavators discovered, immense; indeed it was larger by far than one might imagine for any village. It was, in Cousin's own words, "a graveyard of vast extent."[82]

Why was it so large? Haigneré had good reason to think that a number of insular (and other) pilgrims to whom the cemetery was made available by papal decree, in particular those sick and wearied from their exhausting journeys, died in numbers in the village in the period of its greatest importance and that their interment necessitated the steady expansion of the burial site.[83] Among these debilitated travelers were lepers, who came to Wissant in order to visit nearby healing shrines, including Notre-Dame of Boulogne.[84] The cluster of diseases called leprosy was coming to be regarded as a condition which resisted saintly intervention, but the old idea had not died out.[85] Wissant's own leprosarium, known as the Gazevert and in existence in the thirteenth century, would have served as a way station for other frail pilgrims in addition to lepers, if it was like other hospices in the region.[86]

Equally vulnerable in the circumstances were many of the English abjurers to Wissant. They arrived in an already-weakened state of health from the character of their travel to Dover, bareheaded, barefooted, and unsheltered along the way. For those who were delayed by weather or local political conditions in boarding ship and thus had to bear the additional burden, if I am right, of incarceration in Dover and the ritual of entering the sea before embarking, the situation was even worse. And the final and besetting terror was the journey across the Channel, which, while short in terms of distance, was fraught with danger from seasickness, gales, and fog, the last two of which often forced departing ships back to Dover. How many of the unfortunate abjurers died penniless in Wissant can never be known, but the vast cemetery, so uncharacteristic of a medieval village, offers a grim hint that over the years England's abjurers made a significant contribution to the burials there.

Thomas Weyland, the disgraced Chief Justice, was not one of those who perished in Wissant. Although he was already weak and ill from starvation when he set out on his nine-day walk to Dover in the winter of 1290, although he made his journey without the amenities of decent raiment, shoes, or refuge, and although, given the low incidence of shipping out of the Channel ports in February, it is a good bet that he had to wait at Dover Castle and wade out into the frigid sea before a captain chanced to brave the elements and ferry him to the continent, he survived. Would this once-esteemed man have been treated with such indifference in Dover? Was there no compassion for him in his misery? Or, rather, would anyone—any Englishman—take the chance that the report of an act of kindness toward the fallen Chief Justice might find its way back to an enraged Edward I?

At least Weyland knew French and could read and write. He could communicate with those who followed after him to Wissant and get money from them. The former Chief Justice could speak with other men of importance passing through Wissant. He could correspond with family and friends back home, where his son of the same name was feverishly trying to obtain the king's grace to reclaim his father's confiscated property.[87] With the proper instruments the exiled Thomas Weyland could even draw resources from traveling merchants. Two years after his arrival in Wissant as a broken man, the former Chief Justice had risen above acute illness and despondency and was residing in Paris. Thomas Weyland was a "lucky" man, and as we shall see later on, his life story did not end in exile in the French capital.[88]

John de Balliol, the deposed king of Scotland, was destined to abjure as a political exile after Edward I took him captive. For a while the English monarch was content to keep his prisoner incarcerated in the Tower of London, granting him the occasional privilege of short-distance travel and hunting under guard. But in 1299, Edward agreed to turn John over to papal authorities in France. To obtain this mercy the former king abjured England and was sent to Dover to take ship. Although part of his treasure was confiscated, he was allowed to retain ample resources for his life to come in France. He disembarked, as one would expect, at Wissant, from which he at once moved on. Although it long remained a question as to whether on his own or with French connivance John might return to Britain, in fact he spent most of the rest of his life in honorable retirement at family estates in Ponthieu.[89] Like Thomas de Weyland, old King John was a fortunate exile.

AFTER WISSANT

For the ordinary spring and summer arrivals in Wissant who needed sustenance beyond what could be supplied by their companions or begged and who could not speak French or read or write any other language, including their own, fortune was rare. There were nonetheless a few opportunities, as I remarked earlier. The need for seasonal and occasional hired labor in the region has been well documented by Carola Small.[90] The tasks included clearing stones from fields and weeding in the spring, and drew on male and female transient labor. Ten women, to give just one example, were hired in 1304 by one estate overseer to help in doing this work. Extra labor beyond that of native serfs, tenants, and the permanent work force was recruited in springtime for loading marl (lime-rich mud used as a fertilizer) from the pits where it was dug and for spreading it on the fields. Plowing was a specialized task, and since the extent of fields to be plowed did not change very much from one season to another, it was unusual to hire extra plowmen, but in rare cases (the untimely death or injury of one of the village plowmen, say), overseers might find a replacement from a labor gang. Extra sowers were often needed. And harvesting and threshing, along with putting up the harvest in barns and turning the grain (to avoid rot), were the most common farm jobs offered to labor gangs in the fall.[91] Bronislaw Geremek documented the presence of immigrant labor in the agricultural sector in jobs like the above as well as in the repair of fortifications and canals, dikes, and bridges.[92] Wissant lay close to dike and bridge country.

Yet it should also be noted that, valuable as this extra labor was to reeves and stewards at crunch times, the native labor force expressed resentment at other times, for migrants (non-residents) sometimes, like other "reserve" workers, displaced locals by accepting lower wages.[93] In England, access to migrant labor was sometimes forbidden, and those who housed such laborers faced fines.[94] Moreover, seasonal labor was precisely what its name implied, temporary; migrants had to find ways to supplement their incomes and obtain lodging in slow or off times. Churches were sources of alms, and hospitals were places, at least in theory, of succor.[95] Migrants' own experience and conversations with veteran crew members would provide them with vital information about the most welcoming sites—or the least unwelcoming.

The vast majority of seasonal and immigrant laborers in northern France and Flanders were not English exiles. Rather, the latter joined and blended in with already existing groups of men and women, some natives, some voluntary immigrants, some exiles, all of whom were on the move looking for work.[96] As these men and women traveled they came, for a time, to be under the authority of the work gang supervisors who acted in the name of estate managers and lords. This authority implied responsibilities of a considerable weight, which evoked the very nature of the exiles' and perhaps other immigrants' coming to France. It was incumbent on overseers, reeves, and seigneurs to police the foreigners, to accompany them from place to place until the latter finished their employment. A group of foreign workers might even be obliged to make a declaration of their good intentions—or, at least, their willingness to be watched—by announcing their presence in some way, such as sounding a horn. It should come as no surprise that foreigners who were observed committing crimes could be treated like wild beasts when apprehended: that is, subjected to summary execution.[97] The word *étrangers* has a variety of meanings, but nineteenth-century scholar Louis-Charles Bonne, to whose work in this matter I am referring, was discussing "véritables étrangers, c'est-à-dire ceux qui étaient nés dans un autre royaume." In whatever manner such foreigners died, whether in peace and law-abiding or as the direct or indirect result of criminal activity, their possessions became the property of the king or of those lords in whose jurisdiction they met their end and who enjoyed this princely right.[98]

Many women, in particular the younger women exiles, had a different kind of work available to them, again already alluded to: prostitution. Of course, some of the abjured Englishwomen who disembarked at Wissant or other ports had already been prostitutes in England, not unlike one Edith Stoker. Sometime around 1287 in Bristol, Walter Blakers killed Henry Leverych. Walter fled the scene and was outlawed. Edith, who was identified as a prostitute, confessed in sanctuary that she had held Henry while Walter murdered him. She had no chattels and abjured.[99] It is probable that Edith departed England at Bristol for Ireland and either plied her trade there or tried for a fresh start.

Most other abjuring women in Edith Stoker's predicament, penniless, departed Dover and would have been able to pick up information in those taverns of Wissant catering to English folk about brothels in nearby towns and further afield. The slide into this life in France and Flanders, either by choice or necessity, was fueled in part by the fact that prostitution and brothel culture were flourishing and that "foreign" women were prized in towns that served travelers and businessmen.[100] Not even so dedicated an eradicator of sin as Louis IX could root out prostitution in his domains, though he tried and was admired for trying to do so by later legal commentators who lauded his legislation when they made reference to it.[101] Some towns in the north (Valenciennes and Saint-Quentin are examples) and elsewhere also opted to outlaw brothels and prostitution and to banish those who kept bawdy houses or engaged in the sex trade.[102] But most authorities settled for regulating or licensing prostitution in various ways,[103] saving banishment for abjurers and convicted felons such as rapists or would-be murderers—for instance, the woman who tried to poison her husband by feeding him a toad.[104]

The network of brothels in the towns of Flanders and northern France in most periods was staggering. Bruges, a town of about 45,000 with many international merchants always passing through or staying over on business, had an average of about twenty-five brothels in operation in any year in the first third of the fourteenth century.[105] Many of their international customers were English merchants. For them, an English sex partner after a long trip in foreign lands allowed for conversation. For other customers—natives or international—an Englishwoman was attractive in part because she was different, a bit exotic. But the presence of foreign prostitutes could also be resented, as one disgusted observer's exclamation in Forez in eastern France makes clear: *Vil puta d'etrangi terra!*, "Foul whore from a foreign land!"[106]

Prostitution as a business had its fair share of violence. Most was inflicted on prostitutes by the authorities, customers, pimps, or other prostitutes as the result of competition for customers or for attention from pimps. Violence extended to customers as well, perpetrated by prostitutes who had suffered abuse at their hands or by pimps who avenged the women's injuries. In 1386 English Betty (Inghelsche Bette) scarred another prostitute in the stews where she worked by hurling a stone goblet in her face in a fit of anger that got her dragged before a magistrate in brothel-glutted Bruges.[107] Abortions prevented many unwanted pregnancies from coming to term, but in cases in which babies were born, there could be terrible effects for the children. Two thirteenth-century *Britones*, women from Britain or Brittany, strangled their babies in Aurillac in the Auvergne, where I would suggest they were working in a brothel. Their deed became known, and both were executed by burning.[108]

Some aspiring English prostitutes in France became madams. Men sometimes owned the brothels, employing madams to hire the sex workers and manage them for a regular wage or, in the best of financial circumstances, for a part interest in the enterprise, expressed as a fixed percentage of the women's take.[109] Alternatively, men provided protection or enforced the madams' orders to stubborn employees. Perhaps this was the case for an Englishman named Henry who, I would surmise, abjured England and was followed by his sister, Margaret. In 1300 he was residing in the digs his sister had managed to obtain in Paris. Margaret acted as the madam for the brothel for which the residence doubled. But her career was cut short. On 29 April 1300 Margaret, who had not left England as an abjurer, was arrested for keeping the brothel, which was in the bailiwick of the monastery of Sainte-Geneviève of Paris. Only now was she obliged to abjure, but in her case from all the lands under the jurisdiction of the monastery, on pain of being burned (or worse!) if she returned.[110]

In a number of cases England's exiles, it has been supposed, lost no time in turning to violent crime, alone or in concert with others.[111] This was a pattern of behavior among such people that has been detected elsewhere in contemporary Europe.[112] In Trevor Dean's words, "When strictly enforced, exile was a fearful punishment, pushing exiles into destitution and banditry, cutting their contacts with family and friends, and exposing them to the unpunishable violence of bandit-catchers."[113] How did it begin for those among the English exiles who took to crime? Guarded conversations in Wissant's taverns started the process a good many times with hints that a criminal band was recruiting. This would have been the opening gambit in bringing exiles into existing criminal circles or in constituting new ones. Prying eyes and attentive ears, however, were everywhere. Foreigners—Englishmen, but not solely Englishmen—became more suspect in the French Atlantic ports as the character of relations between the realms began its plummet toward the end of the thirteenth century.[114] Later, during the early phases of the Hundred Years' War, this suspicion was even worse: English residents began to be expelled even from inland towns like Agen.[115] Truces could not induce English students to attend the University of Paris in the numbers that had flocked there in the late thirteenth century.[116]

Initial contacts, if they were to be successful, necessarily included instructions about meeting later in more confidential settings, away from police plants and from drunks who might repeat what they overheard. To protect his goods at Calais the count of Artois, as his fiscal account for 1303–4 informs us, sometimes sent his own undercover detective—the account uses the word "spy" (*espie*)—to the port.[117] If he smelled out a thief, he was supposed to turn him over to the proper public authorities in what was, in fact, a town with long-standing monitoring of prostitutes, hooligans, gamblers, and habitués of taverns.[118] Just as in Calais, with wealthy travelers passing through and expensive goods in transit, Wissant would have been a well-policed and at times spy-infested village, in contrast to the situation of typical medieval rural settlements,[119] and would have had similar undercover men keeping an eye on foreign transients of mean condition. Protecting the vast sums of money accumulated in the village under the aegis of the head of the customs service (*custumarius*) from duties on horses, saddles, harness, wool, and the like and guarding the specie that was transported inland to the count of Boulogne and other aristocrats, who counted the customs and rents as part of their income, were two additional necessities for vigilant official eyes.[120] The fragmentary illustrated thirteenth-century verse life of Thomas Becket, now known as the *Becket Leaves*, depicts one such agent, a certain Milo, the count of Boulogne's man, whom the archbishop mistakes for the collector of passage money. Milo appears with a fat purse.[121] Wariness was the watchword in a village where such people had to do lucrative business.

A singular incident of violence might have brought any one of the English exiles to abjuration in the first place. Other exiles, however, had been habitual criminals before they arrived in France and could choose to resume their criminal careers.[122] The problem of eking out a living in the new environment was so profound that some of the former may also have decided that they had no choice, indeed that they had no chance of survival except by pursuing criminal careers. Piracy was a possibility, since it was not hard to pick up hints in a polyglot port that there was money to be had smuggling or overpowering crews transporting valuable goods to or from Wissant. Nonetheless, it was less dangerous to operate away from the well-surveilled village.

French royal records and the documentation of seigneurial jurisdictions with capital justice provide quite rich information on all the activities I have imagined.[123] They retell the stories of any number of exiles' misspent lives—English and non-English, too—and describe every species of felony perpetrated by them in France. A bastard, Galhard de Montlaur, who abjured the English-held duchy of Gascony for France on account of a homicide committed in Bordeaux around 1300, represents a type of criminal, the veteran of violence, willing to use more violence either to his advantage or for the perverse pleasure of exercising power over new victims in France. Our Gascon bastard committed thefts, rapes, murders, and "many other terrible crimes" (*plura alia enormia crimina*), or at least the allegations that he did so were deemed worthy of investigation. One could interpret much of his behavior, if the allegations were just, as an expression of rage over his overall powerlessness as an exile—his poverty and lack of friendships—in comparison to most of the people with whom he now came in contact. Or perhaps his example simply reveals the obdurate resistance of his pathology to exploiting the second chance provided by exile in a morally reconstructive manner. If local authorities could hunt him down and establish the justice of the charges against him, they were to punish him and no doubt countless others like him in other cases, in an exemplary fashion (*taliter puniatis, quod transeat ceteris in exemplum*).[124]

On occasion one comes across similar *solitary* figures, such as an English thief on whom justice was done in the lands of the count of Artois, according to the count's fiscal accounts of 1303–4, for having stolen wool (*Pour justice faire d'un Englés qui avoit emblé laine*).[125] But English criminals in France more often seem to have joined gangs.

When they did so, they opted for those already including Englishmen as members. Alternatively, two or more English exiles would join a gang together. Like all people, except the most secluded hermits, the exiles craved social support and camaraderie, which might be cultivated with more rapid success when communication was easy with at least one or two other members of the gang. Camaraderie, if not the goal in joining a gang, was at least one potential result.[126] On the other side, law-abiding subjects lived in terrible fear of gangs.[127]

This desire for social support and camaraderie was analogous to the impulse that led many immigrants to seek shelter in neighborhoods already populated with a few of their countrymen in larger towns, neighborhoods whose thoroughfares and byways in time came to bear the "ethnic" names of the incomers. Paris was in many ways a town of immigrants, of whom the English made a substantial number.[128] There were *rues* of the Bretons, Normans, Flemings, Picards, and English.[129] To be sure, the ethnic composition and quality of neighborhoods changed over time in the Middle Ages as it does now, and sometimes governments "cleansed" neighborhoods of targeted populations. Not one of the hundreds of *rues des Juifs* in France had any Jewish residents from 1306 to 1315. Nevertheless, *la rue aus Englès* in the bailiwick of the abbey of Sainte-Geneviève in Paris, which may have obtained its name from the concentration of English university students residing there in the thirteenth century, continued to attract English immigrants until the Hundred Years' War, such as one Master William of Pancras (*mestre Guillaume de Paincris*), by his title a University man, who resided there in 1300.[130] That William was from the island kingdom is obvious from his toponym, which was distinctively English at the time. The ancient martyr Pancras or Paincras gave his name to several places in southeastern England, because it was to him that Augustine the Lesser dedicated the first Christian church he founded in Britain after Pope Gregory the Great sent him there as a missionary in 597.[131]

Paris, given its enormous population, was also a favored haven for gangs whose modus operandi was to strike in the countryside, on the roads, or in smaller towns, before retreating to the relative anonymity and therefore safety of the city.[132] In Paris, they could blend in with the crowds, rest up from their pillaging in safe houses (hideouts), fence stolen goods, enjoy and dissipate their profits in taverns and with prostitutes and friends, and recruit new members.[133] Getting lost in the crowds could be a quite active process. A false tonsure was a possible disguise in a city alive with clergymen. Clerical haircuts were in general forbidden to laymen for precisely this reason: they could facilitate acts of fraud. However, if authorities for any reason came to doubt the validity of a man's tonsure, there was hell for him to pay when he was ordered to but could not read Latin.[134] If an exile could obtain it, clothing appropriate for a knight might predispose observers to ignore or downplay circumstantial evidence that should otherwise have raised suspicions about him.[135] Yet, many were suspected, and then came the questioning.

What could questioning accomplish? Gang members, once caught, tried to hide their identities, either by giving aliases or by refusing to name themselves.[136] A slip of the tongue, the use of a suspect's real name rather than his alias by an accomplice, might be decisive, since many jurisdictions, Valenciennes, Saint-Quentin, Hamburg, and Lübeck among them, exchanged with other nearby authorities lists of the names of men and women whom they had banished. The object of these lists was, sometimes, to prevent exiles' entry from the jurisdictions they had abjured. This goal received explicit expression in a statement dated 1227, issued by the municipality of Cambrai.[137] Probably more often, however, the lists were prepared and archived so that they would be available as written evidence, should the circumstances arise, in any later adjudication of the exiles. The finding of a man's or woman's name on a list, if such a person subsequently committed a crime, would bar access to another abjuration and would also justify capital punishment.[138] The lists that have been discussed in the best scholarly literature are all from northern Europe, but if my reading of Nicole Gonthier, who used these sources, is correct, she believed that such exchanges occurred in many other regions.[139]

To the extent possible, of course, certain exiles involved in crime took pains not just to distract peoples' suspicions but to destroy the evidence of being abjurers. Some continental abjurers who were branded on a finger severed the digit themselves or had their comrades do it for them. Certainly authorities expected such attempts at dissembling.[140] We can infer this from the fact that so many criminals who were apprehended in France (and elsewhere) were missing fingers and that authorities had come to expect the trait in captured felons. One such criminal was three-fingered Philippot (Little Phil) Cavillon; another was Perrin-Quatre-Doigts (Pete-Four-Fingers), whose career has been discussed by Bronislaw Geremek. He was a late fourteenth-century example of an abjurer of a jurisdiction who appears to have had his finger severed in order to conceal the mark of his prior exile for felony.[141]

If they were suspected of being gang members, English offenders arrested in France were encouraged to identify their partners in crime under what one would now call torture. This was also the case for native thieves who were suspected of being members of gangs, such as one Abbeville captive who was put to the question (the locution for "tortured") in order to obtain information on "all [other] thieves, church robbers, [and] destroyers of houses [burglars]."[142] A legitimate question that arises out of this observation is how strong gang members' loyalties were in general and among immigrant gang members in particular. For working together in committing crimes, disposing of and apportioning the profits from such undertakings, and socializing with their fellows could generate animosities and jealousies as much as comradeship, even for those of the same origin or from similar backgrounds. It could do so even when the fundamental basis of interaction was not partnership in crime after all. Consider the example of a group of Englishmen who, in various capacities, came before French authorities in 1333. On 14 February one of them, Jehannot Lenglais (Johnny the Englishman), was released from jail on pledge that he would show up when his case came before the magistrate of Saint-Martin des Champs of Paris. Johnny was under suspicion of wounding another Englishman, Guillot (Little Guy) Lenglais, who had a job in the local watch. Is it certain that these men were of English origin? Although the epithet *Lenglais* alone is insufficient to prove this, since in many other cases it served as a surname,[143] in this instance it is certain that both men were native English. For, pledging that he would see to Johnny's appearance in court when he was called was his acquaintance or friend, a menial laborer (*gangne-maille*), Jehan Poule-Cras (John Fat-Hen), who, it was noted, was also an Englishman. The other pledges were Robin Lenglais (Bobby the Englishman), Thomas Lenglais (Thomas the Englishman), and Jehan Lenglais (John the Englishman).[144]

Suspicion of strangers and foreigners was a general if not universal European sentiment in the High Middle Ages.[145] English foreigners in Paris, like immigrants, itinerants, and exiles from other regions (Brittany, Lombardy, and Lorraine provide examples), often ran afoul of the law whether gang members or not. It was proverbial in other regions of France that Bretons were thieves. It was a miracle (*res miranda!*) when one, the later Saint Yves, turned out *not* to be a felon.[146] There was no miraculous revelation, though, in 1278 for Agnes of York (*Agnès d'Evroic, engelsche*). She was English. She was a thief. She was arrested for the crime in Paris.[147] A Lombard also fulfilled the stereotype of the dangerous stranger. The accused child rapist was at large in the city before being apprehended in July 1333.[148] And so it went: in January 1333 a German skinner landed in a Paris jail after wounding an Englishman named Richard Bantene in his side.[149] A Lorrainer who beat a groom on the head with a board was taken from the Parisian streets and put into custody in October 1336.[150] In September 1337, a group of English travelers (one a visiting cleric) vented their anger with savage blows on a French local or locals and also landed in jail.[151] And another Lombard, who abused a Paris streetwalker by beating her and humiliated her further by chopping off her hair, was brought before the bar in January 1338.[152]

Immigrants of the same origin also got into nasty scrapes with one another, further feeding the stereotype, as the case of Johnny the Englishman earlier suggested.[153] Paris, with its poor, often unassimilated and numerous immigrant groups, was beset with such encounters. In the late winter of 1333 a group of Englishmen came to blows, sullying the reputation of the English immigrant community in the city's bailiwick of Saint-Martin des Champs.[154] But, of course, Paris was not unique in this respect. North and south, it was the same. In Ypres in Flanders one Lambert, an Englishman, brutalized another soul within an inch of his life in 1313.[155] Lambert was fortunate enough to get away from the authorities with his own life, but his misdeed would have done nothing positive for the reputation of English immigrants.

Many years earlier, a group of Englishmen stopped over at one Bertrand de Carpentras's house in Beaucaire in southern France. The sojourn occurred around the year 1240, since it is noted in the surviving records that the incident about to be described occurred while Raoul (*Radulfus*) de Salenchino was the city's chief agent of royal authority, the *viguier*, which can be dated to this period.[156] Bertrand let rooms to travelers, and he put these men up (*de quibusdam Anglicis qui in domo ipsius Bertrandi fuerant hospitati*). In this instance it was a mistake. The Englishmen were suspicious characters, but the innkeeper had little standing with the authorities, who were reluctant to take up

Bertrand's cause after the sojourners' alleged beating of him and other members of his household (*qui [Anglici] Bertrandum et familiam ejus in domo propria verberaverant*) brought him to the *viguier*'s attention. The *viguier* demanded a high pledge from Bertrand to pursue the case and pledges from the suspicious English travelers as well, suggesting that responsibility for the altercation was not clear cut. In the end, the pledge, ten French pounds, demanded of Bertrand was too high for him to pay, and he offered a silver cup that he had purchased for sixty-three shillings. This was never returned, indicating that the *viguier* did not believe his accusations could be sustained or else that he thought Bertrand shared the blame. Years afterward, the innkeeper accused the *viguier* of fraud for retaining the pledge and tried to persuade King Louis IX's *enquêteurs* (investigators of corruption) to compensate him for his loss, which is why we are privy to so much information on the incident. Whether he succeeded in his suit is unknown.

Documents for the year 1334 reveal another criminal gang—a large band of thieves—who counted an Englishwoman among their members. This was rare: gangs were most often male in composition. The woman in question went by the name of Ysabellot, a diminutive of Isabelle/Elizabeth. Betty might be the best translation. Betty the Englishwoman (Ysabellot l'Engelsche) was held as a prisoner in Rouen on suspicion of theft when she entered the records. Held along with her were Jehannot (Johnny) Rauche de Preaux, Jehannot (again, Johnny) Herpin de Saint Joire, Michiel Farmant, Jehan Augustin, Perrot (Pete) Rose, Borchier Jehannot (Johnny the Butcher) Aguillon, Guillaume Fremont, Jehan le Teillier (the Slasher), and Jehan Haust rès. It must have taken time to round up the gang, for 169 days' worth of bread had been purchased for the prisoners' sustenance.[157] The average length of stay in prison for the ten captives was therefore almost seventeen days. Of course a few must have been incarcerated longer, as one or another of the prisoners betrayed his (or her) comrades who were subsequently hunted down. Honor among thieves had its limits.

RICHARD THE ENGLISHMAN AND HIS GANG

Still another vicious criminal gang with English immigrants, exiles, and fugitives that operated in France two years later (1336) highlights many of the points already made.[158] The *prévôt* of the town of Château-Landon, a town now in the *département* of the Seine-et-Marne, took the confessions of various gang members in the presence of ten other citizens on 15 April 1336. The first was a certain Alexander. But this was an alias. He was otherwise known as Richard the Englishman and as Richard *de Veneys*, and he disguised himself as a knight. A second gang member, Johnny (Jehanneton) David, also confessed to an alias, Jake or Jimmy (Jacquet) Carmadin. A third, who acted as Richard's servant, was known as Ralphie (Raoulin). The main charge revolved around their complicity in the murder of one Odart de Courtchamp, which took place at Ouzouer-sur-Trezé (Loiret). The *prévôt* sent authentic copies of the confessions to the royal court of Paris for review. What had he and his suitors discovered?

Richard, in whatever manner he was persuaded to do so (the official assertion that judicial torture was not used could be true), confessed that he sometimes called himself Alexander Bonneville, a name he used because it evoked his native land in the diocese of Winchester in England. If he was telling the truth (and it seems an odd thing to lie about), Bonneville is the French form of Godstone which was in the medieval diocese of Winchester and lies within the boundaries of the present county of Surrey. The name goes back to the eponymous OE "Goda's town," but in popular parlance it was thought to mean "Good Town," hence the choice of Bonneville.

Richard was talkative and a little brash—or he was terrified. Back in England a wealthy local man had left ten silver marks to each of four religious houses (*colleiges de religieux*). Richard's father was the wealthy decedent's executor. He entrusted his son with the task of transferring the legacies to the religious houses. But Richard saw an opportunity and fled to Paris with the money. Given Godstone's location, Richard would have used the port of Southampton to take passage to the continent. When he reached Paris, he gave the money to a certain John the Englishman for safekeeping. He must have learned of these contacts from Englishmen he met at Southampton and/or en route to Paris. Then he started going by the name of Alexander. It was the summer of 1335, and Richard, as I shall continue to call him, stayed in Paris under his assumed name until 29 September, the Feast of Saint Michael Archangel. He confessed that he then partnered with another criminal, Little Phil (Philippot) Cavillon. They traveled to Provins (Seine-et-Marne) in Champagne where they heard tell of a wealthy resident's or business's hoard and made plans for a robbery. But the plans failed: when they broke in, they were unable to crack the strongbox and so returned, disappointed, to Paris.

Further into the confession Richard ratted on Johnny David, accusing him of joining in a trip from Paris to Orléans (Loiret) where they robbed a priest of two gold coins and twenty shillings in change. This was the beginning of a crime spree. From Orléans they went to Saint-Jean-d'Angély (Charente-Maritime), and along the way they fell in with another Johnny, a serving man (probably at an inn), who turned out to be a thief. He robbed pilgrims. Gangs also targeted pilgrims. Such appears to have been the case with a three-person band of thieves, two men and one woman, who were apprehended after attacking and killing a pilgrim in Aurillac, in the Auvergne, around 1240. They were strangers to the area, as Richard and Johnny David would have been in their travels. Neither their names nor aliases were uncovered after they were caught, tried, and executed by hanging, the murderess between her two male companions.[159]

In any case, Richard and Johnny David joined forces with Johnny the accoster of pilgrims and split the profits (ten shillings) among themselves. This Johnny's modus operandi was distinctive. He drugged the pilgrims, in all probability by serving them drinks with the powders that Richard mentioned to his interrogators. This technique would be used again, to worse effect, as Richard would confess, but it was not unique to the serving man Johnny or this gang. A few years later in 1340 still another Johnny (Johannin de la Vente) was prosecuted for a theft in the *pays d'Auge* in Normandy; he too had drugged his victims with sleeping powders or was accused of having done so.[160]

The next leg of their journey took them to the famous pilgrimage center of Rocamadour (Lot) and thereafter to Millau (Aveyron) and Montpellier (Hérault). The band made a good haul. At an inn in the first town Richard managed to steal a gold coin and seven silver pennies from the pilgrims who were visiting the shrine of Our Lady (the Black Madonna) of Rocamadour, whose miracles so captivated the medieval imagination.[161] Perhaps they did not captivate the thieves' imaginations in the same way, however, for robbers mentioned in the miracles often received severe divine retribution.[162] But fear of this, if they had any, did not stop them. At Millau the band got their hands on two gold coins and two shillings in small change from two unlucky merchants. They passed through Montpellier without committing any crimes. But at Nîmes (Gard) they resumed their thieving ways, robbing a priest of eleven florins and other monies minted in Florence.

By now, as they turned north, they were on one of the great commercial routes, following the Rhône. Robbing a priest who had Florentine money already indicates the "international" flavor of the travelers with whom they came in contact. They stayed in Avignon (Vaucluse) for two days before setting out for Mondragon (also Vaucluse). One of the Johnnies came upon a German, from whom he stole six *gros tournois*, the commonest currency in France besides the penny coin. He turned over the take to Richard for safekeeping, which makes me believe that the Johnny in question was Johnny David, who had a lengthier experience of trusting Richard than a newcomer to the gang could have had.

One after another the band found victims as they continued on the long return trip to Paris. At Saint-Vallier (Drôme) the victim was a priest, the take five florins. They fell in with another priest and a Gascon on the road from Condrieu (Rhône) to Lyon (Rhône) and thence Décize (Nièvre) and took four gold French coins and a gold florin from the cleric. I surmise that there were serious suspicions following this series of thefts. So the band proceeded with considerable dispatch and put their criminal activities on hold. But after passing through Nevers (Nièvre) and Montargis (Loiret), they reached Corbeil (Essonne) and resumed their robberies. Richard stole two florins and another gold coin from a merchant before setting out for Paris.

The travelers must have felt relieved that they were back in the relative safety of the great city. The problem was one of the others whom Richard later implicated in the band's criminal activities: Little Phil Cavillon. Little Phil's own behavior had aroused the suspicions of Parisian authorities. When Richard returned to Paris and resumed hanging around with him, he brought suspicion on himself. The authorities took him into custody but could prove nothing. Richard decided to leave the city. He and Johnny David, along with Richard's servant Ralphie, hit the road once more. They headed for Orléans first, where Richard and Johnny had started their previous spree, and from there the three of them traveled to La Souterraine (Creuse). They made a tidy profit, stealing seventy-six florins. And then they got bolder. Money was great, but there were some nice goods to be had as well. At Saint-Esprit (though which one of the many towns and villages of this name is unclear) they stole a belt and coin purse, as well as two silver shillings. At Saint-Rambert (Loire) the trio broke into a strongbox and took three French gold coins, small coins of lesser value, three pairs of kerchiefs, a silver spoon, two silver visors, a woman's surcoat trimmed in rabbit-belly fur (very soft), and an unlined doublet. Ralphie was bolder still. At the inn he stole a horse, which he was to ride in the course of his travels all the way to Vienne (Isère) before abandoning it.

Soon the gang arrived in Pierrefitte (Loiret) after passing through Marcilly-lez-Neuvy (also Loiret). There they met Odart de Court-champ who, knowing no better, accepted them as traveling companions. This was a Saturday, 2 March 1336, and the group continued to travel together until Tuesday. On that evening they took shelter at the house of one Henri, a hostler with a quite appropriate epithet, *Potafeu*, Beef Stew. The hostelry was in Ouzouer-sur-Trezé. All four men took beds. Odart went to his first, after a meal but before the others had finished rubbing down their horses. After they came in they too went to bed. Late in the night the gang went over to the sleeping Odart's bed. Richard admitted to his interrogators that he had drawn a knife. He struck Odart but he did not kill him. The victim fought back and managed to turn the knife enough to wound Richard in the hand. As they struggled Richard succeeded in using his foot to hold down Odart's hand, which now held the knife. Then the others joined the fray. Johnny David struck Odart with his own knife.

Odart was senseless by now, but was he dead? Ralphie procured some horse harness and the trio lifted their victim up and then lowered him down *en unes chambres aysiées*, a euphemism for the public privy (obsolete modern French *cabinet d'aisances* and English "house of ease"). Then the scavenging began—four royal gold coins from Odart's purse, two other gold coins, and three silver pennies. The victim had disrobed to go to bed, so Richard took his money belt and a good striped robe which was in his pack. Ralphie helped himself to the short riding jacket the unfortunate man had worn on horseback. There was other loot, too, including several royal letters. Odart was a crown messenger. Some of these letters they burned. Others they kept. A potential forger could use genuine models in his work. And then they set out. As before, the victim's horse was taken along as booty. It was fawn-colored and had a cropped ear, which made it easy to identify. All this Richard confessed—and one thing more. He confessed that he had had sexual relations—had played *sodomitement*—

with the three other members of his gang who had gone on this spree.[163]

It was not enough to hear Richard's confession. The interrogators obtained similar narratives, differing in the slightest details, from Johnny David and Little Ralphie. In fact Johnny confessed first, that is, even before Richard. The interrogators also recorded that sometime after Ralphie confessed he changed his story and denied everything. This was a remarkable case, but since it involved the murder of a royal courier and the destruction of royal letters, it was, as remarked, sent for review to the court of the chief royal administrator and justice-official, the *prévôt*, of Paris. Alexander or Richard the Englishman, if he preferred, was to be interrogated once more by a rather more elite panel of knights and lords. An irony is that one among them would be executed a few months later for corruption, but for now his role was that of a champion of justice.[164]

During the course of the inquiry, the accused would have been held in the prison of the *Châtelet*, the suite of buildings that headquartered the *prévôt*.[165] The prison was dismal. It included a dungeon for felons of the most serious sort, from which escape was almost impossible. Indeed, prisoners were lowered by rope into this dark pen. One purchase of rope for this purpose is recorded in the accounts of a former *prévôt*.[166] The place was dank, given the water-table of the Ile de la Cité, and was referred to as *la fosse*, which in Old French bears connotations of ditch, pit, and grave as well as dungeon.[167] There were no windows or doors to break or to squeeze through and no stairways to reach in order to effect their escape if inmates thought to attempt one. Prisoners who were accused of less heinous crimes and whose kinfolk or friends paid for the privilege might secure aboveground cells in this period.[168] But this option would not have been made available to these gang members. After being retrieved from this holding pen, Alexander/Richard was implored to swear on the Gospels to confess, and without any coercion or torture (it was claimed) he admitted to everything once again. Everything except one thing: he withdrew his confession of sodomy. In the course of his incarceration in the prison-pit he must have learned from other inmates of the potential punishment, which in northern France was intended to fit the crime.[169] For their first conviction sodomites were supposed to have their testicles (*coüilles*) severed; for their second, the penis itself; execution by burning was mandated for those convicted a third time.[170] Richard's many other capital crimes obviated this precise succession of punishments, but if his confession to sodomy stood he would be "unmanned" one way or another before his execution. He was trying to prevent this humiliation of his body.

In fear, Johnny David, a.k.a. Jake Carmadin, reaffirmed his confession and accused several other men of committing crimes. The clerk of the *prévôt* of Paris dutifully kept notes as to these other men. Then Ralphie had his chance. He had confessed in Château-Landon. Then he had recanted. Now in Paris he confessed again, acknowledging his complicity in the murder and giving details as to his fetching of the horse halter and their mutual placing of Odart in the common privy. He insisted over and over again that Odart was dead, undeniably dead, when they accomplished the deed, a hint that his accusers were repulsed by the possibility that the royal courier was still alive and had drowned in urine and feces. And, yes, he added, he had ridden Odart's horse away after the crime.

Was it enough, all this information? Johnny had opened the way to telling about more crimes. And now there was no stopping the members of the gang. Richard told about how it all started, with his stealing of the legacies in England and delivering the money into the hands of John the Englishman, a horse merchant in Paris, for safekeeping. He did not accuse John of complicity; indeed, he exonerated him of all knowledge of the crime he had committed. Not so with Little Phil Cavillon, against whom Richard also turned. Who was Little Phil? For one thing, he too was an Englishman. For another, it was discovered that he had been exiled from England for homicide. In other words, Little Phil Cavillon was an abjurer. But he had evidently managed to obtain a second and maybe a third abjuration somewhere on the continent after his exile and then hide them, for he was missing his index and middle fingers and therefore any physical evidence of one or the other having been branded. Richard said more. Little Phil had told him how to make sleeping drugs like those Richard had begun to use in his thefts. He told the interrogators the source of the knife, the murder weapon. Another Englishman provided it. There was nothing necessarily conspiratorial in this. Being successful at theft Richard might have bought the knife. He may have found it easier to deal with an English-speaking cutler he was referred to than with someone else.

It was determined that he had used drugs on Odart. Where did he obtain them? Richard responded by reporting on a shop, an *épicerie* in Nevers, where he paid ten pence for the powders, but he could not recall the shopkeeper who had concocted them for him. How did he administer them? Richard told his high-born questioners that he slipped the powders into some oil with which Odart seasoned his soup during the meal he had before bed. As if the confessions were not enough the court received other evidence, including some of the recovered money, robes, and other stolen goods found in the gang members' possession and the horses they were riding when they were apprehended. One, Odart's fawn-colored mount with the distinctive cropped ear, must have been decisive in the case against them. It was expected that the animals would be sold to recover some of the costs of the investigation leading to the extirpation and extermination of the gang.

CHAPTER 5

Returning Home

L ITTLE PHIL CAVILLON, the murderous three-fingered English abjurer whose misfortunes contributed to the story that concluded the last chapter, never returned to his homeland, Blessed Albion. But let us suppose for the sake of argument that he had succeeded in illegally reentering the realm years before his name appears in the surviving French records. In England we shall also assume he reverted to a life of crime. Espied in the commission of a felony, say, theft, we can imagine him fleeing to sanctuary. Who was this man? He would not have admitted that his missing digits, if they had already been severed at the time, were evidence of prior abjuration(s) elsewhere. Philip might have been his real name but the French-sounding Cavillon was in all probability an alias—and unless he had considerable linguistic skills, he would still have sounded English, at least from time to time. Would the authorities suspect that he was an Englishman who had once abjured England? How would an investigator have set about finding whether some Philip somewhere had foresworn the realm within the appropriate period for the current felon's age (a year, five years, ten years before)?

Now, let us grant his interrogators the benefit of an extraordinary stroke of luck. A man recollects that he once saw a Little Phil (*Philippus le Petyt* in the English legal records) who abjured from the town where he, the man, once lived. The London felon now seeking to abjure resembled this other Little Phil, but it was a long time ago, and the witness to the earlier abjuration, though the event was memorable, could not be certain of the identification. How much time and money would officials spend on bringing depositions to London in hope of identifying their captive as the same *Philippus le Petyt?*[1]

Or what if Philip, too, was an alias that Cavillon used, and no witness popped up to identify him? What then? It would have been so easy to lie in answer to direct questions such as "Where were you born?" and "Where did you grow to manhood?" Perhaps he would have broken under pressure, for consider another—genuine—case. It was supposed in 1328 (though evidently not sworn, just suspected) that a captive who called himself Adam of Pickering resembled a man whose place of origin was enrolled differently on an earlier list of abjurers. Was he the same man? Adam seemed to think that the authorities had found him out and possessed all the proof they needed. With no payoff to be had from dissembling, he admitted he was the very man. Our Little Phil Cavillon might also, like Adam of Pickering, have capitulated in our hypothetical scenario, but even in Adam's case, the justices took no chances: they summoned and consulted the coroner under whose supervision the list of abjurers was made. Only after he confirmed Adam's identity did they order the returnee's execution by hanging.[2] This suggests that if no evidence had been garnered to confirm Adam's confession or if he had stood mute, the justices would have been hesitant to condemn him to the gallows. Such judicious hesitation did not always manifest itself in similar cases.[3]

Nevertheless, if the officials had hanged Adam without the confirmation of the coroner's identification and if evidence later surfaced that he was not an illegal returnee—what then? Would the crown have investigated and exacted retribution on the justices? These officials would have heard stories that troubled them. Blunders with or without tragic consequences were known to have happened before. Had not an innocent woman once been mistaken for an exiled Oxfordshire vagabond and robber, Agnes Daythef, who abjured London around 1253–54? Happily, the error in that case was recognized before it was too late.[4] But officials would certainly have heard stories of men serving in similar positions being fined for not carrying out all aspects of an abjuration investigation with punctilious correctness.[5]

Working, of course, from the likelihood that those exiles who returned without permission to do so just wanted to "go home," a common topos among nineteenth-century novelists, there was perhaps some chance of recognizing abjurers who turned up in their old haunts, but otherwise the likelihood of identification was low. So let us suppose, for the last time in this hypothetical excursus, that the authorities decided to suspend their investigation. Here was a man who identified himself as Little Phil Cavillon. He perhaps had a suspicious-looking hand as abjurers on the continent often did, a French name, and an English accent. Despite misgivings, they were willing to accept his claim that he had been maimed by accident, and so they permitted him to abjure the realm. What followed was the road to Dover, embarkation, return to Wissant, and relapse into crime. Then, later, moving from our fiction to reality, Little Three-fingered Phil was exposed as an abjurer from England by another Englishman, the fugitive Richard of Godstone (Goodtown), alias Alexander Bonneville, and his company, vicious criminals all. He would now suffer his allotted fate.

ILLEGAL REPATRIATION AND ITS CONSEQUENCES

We need not rely on speculation for cases of illicit return from exile and their unhappy immediate consequences.[6] In the reign of King John, and therefore no later than 1216, Walter White (*Albus*, or *Blandus*, Fair-haired) killed a basket maker named Robert. There was, as we shall see, some sympathy or popular forgiveness for Walter. Nothing is known of how he endured on the continent, but a decade after the king's death, Walter was back in England living in peace in the Somerset village of *Stineleg* (literally, Stone-meadow; the vocable *stine*, an alternative rendering of *stone*, is common in the county). Perhaps the basket maker's family forgave him. In France the approval of the victim's family could be one of the conditions for royal permission to return from exile,[7] just as elsewhere and in other circumstances the approval of kin could lead to the mitigation of a convicted felon's punishment to forced pilgrimage.[8] But in Walter's case there is no mention of such an intervention, and it is certain that the crown issued no approval of his return. In time someone reported his presence in the village, and an investigation revealed that his neighbors had knowingly harbored him. The crown levied a fine on the village and directed that Walter, who had accumulated chattels worth two marks, making him solidly middle class, be dealt with as an outlaw, signifying execution without hope of reprieve.[9]

John Wagg, who abjured from Northamptonshire a century or so later, was on the point of suffering the same fate as Walter in 1323. He, too, had succeeded in coming back to England without permission. It seems that he was infirm and wanted to spend his last days at home. Yearning for home was a well-known sentiment among these exiles, as André Réville long ago pointed out.[10] John Wagg somehow made it to his *patria*, but was recognized and then imprisoned in the castle of Northampton to await disposition of his case. While in custody he expired of natural causes. If his hope was to die in peace at home, one could argue that he more or less succeeded, though in a venue and under circumstances not as he wished.[11]

Certainly there were exceptions: if an abjured man returned from abroad without license and could prove he was in major orders when he abjured (we saw earlier how this might happen), he would enjoy benefit of clergy. He would be saved from the hangman but confined under perpetual imprisonment. There are a number of examples. But very good proof, including the ability to read Latin, was necessary to make one's case.[12] Another man who was caught upon his illegal return told the authorities that he had been party to a treason plot and was willing to turn crown's evidence against his alleged co-conspirators. Treason was special; the man's execution was delayed until the truth of his allegations could be determined and a process devised to deal with the interesting issue.[13] The punishments eventually imposed— either on the approver-abjurer or his alleged co-conspirators—would have been particularly horrendous. Outside of treason, however, there was no allowance for an illegal returnee to turn approver and enjoy what few protections the status conferred.[14] In 1337 one tried to. Desperate men will try almost anything. This man appealed a number of men for felony at Newgate. They lost no time in pointing out to the justices that as an abjurer who had returned without a royal pardon, their accuser had no legal capacity to appeal them. After the justices verified the accuser's abjuration on the rolls, he was handed over for execution.[15]

Lest England's law and procedures appear harsh, let us recall a fundamental fact. In most instances illegal returnees had abused a grant of mercy which had secured to them their lives, lives which would otherwise have been legitimately forfeit.[16] The courts of the king of France and the count of Artois, to name two institutions with extensive records, also executed those whom the beadles apprehended and who were found to have been banished yet had dared to come back.[17] In 1267 a thief who had earlier foresworn the bailiwick of Sainte-Geneviève of Paris was caught stealing in an area under the abbey's jurisdiction and was therefore hanged; no other penalty could be substituted and no withdrawal of condemnation was permitted.[18] Indeed, there was no crime in anyone's killing an illegally returned *bannitus*, if the latter's status could be proved in, among many other jurisdictions, the Beauvaisis, the Orléanais, Champagne, and the Lyonnais.[19] Further south, the customs of Béarn recognized the special appropriateness of relatives of the original victim summarily—and without culpability—executing a *bannitus* or *bannita* who showed his or her face in the province.[20] A recidivist in Gascony, one already bearing the branding mark (*signatus* in Latin; *senhat* in the vernacular), was subject to execution even if he or she committed a crime whose punishment could have been mitigated in other circumstances.[21] The customs of Alais, another southern French town, put it picturesquely: people mutilated in their members or blinded and then exiled by order of the courts were never again entitled to a meal within the municipal boundaries.[22]

Such abuse, this coming back to dwell near the scenes of their crimes—to sit down to their meals again—ordinarily deserved, according to the judicial logic of the period, the reimposition and expeditious execution of the death penalty. Laws and practices elsewhere—from Ghent to the kingdom of Poland—adhered to the same logic.[23] As in France there was no crime in killing an illegally returned *bannitus* according to the customary law of Ypres, which governed areas in what is now Belgium and as far south as Saint Dizier.[24] Near Colmar a young man who was banished from the town after killing his stepbrother found the separation from his wife unbearable. He was unaware, however, that she had chosen to leave their home and the unpleasant atmosphere his crime had made for her there. When he returned to Colmar without permission and was apprehended, the authorities had him beheaded. Upon the news reaching his widow, a chronicler informs us, she perished *cum dolore*, or as we might say, "of a broken heart."[25] Judging from a case in 1314, authorities in Metz, to give just one further example, ordered banned criminals who were discovered in the city to be drowned in the Moselle.[26] The practice sounds exceptional, and to some extent it was, but punitive drowning for blasphemy or for the rape of a virgin was not unknown even in the absence of recidivism, as prescriptive and narrative sources from the early fourteenth century show.[27]

To return the discussion to France, I noted in chapter 1 that in 1273, a woman banished from the bailiwick of Saint-Maur-des-Fossés (Paris) was apprehended after committing a crime. When officials discovered that she was branded with the *fleur-de-lys*, her fate was sealed. She was executed and her body dishonored by burial beneath the gallows, which does not mean that she was hanged first. The gallows were the symbol of capital authority, but the execution of women in the bailiwick of Saint-Maur-des-Fossés more typically was by burial alive. And we learn more: it was all performed in a public manner: *hunc casum viderunt omnes de villa*,[28] a point we need to pursue.

The public aspect of justice was not limited to the treatment of *bannis* who reneged on their oaths. Judicial scribes often remarked, indeed emphasized, how other executions, as well as the cropping of the ears of convicted thieves, were showcased to everyone in the jurisdiction served.[29] Seeing a man boiled alive in the marketplace, which was the punishment prescribed for false moneyers in Lille or on one of the Channel Islands (because they had boiled metal to carry out their crimes), was meant to be the high point of a cautionary and memorable public tale, as was the hanging of the condemned man's body *after* boiling in the province of Brittany.[30] Just seeing a giant pot intended for the deed (one was sometimes commissioned expressly for the purpose) was a marvelous warning.[31] The execution of a rapist by drowning, referred to above, was accomplished *turpiter*, by which the chronicler indicated the deserved shame of the crime and of the criminal which justified recourse to this visually arresting method.[32] Such displays, often costly, were also an awesome representation and instantiation of municipal, seigneurial, or state authority, as the case might be.[33]

Nevertheless the perjury—the repudiation of the abjurers' oaths never to return—predisposed authorities to increase the spectacle of their punishment.[34] So although it might be construed as a second grant of mercy that a few towns, including Valenciennes and Saint-Quentin in the north and Saint-Antonin in Languedoc, punished an illegal returnee by cutting off a foot and then sending him or her back into exile, this leniency (graded as such by the salient fact of being less final than the death penalty) was fearsome in its exemplarity.[35] The thirteenth century, as Paul Friedland has argued, indeed saw an increasing "spectacularization" of punishments, which, *pace* Foucault, did not come to a more or less definitive end in Western Europe until the late eighteenth century.[36] Such acts of justice were visible and vivid warnings—a foot was hacked off, seared so the amputee did not bleed to death, and the victim left to crawl or struggle with a stick to the municipal boundary whence he or she was delivered into renewed exile in everybody's sight. Even more creative was the contemporary procedure prescribed in Laon for a second banning: if a miscreant did manage an illicit return he or she was to be buried erect on a succession of three Saturdays for at least half a day each time all the way up to the breasts. At the end of the burial on the third Saturday, officials and crowds of jeering youths *(ribauds)* escorted the humiliated prisoner out of the commune with threats of full burial alive if there was a next time.[37]

Such draconian measures could be mollified for particular reasons and most especially with respect to those who sheltered illegally returned exiles. By right any accessory of this type could be executed—and in the immediate aftermath of a crime, harboring, even by a close family member, did result in the death penalty[38]—but there must have been some sense, in the long aftermath of abjuration and exile, after tempers moderated, that it was just too grievous for close relatives to refuse shelter to a beloved sister or son or father who succeeded in sneaking back home. Perhaps this is why in the Lyonnais the penalty imposed on the harborer of an illicitly returned exile was limited to the loss of a hand.[39] Perhaps, too, the realization among the exiles themselves that their return might result in the mutilation or worse of loved ones deterred the former from trying to come back.

LEGAL REPATRIATION

By now in our story it almost goes without saying that if one returned from exile, it was a good deal better to do so after having obtained license. The proper manner to achieve this, in England as elsewhere, was by obtaining a pardon.[40] Men and women convicted of felonies in the regular courts in England and condemned to die could apply for and sometimes obtain royal pardons, because of circumstances or at a price or both, following conviction. Even those who flouted justice by fleeing and were outlawed had access to pardons for their outlawry on condition that they deliver themselves and stand trial on the original charge or charges.[41] It would have been inconceivable to permit this to outlaws while denying it to exiles who had succeeded at ordeals or submitted themselves to an established form of legal process in sanctuary, confessed their crimes, and suffered the hardships of displacement. It was still the case, as with a pardoned outlaw, that a pardoned abjurer from sanctuary could be compelled to stand trial for his acknowledged crime,[42] particularly if a kinsman of the victim, one with proper standing—a widow, say, or a relative who had witnessed the felony—made a direct accusation or appealed him, in the legal jargon. The pardon did not nullify the abjurer's victim's right of appeal. This limitation was identical with provisions on the continent.[43] Yet, in reality, such post-pardon judicial accusations were rare, a fact that will be explored more fully later.[44]

As Karl Shoemaker has remarked, obtaining pardons for condemned men in custody and for outlaws occurred "with a surprising frequency." It was typically preceded by people in good standing coming forward to pay the crown for its special grace. Even when nothing else is known except that a pardon was obtained by an abjurer, it is usually safe to assume that he or she had contacted sympathetic people of moderate to substantial means or with access to credit. John, son of Siward, a Lincolnshire abjurer for homicide in King John's time, was obliged to pay an enormous but at the time not unusual sum of five marks for his pardon in 1218.[45] How else could he do so but by the intervention of well-off friends or ones willing to borrow money and carry debt on his behalf?

We know that, always excepting a few high-born exiles, the abjurers' typical social and personal networks in England consisted of destitute, poor, or middling folk. We shall return to the fate of these "ordinary" abjurers in a moment. But first let us turn to one or two examples of people of high status who were obliged to abjure. An early fourteenth-century mayor of Bristol, a certain John le Taverner, was one such person. The records allege that John was party to a conspiracy to keep him in office against the wishes of "good and lawful" citizens of the town who desired him to relinquish the position. The records also allege that the conspirators "ejected many [of John's opponents] from the liberty of the town and took their goods and chattels." The situation escalated, and in the course of the dispute the mayor, his son Thomas, and Robert Martyn, a burgess and an alleged co-conspirator, were accused of murdering one of their opponents. All three abjured the realm in 1317.[46] They would have gone to Ireland, given Bristol's location. Evidence of the crown's ongoing investigation into the extent of their property preparatory to its sequestration followed soon after, on 12 February 1318.[47]

Men as well-connected as these would have had little difficulty in reestablishing contact with sympathizers who worked to obtain royal pardons for them.[48] But even so, it took several years to seal the deal. The three men returned to Bristol with pardons dated 28 November 1321.[49] Their pardons notwithstanding, their wrath at having been exiled still burned hot. They wanted to avenge the wrong they felt they had suffered. But it was well to know what a pardon did *not* accomplish. Since a pardon created a "new man," it did not allow a grantee to upset legal or properly adjudicated arrangements (civil or criminal) that preceded the original abjuration.[50] Consequently, many of those pardoned felt frustrated. Richard Tilly, the mayor of Bristol at the time of the three pardons just mentioned, was witness to this frustration and to the ensuing new period of disruption. For in their resentment the returnees found ways to harass the citizens whom they blamed for blocking John from office and for now preventing them from achieving the same preeminence they had enjoyed in Bristol before their exile. The records speak of their wreaking vengeance "immediately" after their return. They were accused in formal depositions taken on 16 March 1324 of "maliciously vex[ing] many good and lawful men of the town by divers grievances and extortions."[51] In a word, they wrongly treated their pardons as licenses for retribution, a pattern that Helen Lacey has also observed among a few grantees of pardons in her study of English judicial mercy.[52]

The case of Thomas Weyland, the former Chief Justice, was less fraught. His hard times had been brutal—starved out of sanctuary and sickened almost to death on the road to Dover in the winter of 1290. But he recovered, and in the initial period of his exile found ways, perhaps through friends who joined him in Wissant, to survive with dignity, if not to flourish. No doubt there was sentiment to the effect that Edward I would have pity and forgive his former Chief Justice. The king was known to have relented in his punishments in other cases when his anger abated.[53] Indeed, it has been asserted that despite his mercurial character, Edward I came across in his own time as in general too forgiving of his enemies.[54] Thomas made his way to Paris where in 1292 he waited for the pardon that would be proof of the king's softened mood. Evidence has not been discovered of when the pardon came or when news of it reached the great French metropolis. But it was granted. Weyland returned to one of his wife's manors and enjoyed a quiet retirement thereafter until his death in early 1298.[55]

The outcome in cases like those of John le Taverner, mayor of Bristol, and Chief Justice Thomas Weyland was predicated on the exiles' establishment and maintenance of communication with partisans of their cause in England. But abroad the vast majority of low-born and undistinguished men and women abjurers were cut off from their social and vocational networks with even greater effect than was the case for outlaws who remained at large in the English woods.[56] At least outlaws might be made aware of their pardons through people who had heard—or heard of—public criers announcing them in the streets and marketplaces of towns where, if the fugitives had not fled, they would have stood trial for their crimes.[57] But "run-of-the-mill" exiles and fugitives to France had gone off to almost another world. As long as they were in Wissant, there was the possibility of receiving an official communication through the resident English royal sergeant. After they left the village, however, how were their friends and families in England to locate them? Indeed, it must be acknowledged that for the most part the break with their native land was shattering and complete.[58] All that most ordinary exiles and loved ones back home had were memories which faded and hopes which were never fulfilled. As far as one can tell, most exiles of other jurisdictions suffered the same sort of loss to more or less the same degree, and some of it must have been reinforced by their relatives' attempts to live down their association with the *bannis*, which could be used as a slur in its own right.[59]

In the previous paragraph I used the phrase "to more or less the same degree." On the one hand, exile from a kingdom, across even a narrow sea, and into a wholly different linguistic community was harder to overcome and perhaps to bear than exile from a continental realm or province or from a town and its hinterland, where isolation and deracination (*dépaysement* is Gonthier's term) was relative rather than close to absolute.[60] On the other hand, recall that municipalities were accustomed to exchanging lists of exiles to establish written evidence that could be used to prevent them from benefiting once again from abjuration if they committed crimes elsewhere.[61] Were lists of those pardoned also exchanged? Were old lists updated by the erasure of names of those known to have been pardoned in nearby jurisdictions? Or was it left to the pardoned abjurer to prove his or her pardon if confronted on the issue? We shall have to take up this issue of proving a pardon more systematically later in this chapter.

To refocus now on the English situation, there were a few opportunities for those whom I have termed ordinary or typical exiles abroad to obtain permission to return to the realm. In the initial period after abjuration friends and/or family were one possibility.[62] They could move with haste and see what might be accomplished even before an abjurer reached the embarkation port. Recall the admittedly unique case of Walter Haket who appeared to be trying to escape but in reality chased down a more notorious felon whom he recognized on the road to Dover. His friends and family promptly rallied and raised ten marks for his pardon.[63] At times, as has been remarked, family members followed exiles to Wissant. Some stayed with them throughout their exile. Others could only remain for brief intervals. Before taking return passage to Dover, however, they might arrange to have information about their success at securing pardons sent privately to the resident English royal sergeant, the priest of Saint Nicholas-Sombres, or a local taverner of Wissant. Gratuities must have been given for the promise to try to get the information to their loved ones. A lucky few exiles may have been able to remain in the port for a time or revisit it in expectation of news through these sources.

Still another possibility existed for exiles who obtained some sort of steady work and managed to establish settled residences in France over time. I am thinking of those abjurers whose specialized skills made them employable in respectable trades. Might not a few of the surfeit of *anglici* and *anglois* remarked by Christopher de Hamel as being in the early Paris book trade have been exiles rather than, as he suggested, all voluntary migrants from England simply drawn by employment possibilities to the more active Paris market?[64] Working in this or another respectable trade they would come into contact with well-connected Englishmen and women—men traveling on business, aristocrats, churchmen, pilgrims, indeed perhaps churchmen and pilgrims in particular—to whom they could tell their "sad" stories. They could hope to. After all, a few—a very few—succeeded in gaining an audience with the English king when he was traveling in France.

Henry III was touched by the tales he was told.[65] Edward I was open to listening to them, too.[66]

The case of Halengrat the Balister is informative—to a degree. Born in Bordeaux, he served Henry III as a royal sergeant in England. But he came under censure for the killing of a certain Adam le Sauser. Adam was also a royal sergeant, one who had been assigned to the personal guard of Prince Edward, the future Edward I, and he appears to have worked with an array of members of Halengrat's family. What rivalries stood behind the altercation leading to Adam's killing, I do not know, but Halengrat abjured the realm upon confessing to the deed and went into exile in France during the mid-1240s. He had the advantage, at least, of being a native speaker of the southwestern dialect. During one of the king's visits to Gascony, the disgraced sergeant managed to reach him and appealed for a pardon in what must have been a convincing way, for Henry III extended his grace for both the homicide and the abjuration. By 1253 the once-disgraced royal sergeant was so far returned to the king's good graces that he was receiving property in England in Henry's gift and was sent on a sensitive and successful mission to his hometown of Bordeaux to help negotiate on the king's behalf a major loan of 1,500 pounds in the local currency.[67]

In another example the king's intervention must have seemed a truly extraordinary gift from heaven. Henry III was in France in late 1254, but was planning to return to England after a visit during which he had cemented his friendship with his brother-in-law, King Louis IX, in one of the many steps toward sealing a lasting peace with the traditional Capetian enemy. He was in Wissant on 21 December, as the Christmas feast approached. Christmastide would have been a time when more ships crossed between Dover and Wissant than was usual for the rest of the cold and stormy season. And a no-doubt despondent Thomas of Sheppel, an abjurer who had confessed to harboring a felon named Thomas Crabbe, was scheduled for passage to Wissant. Thomas of Sheppel's friend, a woman named Alesia *de Warrena*, had gone to Dover, probably with the intention of reuniting with him on the continent. But I assume that she heard tell during her brief sojourn in the port that the English king, though in France, was planning to return and would do so from Wissant. Acting on this knowledge, she secured passage on a ship and apparently arrived before her abjuring friend. She also succeeded in obtaining an audience with Henry III at which she interceded on Thomas of Sheppel's behalf. The king's visit with the French king's family and his own queen's extended family had made Henry happy, very happy.[68] And it was Christmas time. He made the importunate Alesia very happy, too, by issuing a pardon for her friend then and there, on the spot in Wissant.[69] So, by the time Thomas of Sheppel arrived in the French village his exile was over. Did the couple hear mass and offer thanks at Wissant's Saint Nicholas Church? Whether or not they did so, it was a very merry Christmas.

Advanced age gave an "elderly chaplain's" saga poignancy. He had languished in France for years. He had not abjured. He had fled the power of the English legal system because, he said, accusations made against him with regard to a homicide were false and he did not even learn of them until it was too late for him to avoid being outlawed. And by now (1279) he had grown old in France. He longed for a pardon and a return to England. He got word that the king, Edward I this time, was on his travels. The elderly exile managed to reach him, tell of his long expatriation, and plead the frailty of old age. The king was kind, but the case was strange. The old man claimed that he could have had benefit of clergy and vindicated himself, but if so, why had he fled? Perhaps the chaplain was just confused, cloudy in his dementia. Edward beneficently promised him that he would look into the matter when he returned to England, and he kept his promise. Soon after, he issued the pardon.[70]

Another sad story was that of Stephen of Handsworth, a Staffordshire man. He found himself in France because he had abjured after a terrible altercation with his brother on 4 July 1288. It was a moving tale that he told the king, but it would be confirmed by the investigation that Edward I ordered into it. Stephen had spent a year in exile when it happened that the king traveled to France and his itinerary took him near enough to where Stephen was staying, to Condom in the Agenais, so that the latter appealed for an audience. The exile told of how he and his brother Richard were drinking in a tavern in company with Richard's wife, Julia. The town was Hampstead, and the tavern was owned by Geoffrey the miller. All three left in the evening (about vespers). Stephen had a flimsy summer jacket on, but he felt chilled on that rainy July night. Julia had a broad cloak, and Stephen asked if he could share it with her to shelter himself from the rain as they walked along. Then Richard lost his temper. He was jealous of his wife and distrusted his brother. He had a heavy stick and he started to strike her as she was bringing Stephen under the folds of her cloak. Stephen was furious, he related to the king, and tried to restrain his brother, but then Richard turned on him. He insisted to the king that he tried to escape his brother's blows, but Richard kept after him. Stephen caught sight of a Danish axe resting nearby and seized it. He struck back at his brother in self-defense—the blow came down on Richard's head—and brought an end to the assault. A week later Julia lost her husband and Stephen his brother to the wound. Stephen fled. He had not intended to kill, but he was afraid of his possible fate. That was his story. And now, almost a year later, in June 1289, he told it in France to the king of England, for whom it was confirmed by an investigation preliminary to the grant of pardon.[71]

English rulers could grant pardons more or less immediately while traveling in France, as Henry III did at Wissant in 1254, but they typically preferred to initiate the process and follow up later, as Edward did in the case of the elderly chaplain and that of Stephen of Handsworth.[72] But what if the king was at too great a distance or there were other obstacles for the suppliants? In these cases, the latter would have sought out intermediaries, including other English travelers, to carry messages to the ruler. Or, if the king returned to England before contact could be made, it might be possible to persuade English travelers to intercede with him if they could procure an audience or at least to contact kinfolk or friends on their return to the island kingdom and urge them to continue to work for their repatriation. If the petitioners were leading settled lives, they could be located with fair ease if anything came of these efforts.[73] It was a long shot, but an abjurer who embedded himself or herself in new networks of French friends might persuade them either to help finance efforts to obtain a pardon or to put in a good word with a distinguished English traveler when the opportunity arose.[74]

Whatever the scenario, a few rather ordinary abjurers did obtain pardons and return to England.[75] But "few" is the operative word for English exiles and fugitives abroad (or "fewer" in comparison to their counterparts expelled from other jurisdictions).[76] It was outlaws in England and condemned felons in custody in England, not abjurers and fugitives in cross-Channel France, who received the bulk of pardons whose "frequency" Shoemaker otherwise regarded as "surprising." No wonder cases of victims' kin appealing pardoned abjurers of their crimes, a right they retained, were so rare. Almost no ordinary abjurers managed to return, but of the few who did and can be documented, there are some further revelatory stories to be told.

Richard of Oakington abjured the realm from the county of Hereford around 1260 or a little before. Richard was mentally challenged ("in his simplicity"), and he was frightened by a scuffle that he was involved in with Warin le Chaluner of Ledbury. Indeed, Richard thought that he had killed Warin and in his unsettled state of mind fled to the parish church of Ledbury for sanctuary. No dead body was ever discovered, but the confession following upon the altercation persuaded the authorities that a felony had been committed, with the body presumably disposed of, and that the rules for sanctuary and abjuration were met. Richard abjured the realm, but his friends could not believe that their slow-witted companion had committed such an act. The absence of the corpse motivated them to do some investigating on their own. I have grounds for inferring that at least one friend followed Richard into exile to look after him and await word of the result.

The alleged murder victim, Warin le Chaluner, had been deep in debt. This was the key. Richard's friends began to snoop around and discovered that a man answering to Warin's description was dwelling in a different location and had taken up residence there soon after the incident with Richard in Ledbury. The friends confronted the man, who proved to be Warin le Chaluner. They then induced him (one can imagine that the scene was not a pretty one) to return to Ledbury and arranged for a hearing to be held before the sheriff and the coroners of Herefordshire. There Warin admitted that he had gone into hiding "because of his debts for the payment of which his goods did not suffice." The officials pressed him on the far more serious charge that he had "maliciously" fled so that Richard would be accused of his murder and hanged or, given the actual circumstances, sent into exile from sanctuary. He insisted that this had not been his intent. In any case, with Warin le Chaluner alive, a petition was remitted to the crown, and Richard received a royal pardon on 27 May 1260.[77] Richard would have learned the news at Wissant where he was probably abiding with a friend.

Less is known of the case of Alan le Lung of Newbury, who had broken prison, taken sanctuary, and abjured sometime in the 1260s. It is revealing that he had a contact in the royal sergeant, Walter Achard, from the locality where these incidents took place.[78] The escape was by definition an affront to the royal administration and a negative reflection on the service which men like a royal sergeant were expected to provide. Yet, one may doubt whether any prior association with the escapee sullied Walter Achard's personal reputation, for it was at his petition that the crown offered a pardon to Alan le Lung on 5 December 1266.[79] Given his connections, it would not be surprising if Walter found a way to get word to Alan of this favorable turn of events.

It is possible that money changed hands in order to obtain the hearing on behalf of Richard of Oakington and perhaps in order to solicit support from local officials for Walter Achard's request. However, evidence of monetary exchange is limited to promises of payments and receipts of payments *to the crown*. On 30 May 1218, for example, William of Duston pledged to pay one mark for the pardon of Henry of Handsacre, who had abjured from Derbyshire for the murders of Richard and Geoffrey Frost, a father and son. William pledged the mark with the understanding that he would make the payment if Henry could not otherwise scrounge the sum from other sources and remit it.[80]

Patrons did not have to be related by blood or marriage or even be friends of their clients to use their good offices and their money to secure pardons.[81] There was a nasty case of arson and disruption (breach of peace) in Hampshire around 1235 involving a number of men. These common servitors of the bishop of Winchester received sanctuary and abjured. Whether he had encouraged or consented to their actions or whether their actions were misguided—carried out without the prelate's knowledge but in his interest—is unknown. Whatever the case, the bishop did what a lord-patron was expected to do.[82] He paid half a mark for the pardon of Ralph of *la Hes'* and half-marks for both William le Vilur and Adam of Wystle, who were identified as his men.[83] One supposes that they awaited word in Wissant to be communicated to them at the parish church, Saint Nicholas-Sombres, to which the bishop would have sent a personal messenger or a missive.

Those who were able to do so looked to the top rank of society for intervention. We have already seen personal appeals to the king, but it was an acknowledged aspect of the system that if the king was unavailable, queens and princesses should be solicited. In fact, they were expected to make themselves available for appeals for clemency and pass these on to their royal husbands and fathers.[84] It should come as no surprise, to give one instance, that after John of Brankiston obtained the favor of the queen of Scotland he was pardoned. John had abjured England from Northampton and had gone into exile in Scotland. He appealed for the queen's intercession, not because of her Scottish dignity or her capacity to intervene formally or informally in the operation of Scots law. Indeed, notwithstanding the occasional use of the language of abjuration when, for example, during wartime Scottish authorities exiled those whom they suspected of sympathizing with their enemies, there is little evidence that, despite their resort to exile, they incorporated foreswearing as a regular practice of their law.[85] Rather, the queen was an English princess, the daughter of the English king, Henry III, and was known as an intercessor with her father for pardons.[86] The English monarch responded with generosity to his daughter's prayer. He both pardoned John of Brankiston and returned half of his goods, even though pardons did not imply automatic restitution of property.[87]

I imagine that it was through the good offices of prelates that a few men with connections to the church but without benefit of clergy were rescued from exile. Acting the patron was almost part of their job description.[88] In the lists of patrons assembled by Helen Lacey, I count twenty-three prelates who, up until the mid-fourteenth century, are known to have interceded to obtain pardons for felons.[89] I am not saying that any of these men in particular did so for abjurers or fugitive exiles. My point is that it would not have been absurd for exiles who had once had some connection to the church to make appeals to traveling English prelates for succor, any more than it was unexpected for royal sergeants to intercede for brother sergeants.[90] Such exiles as I have in mind were employable in many occupations in France since they could read and write Latin to some degree and with their earnings could establish fixed abodes for themselves. They could also write to churchmen they knew in England or correspond with those they met on the continent and implore them, as members of the same profession, to intercede for them when they returned to England.

It is probable that William of Bugbrooke obtained his pardon through some such effort. The records describe him as a chaplain and tell of how he escaped the wrath of his lover's husband by seeking sanctuary, confessing to crimes he had not committed, and abjuring the realm from Leicestershire in 1270. As the years passed on, he burned to return. On 19 October 1282, twelve years after the abjuration, he obtained his pardon. The process was not smooth. The coroners who supervised the abjuration had died during William's exile, so a time-consuming new investigation was necessary, but he finally succeeded.[91] Less has been recovered on Adam Balle of Lichfield, also described as a chaplain, who abjured for the killing of an unnamed man but was pardoned on 12 December 1294.[92] Had he panicked when menaced by this unknown man, struck him dead, and fled to sanctuary? And then did he repent of his actions, write home, and set the pardoning process in motion from afar?

Some of the stories were poignant, crafted in part no doubt by common expectations—"rhetorical strategies"—of what would work, but not like later French pardon tales, whose drafting by professionals had, in my view, a far more pronounced distorting effect.[93] We have already encountered the poor man who was afraid that he would be accused of suffocating his six week-old daughter when he rode out with her one day in 1242. Ashamed, he tried to evade responsibility, then panicked and fled to sanctuary. Yet after abjuring he broke down and pleaded for mercy (a pardon), claiming that his act was unintentional. The coroner at least agreed to reconsider the matter.[94] In 1260 there was some doubt that John le Chaumpeneys committed the murder to which he had confessed and for which he had abjured the realm. Hugh Bigod, the Justiciar, who was exercising though not monopolizing the pardoning power in the years when the barons controlled Henry III's government, agreed to reopen the case.[95] In 1267 another inquiry was ordered into the process of John, the son of Roger of Fincham, who "sometime ago abjured the realm when he was a minor, out of simplicity and fear," the exact words—the legal formula—that had been used to describe Richard of Oakington who also had not had the capacity to understand what was happening to him. John had not even reached adulthood.[96]

Irrational, all-consuming fear is a recurrent motif in the descriptions of the circumstances that drove young people into exile and could be alleged as a factor in justifying their pardon. One of the Inquisitions Miscellaneous describes a remarkable case which, although it does not involve an abjuration, vividly evokes the fear characteristic of the criminal justice system and of those who had the power to enforce its sanctions. A twelve-year-old boy, following the execution of his brother and mother for felony and harboring a felon, was so frightened by the threats of the local bailiff, who wanted to get his hands on the family's property, that he fled the country and went overseas with what resources he could carry with him. Thereafter the bailiff insinuated the boy's complicity (by his flight?) in the original crimes and got him outlawed. In time and with persistence the youth, named John of Elmbridge, made contact with people willing to argue his case in England. After a successful judicial inquiry beginning on 29 July 1284, he received a royal pardon from Edward I on 17 October.[97]

Another case, that of Alice of *la Venele*, is both poignant and bizarre.[98] She averred that a certain John of Norwich had promised to marry her. Before doing so he wanted to reclaim some property in her name from a group of men (bailiff of Bury St Edmunds Nicholas Fuke, John of Hockwold, and others) who had evicted her. As Fuke's office implies, the property, a freehold, was located in Bury. Alice's fiancé obtained the necessary writs from the Chancery to initiate the prosecution of her claim, but she alleged that before the matters could be resolved, the men conspired to have John arrested on a false accusation of theft, which led to his indictment. She further insisted that their conspiracy had as its goal nothing less than his judicial murder and that her fiancé saved himself only by successfully claiming benefit of clergy. (One wonders whether he was an appropriate betrothed.) Frustrated and not content to leave matters as they were, the men turned their attentions to Alice (or so she alleged) with the intention of killing her. She had no idea what to do or how to protect herself, so she fled to a church and asked for sanctuary. It is hard to know precisely what happened next. She certainly confessed to a felony and abjured. She claimed that she was advised to do so—bad advice, she conceded—though she took the advice because of her hope to seek out the king in Gascony for a pardon and full remediation of all her problems. She pleaded in a formal petition for an investigation in Norfolk (her betrothed's home county) and Suffolk (where Bury St Edmunds is located). This would have been about 1288. Her hopes—or dreams—notwithstanding, she received no rectification of her situation.

THE MATTER OF WAR

One story that involved numerous English abjurers living in France and was chilling in the extreme occurred in 1326. Disputes in Gascony had provoked aggressive displays and the possibility of war between the English and French kings. Edward II, it was reported, was expelling Frenchmen from his kingdom, and Charles IV chose to re-taliate—or so we are told. He ordered the seizure of English residents in France and the confiscation of half their goods, with the obvious intent of holding the aliens to ransom until his political disputes with the English ruler were resolved. Many of the English, in particular the exiles from the island, were desperately poor, and Charles and his advisers perceived no advantage in confiscating their miserable goods, which would cost as much or more to carry out than the campaign was worth. But something had to be done. There was no purchase in holding the poor to ransom, so it was not intended that they be kept in holding pens to await release. Instead, they were to be expelled.[99] The consequences, if this policy were fully executed, would have been devastating to the exiles. (There is an uncanny modern parallel in Cuba's expulsion of its undesirables in 1978 as part of the Mariel boatlift.) There is no evidence so far as I know that they would have been allowed to return to England to live free. As it turns out, the policy seems to have been curtailed once the political disputes between the two kings cooled and the threat of war temporarily abated. But mutual threats of this sort would be made in future years.[100]

One other story that arose from disputes, indeed from war, be-tween the two kingdoms (and between England and Scotland) was repeated again and again around the time the incidents just described took place. It was of abjurers and a few outlaws abroad who volun-teered or were recruited for the English army or navy when it was on campaign. The government of Edward I received, for example, the pe-tition of Gregory of Stradsett who claimed that he had taken sanctu-ary while still underage (he said at age twelve, which appears to have been the cutoff[101]) and that he also, not knowing any better, foreswore the kingdom, even though his crime, theft, was petty—some geese and a hen. Since that time he had grown to adulthood and "had served in the king's war in Gascony." He pleaded for the king to restore him to his peace: in effect, to pardon him. In response the Chancery was instructed to issue a writ to the coroners to have the record of the abjuration brought to the Council ("before the king").[102]

In another case, on 20 March 1318, seven years after Richard Old-ere and his wife Sabine fled the country following a homicide, they, too, received pardons for both the crime and the flight in return for the husband's good military service for the English king in Scotland.[103] This case and that of Gregory of Stradsett in the preceding paragraph are emblematic. What began as a trickle became a flood of abjurers and outlaws seeking and being granted royal pardons for serving in the king's wars or for being willing to.[104] The earliest evidence that this was being systematized occurs in 1294, coinciding with the initial breakdown of the long Anglo-French peace.[105] By the mid-fourteenth century, at the end of our story, one has entered the veritable age of blanket pardons, though the purpose of the grants was not limited to providing soldiers and sailors for the crown's forces.[106] Some English jurists and commentators expressed concerns about the equity of blanket pardons.[107] Such criticisms, although they did not lead in the short term to substantial reform, since manpower needs were acute, were themselves the culmination of decades upon decades of concern about the proper exercise of the pardoning power.[108]

PROVING A PARDON

How did one prove a pardon? This question had to be asked from time to time, as for example of a certain Walter Bukerel, who was known to have abjured but was recognized in London in 1244. He was brought before the London Eyre of that year to answer for his presence in the kingdom.[109] What proof did he have that he had been permitted to return? In truth, the challenge was a fairly easy one to meet. And it mimicked a process simultaneously in use in other circumstances and undoubtedly other jurisdictions. For example, a person who lost an ear not as a punishment for theft but in an innocent way could obtain written official confirmation to help relieve suspicion. A Londoner, John the son of William *de Bosco*, did so in 1276 and thus carried proof that a horse had bitten off his ear.[110] Presumably, one could obtain such documentation for other mutilations that appeared to be similar to those inflicted as punishments by authorities throughout Europe, the list of which was very long—severed tongues and feet, lost eyes, burns (brandings) on the lips, cheeks, and forehead, etc.[111] Similarly, people whom the king of England pardoned, each and every one of them, received a parchment letter of protection, a pardon ticket, so to speak.[112] From at least the early thirteenth century in the English case, the document was supposed to be delivered into the successful petitioner's hands when he or she came forward to receive it in a judicial forum for public declaration.[113] It is an a fortiori indicator of how separated abjurers in exile abroad were that a few of the pardons obtained by friends and families were, because of loss of contact, apparently never retrieved.[114]

A pardon ticket took the form of a letter patent that was to be retained on a returned exile's person *at all times*: "he must be armed with a pardon."[115] I cannot but assume that the requirement was similar for those pardoned by continental jurisdictions. The ticket stood proof, in particular, against administrators' failure or reluctance to expunge a pardonee's name from lists of abjurers which circulated among municipal administrators.[116] If, in England, a recognized abjurer was arrested or got into a scrape or was implicated in a crime and evidence of prior abjuration was suspected or revealed, defense—protection from the peril of execution—was also possible by showing the official scrap of parchment that had restored one to the king's peace.[117] Yet, no action lay with the victim, the pardoned exile, for slander (scandal) if he were slurred as an illicit returnee, as it did in the case of other pardons. The latter created wholly new men, who were not supposed to be publicly referred to as the authors of the crimes for which they were pardoned. The king's grace, the early commentator Giles Jacob (d. 1744) averred, "so far clears the Party from the infamy, that he may have an Action for a Scandal in calling him Traitor or Felon, after the Time of the *Pardon*."[118] Jacob was slurred as a dunce by Alexander Pope in the *Dunciad* ("Jacob, the scourge of grammar, mark with awe, / Nor less revere the blunderbuss of law"), but he was a formidable legal scholar.

The theoretical limitation on the abjurer's pardon, that is, the rule that there was no action for slander against those publicly deriding the pardonee as a felon or illegal returnee, was enforced in practice, as one John l'Angleyse discovered. He had abjured for the killing of a village worthy in Lympne in Kent and spent three years in exile before returning to England after his pardon in 1350. He tried to appeal those who accused him of entering the country illegally, but if I am interpreting the evidence with accuracy, his effort went for nothing as "no grievance was shown."[119] It was important to the safety of the community that people comparable to whistleblowers in modern business organizations and government bureaucracies be allowed to make their suspicions of illegal returnees known without fear of reprisals, even if their accusations proved mistaken.

A parchment pardon ticket, which was supposed to be on one's person at all times, could be lost, worn out, or stolen. A lost or worn ticket could be verified against the Patent Rolls and replaced for a fee.[120] The Patent Rolls also provided a check against the effective forgery of tickets. Both the English and the French were more than a little concerned that imitations of their letters were available from professional forgers.[121] But what of a stolen pardon ticket? It is hard to imagine a more insidious revenge than stealing a man's or woman's proof of being in the king's peace and then accusing the victim of making an illicit return to the kingdom. Yet, the crime was not unsuspected.[122] Victims of such thefts (rare, one supposes) upon being denounced to the authorities would, of course, protest their innocence. It is an open and troubling question whether officials unfailingly responded to the protests with a full inquiry or by asking the central government for a laborious search of the rolls.

The last sentence is not intended to prejudge the situation by implying that the authorities were lax. A case from 1345 shows them very concerned and expressing willingness to investigate an accusation of forgery. In this instance the accuser who claimed victimhood alleged that his enemies had wrongfully gained access to a coroner's roll listing those who had foresworn the kingdom under that official's supervision. The accuser averred that his tormentors had maliciously enrolled his name on the roll.[123] If he was being truthful, one can only hope that the officials entrusted to assess his claim made a thorough investigation.

CHAPTER 6

Epilogue: Atrophy and Displacement

T HIS STORY OF EXILE and of the exiles themselves has provided a distinctive and, I hope, useful entry into many aspects of medieval life, such as criminal process and criminality itself, ideas and practices of punishment and mercy, interethnic and interlinguistic relations, foreigners' involvement in prostitution, and so on. Yet recourse to exile entered a crisis during the mid-fourteenth century. The dramatic title I first intended for this epilogue, "Death and Resurrection," would have overstated both the crisis and its sequel. The final choice, "Atrophy and Displacement," captures the situation better with its implication that certain aspects of the old and weakening system were displaced over a considerable interval of time onto newer or existing forms of dealing with felons while at the same time officials were still avoiding a superabundance of executions.

It will come as no surprise, perhaps, that the reduced reliance on exile in England owed itself to the growth of what many historians call proto-nationalism, in particular that which arose during and from the Hundred Years' War (1337–1453). The spillover from the war may have affected many other jurisdictions on the continent as well, but most of them, France excepted, not in so profound a manner. It is not at all the case that developments in their systems of exile, in particular those of municipalities, share the temporal arc of changes in England. Ghent is representative of these municipalities, despite the fact that its location on the territorial march of the seemingly endless Anglo-French war inevitably influenced the lives of its abjurers. Its Book of Exiles proves that banishment was a flourishing legal process for many decades after the close of the Hundred Years' War.[1]

Indeed, if we possessed the sources, we could probably expect to find that many of the male exiles from Ghent during the war had found employment as soldiers in the contending royal armies and many of the females as camp followers.

My inclination is to think that it was the Wars of Religion, not the Hundred Years' War, which in continental jurisdictions more significantly increased the political tension around exile. It is to be expected that sectarian Protestant jurisdictions delighted in dumping their felons in Catholic and rival Protestant territories, although no one really wanted to receive such felons, stained as they might be not only with criminality but with heresy as far as authorities in the lands of exile were concerned. Yet, despite the obvious concerns, resort to exile was tenacious. Here one must differentiate the expulsion of religious dissenters merely as religious dissenters, like the English-forced abjuration of certain contumacious Roman Catholics into exile during the early phases of the Reformation, which was really a species of political exile.[2]

Despite these speculations, for the two territorial monarchies at the center of our story sending one's confessed criminals to the other country atrophied for different reasons. And irrespective of the profoundly medieval inclination to maintain the law unchanged—to preserve its integrity, as it were—forces conspired to bring the system of extra-regnal abjuration between the two countries almost to an end by the close of the Hundred Years' War. In the first place, such deportations were tantamount to acts of belligerency during the war. No doubt previous military conflicts between the two realms generated this or similar sentiments, but the Hundred Years' War was special. More than any previous conflict between the two kingdoms, it encouraged the hardening of rival identities, French and English, identities which were there already *in nuce* but grew ever more exclusive as time went on and hostilities and distrust persisted. It was this same proto-nationalism that in perfect parallel led to the severing of ties established in the wake of the Norman Conquest between the English alien priories and their mother houses in France. The whole set of relations crumbled after 250 years during which neither kingdom seemed to detect *serious problems* with the ties.[3] Problems? Yes. Men were already wondering aloud whether Englishmen and Frenchmen could endure living under the same roof of an alien priory before the advent of the Hundred Years' War.[4] But unsolvable problems? No. As the war ground on, however, it became more and more a corrosive solvent of structures once binding France and England. We need think only of the probable effect of the threats of mutual mass exile of the subjects of one realm to the other.[5]

Hostilities bracketed periods of demobilization during the war. English troops who were demobilized in France lived off the land. French who were demobilized during the truces savaged their own people, but the root cause of the existence of the indigenous marauders was always known to be the English war. Demobilized troops were a scourge.[6] Perception of the deportees, while the system of exile endured, was harsh enough. How much more unforgiving were perceptions of them when it became known that the exiles and potential exiles, felons all, were volunteering for and being recruited to England's armies for the sake of pardons and then demobilized in France during the truces? Fear of Englishmen among the French population rose to an intensity not matched or exceeded until the aggressive and lethal rivalries of the Napoleonic era.

Yet, Frenchmen loyal to the Valois also feared that some of their own countrymen were capable of being seduced into betraying the fatherland by funds funneled through English secret agents.[7] In 1340, Jacquet de Meri was detained at Pont Audemer for forty-three days on suspicion of spying for the English.[8] The French authorities also suspected Englishmen otherwise living peaceably in France of diverse intrigues. As Jonathan Sumption has written, "The French government's fears were by no means absurd. Englishmen living in France did occasionally act as spies and guides."[9] So, too, did Englishmen who for various legitimate reasons were given safe-conducts by the French to carry on diplomatic and related business during the war.[10] The same year that Jacquet de Meri was arrested for betraying his countrymen, Bobby the Englishman (Robins l'Engloys) was captured in a boat while trying to reach an English encampment with the information he had gathered.[11] Suspected spies could be executed by summary military justice, but they could also be held and tortured in the hope of obtaining information to break up spy rings. Or, like captives of war, they could be spared to deter the other side from taking reprisals on prisoners under the *lex talionis* or to negotiate ransoms (the promises exacted being ratcheted up by the threat or reality of torture).[12] Perhaps best of all, spies who were unmasked (and there were plenty of spies operating on either side[13]) could be subjected to alternating blandishments and threats that might induce them to play the role of double agents. I do not know what the French expected to get out of Jacquet de Meri by holding him for forty-three days or from Bobby the Englishman by keeping him in custody in the *pays d'Auge* for 166 days. I do know that English spies—professional and ad hoc—were very much at large in France, that suspicions that they were had a caustic effect on social experience there, and that the French held the English responsible.[14]

To the French in France the English were mud, dirt, the foamy spittle that gathers at the corners of the mouth (*boe, boue*[*s*]).[15] Or just "English." In Valois-held territory in this period, the designation itself was an actionable slander if used by one Frenchman against another. It conjured all the crimes that English troops, either on active duty or temporarily demobilized, committed, were accused of committing, or were thought capable of committing in late medieval France.[16] An ugly parallel is the way that the word "Jew," stereotyping avarice, was used for centuries by Christians to smear other Christians, especially canny merchants, tight-fisted bankers, and hard-bargaining pawnbrokers.

In England the problems of sustaining the exile system in the fourteenth century were multiple. In the periods of hot war, how were authorities supposed to deal with groups of men who had abjured and in earlier times would have been entitled to go into exile but for reasons of advanced age or physical impairment could not now be pardoned to serve in the army? How were the same authorities to handle the women's cases? Truces came often enough and lasted long enough that recourse could repeatedly be made to a revived if slightly crippled exile system, a fact that explains why one can find cases, diminishing in number, to be sure, of deportation to France in the late fourteenth and early fifteenth century. But the on-again off-again system was in shock from other factors as well.

For one, when the English king laid claim to be king of France, he was in the strange position in his French localities of heading up a wartime territorial (or, as the French would say, occupying) administration which, insofar as it operated at all, should have employed abjuration in appropriate situations to exile men and women to England. But what sense did it make to exile a person from England to France or from France to England, if one and the same ruler was the immediate lord of both? Perhaps the days of abjuration between Normandy and England before 1204, when they shared a common ruler and instances of similar jurisdictional tangles, could have been invoked as precedents. A technical point, however, further complicated the situation in the early phases of the Hundred Years' War: English writs had to be rewritten, a culturally dreaded task, for it carried the possibility of creating new law without the time-consuming cultivation of consensus through parliamentary assent which was typically required. Any modified or new royal writ now had to specify whether it was issued in the name of the Englishman who was king of England or in that of the same man who invoked his claim to be king of France. And every one of the tiniest features of language had to be adapted so that there were no internal contradictions and no other lack of clarity in the writs. Perhaps this interval of instability in administrative practice—when many mistakes were being made and many means were being devised to correct them and prevent them in the future—did not last long. But it made for confusion, for delays in the exercise of justice and for the inefficient transfer of property in 1346,[17] a time when the English crown, thinking that its decisive victory was in sight, was articulating exalted claims of its majesty.

How different the exile system had been in the thirteenth century, how much like a well-oiled machine, even as far as the efficient movement of persons. Shipmen at Dover knew their duty. Officials—the English sergeant and the French authorities—knew theirs at Wissant. But after Wissant as a port was hobbled by the English military assault in the mid-fourteenth century and its harbor permitted to deteriorate, one could ask what obligation shipmen at Dover continued to have to ferry felons across the Channel. Wissant's partial recovery in the decades after its sacking and burning raised the possibility of greater regularity in transporting abjurers there. This in turn, like the periods of truce alluded to in the previous paragraph, checked the full abandonment of the system of exile in England. But it could not assure its survival, let alone its vibrancy.

Could the obligations of the Dover shipmen be adjusted, with the crown laying responsibility on them to transport exiled felons to English-held Calais or some other port instead of Wissant after the ravage of the latter and the displacement of much of the French village's seaborne traffic? Perhaps there was some pressure in this regard, but I doubt that it became the Dover shipmen's recognized duty. The men of the Cinque Ports were prickly about their rights vis-à-vis the crown, as examples of disputes described in chapter 3 demonstrated.[18] Katherine Murray associates their liberties consequentially with their "arrogance."[19] Yet, as with other issues, this begs for further research.

An additional obstacle to the establishment of a regular Dover–Calais exile conduit to France was the fact that the movement inland from Calais of those abjurers who disembarked at the port would be resented by natives even in times of truce. The unwalled village "boundaries" of Wissant presumed the expeditious dispersal of abjurers into the hinterland, where Englishmen and women could join other of their exiled countrymen already employed in migrant rural work gangs, brothels, and other vocations. As long as the English held Normandy (to 1204) and had military access to the French royal domain through that province and because there had been no serious coastal military activities near Wissant since 1217, there was never much pressure to wall the village. Calais was less a village and more a town, and once it came into English hands in 1347, its ramparts were augmented. The thick "solid limestone walls" were also protected by towers and well-secured access gates.[20] It was not a space that seemed to invite routine dispersal of large numbers of transients. And there were very few English workers of any sort outside the walls anyway, given persistent French suspicions of their presence in the kingdom during the Hundred Years' War.[21] Even those few abjurers to Calais who managed to penetrate the French interior were liable, poor as they were, to be targeted as vagabonds in an economic environment which, because of the dislocations of war and the beginning of the plague cycle, encouraged vicious hostility to vagrants.[22]

Meanwhile, constriction in the application of the system of extra-regnal abjuration and a steady increase in the number of hiatuses in its use became facts of life. Perhaps the system held on longer where a plausible alternative to France could be designated as an exile destination. Exeter's abjurers in the late Middle Ages must have emigrated to Ireland,[23] and the Cinque Ports and their limbs could facilitate seaborne exile to Scotland. The late medieval collection of customs for Faversham, one of the Cinque Port limbs, indeed, makes specific reference not to France but to Scotland as the abjurers' destination in those days.[24]

So what did happen as the exile system withered on the vine, slowly and in spurts, but inexorably? The solution was not regularized until much later. The vast majority of abjurers in the long thirteenth century were men and women who were successful recipients of sanctuary. There were classically two types of sanctuary—general and chartered. All of the discussion until now in this study has been about general sanctuary. Chartered sanctuary was somewhat different. England's chartered sanctuaries were small territorial units associated usually with major monastic and episcopal churches, such as Westminster Abbey, Battle Abbey, Durham Cathedral, and York Minster, and limited in number to twenty-two, supposedly by the Conqueror but in reality by local custom.[25] There, under ostensibly regimented conditions, transgressors who could not pay their debts could live until families or friends discharged those debts. Some inmates never left these asylums, which were akin to villages.[26] But chartered sanctuaries classically were not available to felons.

Much as the petit jury system, however—twelve good men and true—got started through administrative innovation in the early thirteenth century by frustrated judges and administrators who could no longer send the accused to ordeals, it may be that coroners with the connivance of sheriffs and judges conceived of the idea of sending abjurers into internal exile to these chartered communities. Long after the fact, this policy was affirmed in 1530, by statute, when general sanctuary was suppressed; it was further justified by the assertion that there were national security reasons to suppress extra-regnal abjuration, including the fact that many able-bodied seamen and potential soldiers among the exiles were thus lost to the military service of the crown.[27] The policy was reaffirmed in 1536, also by statute, after the English break with the Roman church.[28]

The new system inexorably contributed to a documented chorus of criticism that the chartered sanctuaries had become dens of iniquity replete with all manner of criminals, from the least dangerous to the most rapacious.[29] The porosity of these communities (they could hardly be called "gated" in our modern terms, even if they had symbolic gates and erect boundary crosses[30]) transformed them into safe havens for predatory lowlifes, or so the critique ran. The crown's adoption, confirmation by statute (1529), and regularization of the continental practice of branding abjurers was helpful, I think it is reasonable to suppose, in deterring some of these felons from carrying out criminal acts in the last years of traditional sanctuary with its more frequent exile to Scotland or, later, outside the chartered sanctuaries.[31]

Let us recall that in thirteenth-century England there was very little expectation that abjurers who disembarked in France, the overwhelming majority of such persons, would ever return to England—and expectations mirrored fact. If branding of abjurers was inflicted at all in England in our period, it had been rare and was therefore of little importance in the overall scheme of things. Innovations in the later Middle Ages—more exile, as suggested by the customs of Faversham, to the far north (from which re-entry into England was relatively easy) than to France or exile to chartered sanctuaries *within the realm*—constituted another matter entirely. Now the abjurers lived close to or among their own countrymen and women, and their own countrymen and women needed to be satisfied that recidivists would not escape the determinative punishment of execution. The situation now was much more like the continent's had always been. The new or dramatically increased practice of branding abjurers in England and the statute that regularized it in a sense provided the island kingdom's crime-fighting arsenal with the time-honored continental answer to illegal return.

Authorities in England opted to brand foreswearers on a finger, a practice that had earlier been mandated by a statute of 1487 for felonious clerics, who were marked on their left hands **T** or **M**, thief or murderer, and were then confined to monastic or episcopal prisons.[32] In the case of abjurers, the mark was an **A** for abjurer, but the authorities, concerned lest those so marked cut off the designated finger, inflicted it on the offender's right-hand thumb. [33] Why the thumb? Knowledgeable about practices across the Channel, English authorities were trying to prevent their abjurers from obtaining second or third opportunities to foreswear by cutting off their branded fingers, as sometimes occurred on the continent. After all, who could prove that the loss was other than accidental? But the likelihood of self-inflicted amputation was drastically reduced by branding a thumb, for the loss was far more consequential. Thumblessness incurred severe diminished utility of the hand even when the digit was removed only down to the first joint. At the second, the decline in utility was and is "disastrous."[34]

Severing the *right-hand* thumb was even more consequential. Societies like that of medieval and early modern England and Europe in general privileged right-handedness. This has long been inferred from the fact that *sinister* (left-handed) in Middle English and its cognates in the continental vernacular languages signified deceptive, malicious, unlucky, dishonest, and corrupt. *Dexter* (right-handed), on the contrary, evoked auspiciousness and protective power and might. A dexter (alternative spelling, destrer) was the knight's steed, always led by the squire on the right side.[35] A man who could count on the right hand of God for strength need fear nothing, said a medieval proverb (*Nullum formidat / cui robur dextra dei dat*).[36] So the high biological propensity toward right-handedness in human beings, estimated at 70 to 95 percent in various studies of modern populations,[37] would have been complemented in earlier centuries by the social discipline of enforced right-handedness, which is effective if imposed in early childhood. This is why medieval Bretons, to give one illustration, specified that convicted forgers have their right hands severed: almost all, perhaps all, such felons would forever be precluded from resuming their profession.[38] Medieval authorities also knew it would be hard for a thief who was branded on his right thumb to sever it and still play the cutpurse.[39]

Despite the new measures in England, inmates continued to be accused of sneaking out of the chartered sanctuaries to commit crimes on the highways and in the cities, towns, and villages nearby. And they did so or were accused of doing so even though, according to statute (1536) and like extra-regnal abjurers of old who returned without permission, they faced the death penalty if captured outside the precincts.[40] Moreover, despite or even because of new methods of government control, such as the branding, many churchmen resented the transformation that chartered sanctuaries underwent de facto and then de jure at the end of the Middle Ages. I raise the possibility of a causal connection, since the criticisms threatened to provoke the government into more and closer oversight of the chartered sanctuaries, with a potential loss to ecclesiastical jurisdiction. Only a few years after Henry VIII's statute of 1536, a series of hammer blows culminating in a 1540 statute reformed or put the finishing touches to the reform of the chartered sanctuaries, eliminating most, re-siting seven of them, forbidding them to felons, and otherwise restricting them.[41] Of course, there was some temporary turning back of the clock under Queen Mary (1553–58), given the "Catholic" character of sanctuary privileges.[42] But in time chartered sanctuaries came to constitute simply an alternative—a tenacious alternative, to be sure—to the kingdom's debtors' prisons.[43] Other services were so inconsequential as to be abolished by statute in 1623.[44] And yet abolition did not come soon enough to prevent the influence of the law of sanctuary in watered-down form from jumping the ocean to the English colonies in North America. But that is another story.[45]

With the abandonment of the internal exile of felons to chartered sanctuaries in England, what "should" have happened was the creation of yet another alternative to extra-regnal exile. New alternatives were devised and old ones sustained in importance, as I note below. What emerged from this, together with the general atrophy of abjuration dating from the Hundred Years' War, was a precipitous decline in legal foreswearing for both the punitive and merciful purposes it had served in thirteenth- and early fourteenth-century England. One continues to come across occasional references to abjuration of the sort that has been the focus of this book well into the early modern period. Sometimes these references point to archaic usages either unrelated or only marginally related to general sanctuary, which was always, as long as it existed, the chief source of the abjuring population.[46] More often, however, these references, in particular the allusions to extra-regnal abjuration, are evidence that the principles behind an obsolete or "decayed" system long remained "good to think with" in the intellectual world of the jurists and the lawyers. What, for instance, could one infer by analogy from now-bygone practices as to the legitimate scope of coroners' authority, licit community vengeance, or the permitted extent of mercy?[47] One is reminded how often and evidently how enjoyable it was for Tudor and early Stuart English lawyers to ruminate on alienage by reference to the legal status of Jews, even though no Jews had resided in England or enjoyed the status since the expulsion of 1290.[48]

A CONCLUDING WORD

Western societies argue back and forth about the need for the death penalty, sometimes propelled by logic, sometimes by political and social crises. On occasion, indeed, when rage over crime has led to draconian legislation, it was followed quickly by legislative, judicial, or administrative restraint.[49] Many Enlightenment thinkers argued more systematically against the "barbarity" of capital punishment,[50] but it was not until the close of the eighteenth century that this had the effect they hoped it would. *Albion's Fatal Tree* may exaggerate, or so certain critics would allege.[51] Yet, there is no reason to doubt that the eighteenth century was witness to an enormous number of executions in Britain after what appears to have been a less regular and widespread use of the punishment in large parts of the seventeenth century.[52]

Among the moments of crisis that have provoked governments to pass draconian laws, one can count the fear of invasion facing the French revolutionary leaders in the early 1790s. In this period "revolutionary justice," the climacteric phase as opposed to its preceding idealistic early phase (1789–90), gave rise to the Terror.[53] The question is not whether such sanguinary violence—liberty or death—was "necessary." The authorities at such times certainly argued that it was, the alternative supposedly being the triumph of counterrevolution.[54] My point is merely that such crises have often encouraged spikes in the infliction of judicial executions.

Western Christians in the High Middle Ages went through such phases, too. But most of the time in most of their polities, people wished not to—or at least did not—endure such high levels of executions for long. Exile was an available as well as a viable alternative and served many other purposes as well. Sometimes, though less prominently in England, it simply provided an alternative in the litany of prescribed cruel punishments, short of the death penalty, rather than as an alternative to it. At other times—and here England is representative of a universal European usage—it was a form of mercy for thousands of confessed felons who found shelter, metaphorically and literally, in the sanctuary of the church. Yet, at the close of the Middle Ages and at various later points outside of England, long-accustomed applications of exile again temporarily lost their viability either as punishment or mercy.

Traditional—*medieval*—forms of exile on a large scale having become untenable, the situation vexed rulers as to how to proceed to achieve justice in their lands. In other words, because of the technical impossibility of sustaining the traditional practice of exile, alternative ways needed to be found—some revived out of ancient precedents, some innovative, some tweaking the traditional model—whereby capital punishment was not inflicted with the frequency otherwise mandated by the laws. These included easier or cheaper access to pardons after judicial conviction, galley slavery in the Renaissance Mediterranean, transportation to penal colonies in the British, French, and Portuguese empires, the Siberian exile system under the Romanovs, and long-term and life imprisonment, perhaps at hard labor, in many polities.[55] Human beings kill a great many other human beings judicially, and they have been doing so for a long time—but rarely as many as they claim the right to kill. This restraint has typically been permitted by systems of otherwise almost unspeakable harshness.

Notes

Notes to Introduction

1. For example, Cassard in *L'age d'or capétien*, p. 5.
2. Matthew, *English and the Community of Europe*, pp. 13–14. *Littérature latine et histoire du moyen âge*, p. 38 no. 19 ("privilege accordé par Louis VII à deux étrangers [anglais de Londres et Colchester] établis en France [1175]").
3. The literature on these subjects is scattered, but works of relevance laying their stress on England and France and occasionally putting their findings in broader contexts include the following: Gabriel, *Garlandia*, pp. 1–26, and Verger, "L'Université [de Paris]," pp. 10–11, on English students and teachers in Paris; Slivinski and Sussman, "Taxation Mechanisms and Growth," p. 29, with information on wealthy English residents of Paris ca. 1300; Lloyd, *English Wool Trade*, pp. 14, 19, 21, with references to English merchants in France and their precarious situation during diplomatic crises; Cuttino, *English Diplomatic Administration*, index, s.v. "envoys," cataloguing English diplomatic missions to France; and Williams, *Cistercians in the Early Middle Ages*, pp. 31–40, on attending the General Chapter.
4. Sumption, *Pilgrimage*, pp. 182, 198–203; Sigal, *Les Marcheurs de Dieu*, pp. 58–67. See also Vincent, "Pilgrimages of the Angevin Kings," pp. 12–45.
5. Reyerson, "Medieval Hospitality," pp. 40–43; Williams, *Cistercians in the Early Middle Ages*, pp. 36–38; Gabriel, *Garlandia*, pp. 5, 42.
6. Trotter, "(Socio)linguistic Realities," pp. 117–31.
7. Lodge, "Language Attitudes and Linguistic Norms," pp. 73–83; Iglesias-Rábade, "The Multi-Lingual Pulpit," pp. 479–92. See also Trotter, "Not as Eccentric as It Looks," pp. 427–38.
8. Labarge, *Medieval Travellers*, p. 24.
9. Hunt and Murray, *A History of Business*, p. 104, and Kaeuper, *Bankers to the Crown*, pp. 209–10, 226–27.
10. F. Donald Logan, *A History of the Church*, p. 1.
11. Rashdall, *The Universities of Europe in the Middle Ages*, 3, pp. 374–75, See also Schwinges, "Student Education, Student Life," p. 227.
12. Coulet, "Inns and Taverns," pp. 468–77; Reyerson, "Medieval Hospitality," pp. 40–43.
13. Hunt and Murray, *A History of Business*, pp. 67–69. See also *Kunera—Database for Late Medieval Badges and Ampullae* (also referenced in Gaposchkin, "From Pilgrimage to Crusade," pp. 58–59 n. 73); and Koldeweij, "Notes on the Historiography and Iconography of Pilgrim Souvenirs," pp. 194–216. Cf. *Exhibition Catalog: Medieval English Pilgrim Badges*, pp. 1–18.
14. Cohen, "Roads and Pilgrimage," pp. 321–41.

15. For an excellent sense of these necessities (and for further references to pursue the subject), see Rouse and Rouse, "Expenses of a Mid Thirteenth-Century Paris Scholar," pp. 207–26.

16. The bibliography on prostitution in medieval France and elsewhere is now extensive. Most relevant here are Rossiaud, *Medieval Prostitution*, and Otis[-Cour], *Prostitution in Medieval Society*. See also Bullough and Bullough, *Women and Prostitution*, and Karras, *Common Women*.

17. Power, "*Terra regis Anglie*," pp. 189–209.

18. Matthew Paris, *Chronica majora*, 4, p. 45; the quoted phrase is from Tyerman, *England and the Crusades*, p. 104.

19. Cf. Treharne, *The Baronial Plan of Reform*, pp. 78–79.

20. *New Cambridge Medieval History*, 5, pp. 279–305.

21. See Géraud, "Les routiers au douzième siècle," pp. 125–47; Géraud, "Mercadier. Les routiers au treizième siècle," pp. 417–47; and Seward's *The Hundred Years' War*, which, although written for a popular audience, is dependable and, as its subtitle *The English in France* indicates, has this theme as one of its motifs for the fourteenth and early fifteenth centuries.

22. Bell, Brooks, and Moore, "Credit Finance," p. 111.

23. Kaeuper, *Bankers to the Crown*, pp. 227–48.

24. Gonthier, *Cris de haine et rites d'unité*, pp. 69–70.

25. Mundill, *England's Jewish Solution*; Jordan, *The French Monarchy and the Jews*, pp. 183–84; Jordan, "Administering Expulsion," pp. 241–43.

Notes to Chapter 1

ABJURING THE REALM

1. Peters, "Prison before the Prison," p. 11.

2. Mellinkoff, *The Mark of Cain*; idem, "Cain and the Jews," pp. 16–38; idem, *Outcasts*, 1, index, s.vv. "Cain and Abel."

3. Shoemaker, *Sanctuary and Crime*, p. 135; Stewart, "Outlawry as an Instrument of Justice in the Thirteenth Century," pp. 49–51. Lacey, *The Royal Pardon*, pp. 12–13, 37, has only a few words to say on abjuration of the realm and, in my opinion, wrongly assesses its importance.

4. Hurnard, *The King's Pardon for Homicide before A.D. 1307*, pp. 173–74, notes these other forms of mitigation. See also Dean, *Crime in Medieval Europe*, pp. 134–35.

5. In the texts I am exploiting, *abjurare* almost always refers to legal foreswearing of the realm or of another jurisdiction, although it could be used more loosely in political contexts (p. 137), to describe the promises made by couples to refrain from inappropriate sexual commerce (*Registre de l'officialité de l'abbaye de Cerisy*, p. 110 no. 138b; "Visites pastorales de maître Henri de Vezelai," p. 466), and to define the vows made to eschew heresy. *Extrajurare* and *ejurare* are fairly common alternatives but appear with less frequency than *abjurare* over the course of the thirteenth century. For some examples, see *Calendar of Documents Preserved in France*, 1: *A.D. 918–1206*,

pp. 478 no. 1318; *Curia Regis Rolls*, 3: *5–7 John*, p. 145; *Curia Regis Rolls*, 6: *11–14 John*, pp. 214, 256, 350; *Curia Regis Rolls*, 7: *15–16 John*, pp. 241, 244, 247; *Curia Regis Rolls*, 11: *7–9 Henry III*, p. 574 no. 2861. *Extrajurare* had an important second meaning: namely, to renounce or cede one's rights in land. See *Calendar of Documents Preserved in France*, 1: *A.D. 918–1206*, p. 186 no. 528.

6. See, for example, *Close Rolls, 1259–1261*, pp. 119, 210.

7. See p. 2.

8. For outlawry and waiving and the general background on and practice of licit slaying of outlaws, see Hurnard, *The King's Pardon for Homicide before A.D. 1307*, pp. 89–92; Stewart, "Outlawry as an Instrument of Justice in the Thirteenth Century," pp. 41–42, 46. See also Sartore, *Outlawry, Governance, and Law*, and Timothy Jones, *Outlawry in Medieval Literature*.

9. Sartore, *Outlawry, Governance, and Law*, p. 11; Zaremska, *Les bannis au moyen âge*, pp. 40–42; Jacob, "Bannissement," p. 1044.

10. Pugh, "Early Registers of English Outlaws," pp. 319–29. For the snippet of mid–thirteenth century verse, see *The Treatise (Le Tretiz) of Walter of Bibbesworth*, pp. 88–89.

11. Stones, "The Folvilles of Ashby-Folville," pp. 117–36; Bellamy, "The Coterel Gang," pp. 698–717. In general on the Robin Hood legends, certain versions of which represent the outlaw leader as aristocratic, see Keen, *The Outlaws of Medieval Legend*.

12. *Somersetshire Pleas . . . (Close of 12th Century–41 Henry III)*, p. 298 no. 1108; *London Eyre of 1276*, nos. 84 and 97. These cases (dated respectively, 1243, 1257–58, and 1258–59) represent both men and a woman as fugitives and, insofar as one can tell, poor, although the phrase "no chattels," used in these cases, is not an invariable marker of poverty (cf. pp. 36–37).

13. For a few examples of such people—fugitives abroad—showing up in the records, see *Calendar of Inquisitions Miscellaneous*, 1, p. 385 no. 1331; *Somersetshire Pleas . . . (Close of 12th Century–41 Henry III)*, p. 60 no. 280.

14. *Legal History: The Year Books* (online), Seipp numbers 1330.291ss and 1353.179ass.; Trenholme, *The Right of Sanctuary*, p. 42; Réville, "L'Abjuratio regni," p. 20.

15. See the sources adduced below at nn. 116–17.

16. *Central Law Journal*, 55, pp. 404–05.

17. Mandery, *Capital Punishment*, p. 560.

18. On the fully probative nature of the judicial ordeal I follow Langbein, *Torture and the Law of Proof*, p. 7, but note the (in my view) unpersuasive criticisms in Whitman, *The Origins of Reasonable Doubt*, pp. 101–02.

19. Cf. Forrest, "The Transformation of Visitation," pp. 24–27.

20. Réville, "L'Abjuratio regni," p. 10; Ireland, "The Presumption of Guilt," pp. 243–55; Jenks, "Die 'Assize of Clarendon'," pp. 27–43; Taylor, "*Judicium Dei*," p. 116; Lambert, "The Evolution of Sanctuary," p. 133; Masschaele, *Jury, State, and Society*, pp. 47–48.

21. Hyams, *Rancor and Reconciliation*; see also Lambert, "The Evolution of Sanctuary," p. 136.

22. For this percentage, see Taylor, "*Judicium Dei*," p. 116, and Ireland, "Theory and Practice," pp. 62–67. Comparative figures show continental judges acquitting more than 50 percent of those who went to the ordeal. Among the most important works in the huge and exciting literature on the ordeal are Bartlett, *Trial by Fire and Water*; Hyams, "Trial by Ordeal," pp. 90–126; and Peter Brown, "Society and the Supernatural," pp. 302–32.

23. Cf. Baldwin, *Masters, Princes and Merchants*, 1, pp. 323–32.

24. Shoemaker, *Sanctuary and Crime*, p. 117.

25. Sartore, *Outlawry, Governance, and Law*, pp. 88–90. For examples, see *Curia Regis Rolls*, 6: *11–14 John*, p. 256 (dated 1212); *Curia Regis Rolls*, 7: *15–16 John*, pp. 241, 247.

26. *Curia Regis Rolls*, 6: *11–14 John*, p. 256.

27. Taylor, "*Judicium Dei*," pp. 114–15.

28. Groot, "The Early Thirteenth-Century Criminal Jury," pp. 3–35; idem, "The Jury in Private Criminal Prosecutions," pp. 113–41; Masschaele, *Jury, State, and Society*, pp. 74–75.

29. S. L. E., "Papal Elections," p. 428; Watt, "The Papacy," p. 112. For alternative views, see Ryan, "Less than Unanimous Jury Verdicts in Criminal Trials," pp. 212–13.

30. Ryan, "Less than Unanimous Jury Verdicts in Criminal Trials," p. 212. See also Caviness, "Giving 'the Middle Ages' a Bad Name," pp. 177–78.

31. Shoemaker, *Sanctuary and Crime*, p. 119; Ireland, "Theory and Practice," pp. 56–67; Masschaele, *Jury, State, and Society*, p. 7.

32. Bureau of Justice Statistics, online at http://www.bjs.gov; and Friedman, "Making Sense of English Law Enforcement," n. 16.

33. Dean, *Crime in Medieval Europe*, pp. 10–11.

34. Summerson, "Attitudes to Capital Punishment," p. 125; Dean, *Crime in Medieval Europe*, pp. 10–11; Zaremska, *Les bannis au moyen âge*, p. 72; Gauvard, "Les oppositions à la peine de mort," pp. 134–66; idem, "Justification and Theory of the Death Penalty," pp. 190–208; Morel, "De l'exclusion à la redemption," p. 259.

35. Summerson, "The Early Development of the Peine Forte et Dure," pp. 116–25; Hostettler, *The Criminal Jury*, pp. 25–26; Musson, *Public Order*, pp. 196, 202; Prestwich, *Edward I*, pp. 279–80.

36. Jordan, "A Fresh Look at Medieval Sanctuary," pp. 17–32, with references to earlier literature. Although more than a century and one-half old, Beaurepaire's *Essai sur l'asile religieux* was unknown to me at the time I wrote my article on sanctuary and should be consulted. It is a splendid piece of work, informed not only by the author's own considerable intelligence and research but also by a cache of information supplied to him by the great scholar, Léopold Delisle (p. 57 n. 2). See also Sartore, *Outlawry, Governance, and Law*, p. 74.

37. See, for example, Barmash, *Homicide in the Biblical World*, pp. 71–93.

38. Trenholme, *The Right of Sanctuary*, pp. 2–9. See also Lambert, "The Evolution of Sanctuary," pp. 123–24.

39. Boutillier, *Somme rural*, p. 17; Shoemaker, *Sanctuary and Crime*, pp. 95–108; Trenholme, *The Right of Sanctuary*, pp. 23, 26, 44; Lambert, "The Evolution of Sanctuary," p. 129.

40. Lambert, "The Evolution of Sanctuary," p. 116 and passim.

41. See, for example, *Administrative Korrespondenz der französischen Könige um 1300*, pp. 384–85 and 490 nos. 298 and 464. Sometimes such venues were described as places of ecclesiastical immunity (*immunitas*), such as at pp. 210–11 no. 44.

42. Jordan, "A Fresh Look at Medieval Sanctuary," pp. 17–32. Also, Lambert, "The Evolution of Sanctuary," pp. 115–44.

43. Jordan, "A Fresh Look at Medieval Sanctuary," p. 18, and Shoemaker, *Sanctuary and Crime*, pp. 145–50. And see chapter 6, pp. 142–45.

44. Frampton, *A Glance at the Hundred of Wrotham*, pp. 47–50. Here and elsewhere I have, whenever possible, converted the historical toponyms found in the documents (in this instance *Hynton'*) to their modern equivalents, using the *Historical Gazetteer of England's Place-Names* and the *Henry III Fine Rolls Project* and other standard sources. When identification remains uncertain, I have used italics for the original.

45. *Patent Rolls, 1292–1301*, p. 6.

46. *Patent Rolls, 1307–1313*, p. 425.

47. Toureille, "Larrons incorrigibles," p. 44.

48. Turning, *Municipal Officials*, p. 31; Jordan, "A Fresh Look at Medieval Sanctuary," p. 246 n. 13; Lambert, "The Evolution of Sanctuary," p. 118.

49. *Petitions to the Crown from English Religious Houses*, pp. 245–46 no. 193.

50. Shoemaker, *Sanctuary and Crime*, p. 134, also discusses this case.

51. Réville, "L'Abjuratio regni," p. 31–32.

52. The case is treated in some detail by Shoemaker, *Sanctuary and Crime*, pp. 138–39.

53. For such cases, see Cox, *Sanctuaries and Sanctuary Seekers*, pp. 34–47, and Trenholme, *The Right of Sanctuary*, pp. 75–78; Sartore, *Outlawry, Governance, and Law*, pp. 137–40.

54. For additional cases, see also Trenholme, *The Right of Sanctuary*, pp. 80–81; Réville, "L'Abjuratio regni," pp. 29–31.

55. *Patent Rolls, 1281–1292*, p. 143. Cox, *Sanctuaries and Sanctuary Seekers*, p. 229.

56. *Close Rolls, 1307–1313*, p. 107. For additional examples of breaches of sanctuary, see Shoemaker, *Sanctuary and Crime*, pp. 139–42.

57. Thus, *Curia Regis Rolls, 8: 3–4 Henry III*, p. 279.

58. *Curia Regis Rolls, 13: 11–14 Henry III*, p. 212 no. 986. On the general point, Trenholme, *The Right of Sanctuary*, p. 40.

59. Cox, *Sanctuaries and Sanctuary Seekers*, p. 18.

60. For an estimate of how many thousands, see pp. 25–26.

61. The ten-percent estimate of female asylum seekers is my own, but on the general point, see Shoemaker, *Sanctuary and Crime*, p. 124, and Réville, "L'Abjuratio regni," pp. 25–26. For women as a proportion of accused felons, ten percent or a little more, see Dean, *Crime in Medieval Europe*, p. 77; Bresc, "Justice et société," p. 31.

62. *Eyre of Northamptonshire, 3–4 Edward III*, vol. 1, p. 208 (summarized in *Legal History: The Year Books* [online], Seipp number 1330.406ss). For a similar

case where the injured man escaped after seeking sanctuary, see Cox, *Sanctuaries and Sanctuary Seekers*, p. 237.

63. *Legal History: The Year Books* (online), Seipp number 1324.037.

64. Shoemaker, *Sanctuary and Crime*, p. 134, and pp. 64, 120–22 of the current work.

65. Woolgar, *The Senses in Late Medieval England*, pp. 180–81. Many scholars refer to these artifacts, but in words which are not always consistent with the best evidence—and it is not always clear where their ideas, some quite weird, come from. See, for example, Roth, *Crime and Punishment*, p. 28; Sokol and Sokol, *Shakespeare's Legal Language*, p. 334; Rabben, *Give Refuge to the Stranger*, p. 63; Jones and Johnstone, *History of Criminal Justice*, p. 38; etc., etc., etc.

66. *Eyre of Northamptonshire, 3–4 Edward III*, vol. 1, p.189 (summarized in *Legal History: The Year Books* [online], Seipp number 1330.364ss).

67. Bracton, *On the Laws and Customs of England*, 2, p. 383. Pollock and Maitland, *The History of English Law*, 2, 590–91.

68. Cf. Trenholme, *The Right of Sanctuary*, pp. 38–39; Réville, "L'Abjuratio regni," p. 16.

69. Shoemaker, *Sanctuary and Crime*, pp. 144–45, on Hubert de Burgh; and Brand, "Chief Justice and Felon," p. 46, on Thomas Weyland.

70. *Select Cases from the Coroners' Rolls A.D. 1265–1413*, pp. 86–87. (The case dates from December 1377.)

71. Sartore, *Outlawry, Governance, and Law*, p. 150.

72. Trenholme, *The Right of Sanctuary*, p. 43; Réville, "L'Abjuratio regni," p. 20.

73. *Curia Regis Rolls*, 6: 11–14 John, p. 350.

74. See, for example, the collusion alleged between the coroner's jurors and one William Jurday, who abjured Somersetshire for theft. He was spirited away and hidden in the village of Crandon: *Somersetshire Pleas . . . (12th Century–41 Henry III)*, p. 306 no. 1153. The jurors and the township of Crandon incurred the crown's wrath and were fined for the offense.

75. Summerson, "Peacekeepers and Lawbreakers," pp. 56–76, is partly motivated by this question, even though much of his evidence postdates the period of central concern in the present study.

76. Schubert, *Räuber, Henker, arme Sünder*, p. 100; Zaremska, *Les bannis au moyen âge*, p. 84, also notes the near-ubiquity of individuals being legally *marqué[s] au fer*.

77. In general on French branding practices, see Gomart, "De la peine du bannissement," p. 451; Janin, "Documents relatifs à la peine du bannissement," pp. 420–21; Jusserand, *Les Anglais au moyen âge*, p. 149 n.1; Gonthier, *Le châtiment du crime*, pp. 140–41. Purchases of royal *fleur-de-lysé* branding irons are recorded in the fiscal accounts; see "Un compte de menues dépenses," pp. 24 and 26 nos.174 and 194.

78. Documents recording the purchase and repair of branding irons with crosses in 1280–81, 1293, 1298, etc. are published in *Actes et comptes de la commune de Provins*, pp. 49, 90, 166. See also Bourquelot, "Notice sur le manuscrit intitulé Cartulaire de la ville de Provins," p. 447.

79. *Medieval Popular Religion*, p. 171, excerpting the *Materials for the History of Thomas Becket*.

80. For the case, see *Registre criminel de Saint-Maur-des-Fossés*, p. 322. On the custom of burying women alive, see Gonthier, *Le châtiment du crime*, pp. 161–62.

81. *Établissements de Rouen*, 1, p. 19, and 2, pp. 16–19, article 10.

82. In particular on work-related accidents, see Leguay, *Pauvres et marginaux*, pp. 184–85.

83. Bellamy, *Crime and Public Order*, pp. 67, 181; Woolgar, *The Senses in Late Medieval England*, p. 56.

84. See the early modern annotations to Boutillier's fourteenth-century *Somme rural*, p. 871.

85. For a contemporary articulation of the sentiment, see *Coutume d'Agen*, pp. 58–59, 300. The reference to Bentham is to his *Théorie des peines et des récompenses*, 3, pp. 91–92. See also Bimbenet, "Examen," p. 9, "la marque au fer chaud était un signe caché qui ne se révélait qu'aux yeux du fonctionnaire chargé de le rechercher."

86. Laingui and Lebigre, *Histoire du droit pénal*, 1, pp. 127 and 185 n. 10.

87. C.P. Jones, "*Stigma*: Tattooing and Branding in Graeco-Roman Antiquity," pp. 139–55.

88. *1235 Surrey Eyre*, 2, p. 434 no. 567.

89. Sharpe, *Judicial Punishment in England*, p. 23; Bellamy, *Crime and Public Order*, p. 181.

90. See pp. 126–27, 142–44.

91. *Statutes of the Realm*, 1, p. 88. I have modified the translation. This class of exiles was brought to my attention in Caroline Dunn's as-yet unpublished paper "Prosecuting Ravishment in Thirteenth Century England."

92. *Legal History: The Year Books* (online), Seipp number 1334.147.

93. For the information on approvers which follows, see Musson, *Public Order*, pp. 172–74 and 213–14; Sartore, *Outlawry, Governance, and Law*, pp. 74 and 145–46; Röhrkasten, "Some Problems of the Evidence of Fourteenth Century Approvers," pp. 14–22, and, more comprehensively, Hamil, "The King's Approvers," pp. 238–58, and now especially, Röhrkasten, *Die englischen Kronzeugen*.

94. Hamil, "The King's Approvers," p. 248. For a glimpse into the operation of the process, see Clanchy, "Highway Robbery and Trial by Battle," pp. 25–61.

95. For a possible late and eccentric use of combat, see Neilson, *Trial by Combat*, pp. 154–58. See also Hamil, "The King's Approvers," pp. 256–57.

96. Groot, "The Early Thirteenth-Century Criminal Jury," p. 18.

97. Musson, *Public Order*, pp. 243–46; Hamil, "The King's Approvers," pp. 247–51; Röhrkasten, "Some Problems of the Evidence of Fourteenth Century Approvers," pp. 14–22; idem, *Die englischen Kronzeugen*, p. 192.

98. Hamil, "The King's Approvers," pp. 250–51.

99. *The 1258–9 Special Eyre of Surrey and Kent*, pp. 35–36 no. 54. See also Sartore, *Outlawry, Governance, and Law*, pp. 161–63. A major collection of documents relevant to Hugh Bigod's justiciarship will appear from the Seldon Society as *The Court of the Justiciar of England (1258–60)*, edited by Andrew Hershey. (I

owe this information to Nicholas Vincent.) Here is the advance description of the contents of the volume: "In the Provisions of Oxford the rebel barons appointed Hugh Bigod 'to right the wrongs done by all the other justices, bailiffs, earls, barons, and all other persons'. His court's unpublished records, with over a thousand entries, show Bigod taking such action against the worst excesses of royal bureaucracy . . . including against the king himself. The introduction will address the barons' ideal of justice and law as simple, immediate, and personal, as well as new procedures and the interest of the cases." See http://www.law.harvard.edu /programs/selden_society/pub.html.

100. *Select Cases from the Coroners' Rolls A.D. 1265–1413*, pp. 127–32.

101. *Close Rolls, 1237–1242*, p. 5.

102. *Calendar of Coroners' Rolls of the City of London A.D. 1300–1378*, pp. 130–31. The other approvers, whose fate is unknown, were named Richard of Leicester, William of *Codenorde*, and Adam Waleys. Despite the editorial note at p. xvii, none of these men is said to have abjured the realm.

103. On conviction rates, see Stones, "The Folvilles of Ashby-Folville," pp. 130–31 (also citing Bertha Putnam in J. F. Willard, *English Government at Work*, 3). On the passion for depicting executions, see Morel, "De l'exclusion à la redemption," pp. 259–72 and plates, and Caviness's complex arguments on the representation of spectacular punishments, "Giving 'the Middle Ages' a Bad Name," pp. 175–235.

104. *Pleas of the Crown for the County of Gloucester*, p. 137. Sartore, *Outlawry, Governance, and Law*, pp. 131 and 150–52, makes a similar observation.

105. For the discussion in this and the next paragraph, see Jordan, "Fresh Look at Medieval Sanctuary," pp. 26–27.

106. In addition to Jordan (above, n. 105), see Wright, "The High Seas and the Church," p. 31; Trenholme, *The Right of Sanctuary*, p. 25; Cox, *Sanctuaries and Sanctuary Seekers*, p. 31.

107. See pp. 69–70. See also Wright, "The High Seas and the Church," p. 31.

108. Kitsikopoulos, "England," p. 35, accepting the conclusions of Bruce Campbell.

109. For a variety of estimates, some even higher, see Jordan, *The Great Famine*, p. 191 n. 29.

110. Shoemaker, *Sanctuary and Crime*, pp. 95–108.

111. *Calendar of Inquisitions Miscellaneous*, 3, p. 103 no. 298, dated 1358.

112. In *Select Cases from the Coroners' Rolls A.D. 1265–1413*, p. 58 n. 4, Charles Gross made reference to a roll with eleven membranes, dating from 27 Edward I to 20 Edward II (1299–1327), with twenty-three cases of abjuration in the county of Northamptonshire, which he did not edit.

113. Whitley, "Sanctuary in Devon," pp. 302–13.

114. Bresc, "Justice et société," p. 33, *un monde de bannis*.

115. Gonthier, *Le châtiment du crime*, pp. 134–40.

116. Cf. Zaremska, *Les bannis au moyen âge*, pp. 25–40.

117. Naessens, "Judicial Authorities' Views of Women's Roles in Late Medieval Flanders," pp. 52 (on population) and 59 and 74 (on the Book of Exiles). The

ballincboek records cases starting only in 1472 and running to 1537, so no coeval comparisons of the system it reflects can be made with thirteenth- and fourteenth-century English and French exile for felony.

118. The French royal formulary, circa 1300, edited by Hans-Günter Schmidt, is replete with models, taken from genuine charters, addressing the complexities of exile for felony. *Administrative Korrespondenz der französischen Könige um 1300*, pp. 198–99, 210–11, 230–31, 290, 322, 324–25, 348, 367–68, 377–78, 384–85, 423, 433–34, 490, 502–03, 525, and 528–29 nos. 25, 44–45, 74, 159, 207, 211, 246, 272, 287, 298, 359, 373, 464, 484, 517, and 523. The *Actes et comptes de la commune de Provins*, pp. 22–23, includes a list of *bannis* for 1296 and court cases demonstrating the application of the process in 1304–05, among other years (pp. 201–02). Brochon, *Essai sur l'histoire de la justice criminelle à Bordeaux*, pp. 51–52 n. 5, catalogues references to numerous registers, now disappeared, for the Bordelais. Dehaisnes notes references to the once-existing fourteenth-century rolls of banishments for the county of Flanders, "État général des registres de la Chambre des comptes de Lille relatifs à la Flandre," p. 300 n. 1; see also Warnkönig, *Flandrische Staats- und Rechtsgeschichte*, 3, part 1, pp. 177–78. Zaremska, *Les bannis au moyen âge*, pp. 125–54, uses surviving registers from Central Europe as the main evidence in her study; and Caviness makes reference to German equivalents, "Giving 'the Middle Ages' a Bad Name," p. 198.

119. Various documents of procedure and practice are either edited, quoted, or cited as well as commented upon in Ducoudray, *Les Origines du Parlement de Paris*, pp. 897–98; Gomart, "De la peine du bannissement," pp. 449–64; *Mémoires historiques . . . Valenciennes*, 3, pp. 181–82; "Bannis de Douais," pp. 3–9; Janin, "Documents relatifs à la peine du bannissement," p. 419; Curveiller, "L'étranger à Dunkerque," pp. 28 and 34 n. 30; idem, *Dunkerque, ville et port*, p. 90; *Recueil des monuments inédits du Tiers-État*, 1, pp. 46, 127–28, 132; 3, p. 482; and 4, pp. 174–78, 195–203, 651; *Droit coutumier de Cambrai*, pp. 10–11 nos. xxxvii, xl, xlii–xliii; *Coutumes de Beauvaisis*, p. 736 s.vv. "Banish, banishment"; *Le livre Roisin: coutumier lillois*, pp. 42, 64, 69, 73, 87–90, 96, 100–01 nos. 55, 92, 98, 106, 130–01, 134–35, 146, 151–52; *Lois, enquêtes et jugements des pairs du Castel de Lille*, p. 136 no. 217; Warnkönig, *Flandrische Staats- und Rechtsgeschichte*, 3, part 1, pp. 173–81; idem, *Histoire consitutionelle et administrative de la ville de Bruges*, pp. 365–66, 372 nos. 5, 11, 36, etc.; Cardevacque, "Le bourreau à Arras," pp. 164–65; Pagart d'Hermansart, *Histoire du bailliage de Saint-Omer*, 1, p. 153 (also, Monteil, *Traité de matériaux manuscrits*, 2, p. 214); *Établissements de Rouen*, 2, p. 187, s.v. "*bannissement*"; Bourquelot, *Histoire de Provins*, 2, pp. 417, 435; *Coutume de Saint-Sever*, pp. 38–40; *Très ancienne coutume de Bretagne*, pp. 149–53 nos. 108–11; Grand, "Justice criminelle," pp. 93, 104–05 (Auvergne and its environs); *Fors de Béarn*, pp. 66, 121 articles 178, 36; *Archives de la ville de Lectoure*, p. 52 no. 84; Turning, *Municipal Officials*, p. 24. More generally, Carbonnières, "Le privilège de bannissement," pp. 315–17; Beaurepaire, *Essai sur l'asile religieux*, p. 63; Coy, *Strangers and Misfits*; Zaremska, *Les bannis au moyen âge*, pp. 74–75.

120. Halba, "Le vocabulaire du bannissement," pp. 347–72.

121. McCune, "Justice, Mercy, and Late Medieval Governance," pp. 1671–77. For the "triumph" of this sentiment in France as well, see Gauvard, *De grace especial*, 2, p. 908.

122. The system of exile for felony in France was equally harsh; see Geremek's description in *Les marginaux parisiens*, pp. 22–23. He does not use the word "mercy."

123. Hoffmann, Kahn, and Fisher, "Plea Bargaining in the Shadow of Death," pp. 2313–92.

124. Shoemaker, *Sanctuary and Crime*, p. 119.

125. Giles Jacob, *The Law-Dictionary*, 5, p. 31.

126. Giles Jacob, *The Law-Dictionary*, 5, p. 31. See chapter 4, pp. 100–12 of the current work for a fuller discussion of gangs.

127. Prestwich, *Plantagenet England*, p. 524.

128. An exquisite case illustrates the disdain for such men. Two hundred and seven prisoners awaiting final disposition of their fates in an overcrowded Nottingham jail ca. 1330 petitioned the crown for relief. The justices who were sent to deliver the jail were remarkable in their leniency. One hundred and ninety-eight people, not yet tried, were released outright. They had suffered enough through the pre-trial imprisonment. Of the remaining nine, four more, already convicted, were permitted to purchase royal pardons. That left five, all of whom were condemned to death by hanging. One of these avoided his fate by proving benefit of clergy. The other four were indeed hanged. Who were these people? Whatever the crimes for which they had been incarcerated, what marked them and them alone as detritus was that three were failed approvers and the fourth, Agnes, was the accomplice wife of a failed approver who had already been hanged. What may have been the most lenient panel of justices ever at work in medieval England could not have cared less about saving an approver's life. Crook, "A Petition from the Prisoners in Nottingham Gaol," pp. 212–13, 218.

129. *Pleas before the King or His Justices, 1198–1212*, pp. 81–82 no. 739.

130. Flower, *Introduction to the Curia Regis Rolls*, pp. 323–24, 444–45.

131. Flower, *Introduction to the Curia Regis Rolls*, p. 323.

132. For the possibility of pardon, however, see chapter 5, pp. 119–33.

133. *OED*, s.vv. "rough music." I owe this observation to Nicholas Vincent.

134. In the preface to Zaremska, *Les bannis au moyen âge*, p. 16. See also Gonthier, *Cris de haine et rites d'unité*, pp. 175–78.

135. See chapter 4, pp. 90–91.

136. One should note here the way in recent years a concentration of possible refugees from France to England at the infamous Sangatte camp, also on the Channel, has produced very negative reactions in Britain.

137. I readily admit that the cases I have examined, being drawn from different kinds of data with enormously varying content, fail to meet the criteria required by quantitative social scientists for a proper sample. I believe, however, that the information I have gleaned is sufficient to make plausible statements about the nature and experience of the exile system. If we adhere to the estimate of 75,000 exiles during the period covered in this study, 2,000 cases constitute 2.67 percent of the total.

Notes to Chapter 2

THE ABJURERS, THEIR CRIMES, AND THEIR PROPERTY

1. Cox, *Sanctuaries and Sanctuary Seekers*, pp. 270–307, with gleanings from many of these sources.

2. Brand, "Understanding Early Petitions," p. 103. See also pp. 124–34 of the current work.

3. See pp. 145 and 162 n. 91.

4. Cox, *Sanctuaries and Sanctuary Seekers*, pp. 242–60.

5. Cox, *Sanctuaries and Sanctuary Seekers*, pp. 261–69, with excerpts.

6. See, for example, the "Inquisitiones post mortem," published in the second volume of *Archaeologia cantiana* in 1859.

7. Murphy, "The Key of the County," p. 67.

8. Deller, "The Texture of Literacy in the Testimonies of Late-Medieval English Proof-of-Age Jurors," pp. 207–24; Hicks, *The Fifteenth-Century Inquisitions Post Mortem*; Kitsikopoulos, "England," pp. 24, 29.

9. See Dyer's perceptive discussion in "Poverty and Its Relief in Late Medieval England," pp. 61–66.

10. Frampton, *A Glance at the Hundred of Wrotham*, p. 49.

11. *London Eyre of 1276*, no. 28.

12. Titow, *English Rural Society*, pp. 78–80.

13. See, for example, *Calendar of Inquisitions Miscellaneous*, 1, pp. 173, 307, 409, 473, 492, 494–95, 580, nos. 536–37, 1011, 1437, 1695, 1777, 1788, 1793, 2177; and 2, p. 20 no. 70); *Staffordshire Plea Rolls* 4, p. 72.

14. Examples of messuages only noted: *Calendar of Inquisitions Miscellaneous*, 1, pp. 171, 175, 339–40, 352, 373, 381, 414, 464, 505 nos. 525, 551, 1133, 1190, 1280, 1314, 1459, 1658, 1855; and 2, pp. 82, 234, nos. 328, 942. Examples of messuages, each with ten acres or less: *Calendar of Inquisitions Miscellaneous*, 1, pp. 389, 463, nos. 1348, 1649.

15. *Calendar of Inquisitions Miscellaneous*, 1, p. 475 no. 1701.

16. Strangers and vagabonds: *Somersetshire Pleas . . . (12th Century–41 Henry III)*, pp. 228, 243–45, 255, 257, 260, 270, 296, nos. 747, 819, 824, 827, 884, 895, 911, 960, 1094; *London Eyre of 1244*, nos. 49, 93, 151; *London Eyre of 1276*, nos. 23, 28, 38, 42, 57–58, 90, 186, 242, 263; *Staffordshire Plea Rolls* 4, p. 73; *Staffordshire Plea Rolls* 6 part 1, p. 268; *Calendar of Inquisitions Miscellaneous*, 3, p. 315 no. 832.

17. Fuller, "Pleas of the Crown at Bristol," p. 159.

18. *Somersetshire Pleas . . . (12th Century–41 Henry III)*, p. 270 no. 960.

19. *London Eyre of 1244*, no. 49; *Staffordshire Plea Rolls* 4, p. 73.

20. *Somersetshire Pleas . . . (12th Century–41 Henry III)*, p. 296 no. 1094.

21. *Somersetshire Pleas . . . (12th Century–41 Henry III)*, p. 245 no. 827.

22. *Somersetshire Pleas . . . (12th Century–41 Henry III)*, p. 228 no. 747; *London Eyre of 1276*, no. 90; *Calendar of Coroners' Rolls of the City of London A.D. 1300–1378*, p. 124.

23. *Somersetshire Pleas . . . (12th Century–41 Henry III)*, pp. 228, 244–45, 260, nos. 747, 824, 827, 911; *London Eyre of 1276*, no. 38; *Staffordshire Plea*

Rolls 6 part 1, p. 268. See also Whitley, "Sanctuary in Devon," p. 305 no. 1, 306 no. 20, 307 no. 3, 309 no. 15, 311–12 nos. 14–15.

24. *Somersetshire Pleas . . . (Close of 12th Century–41 Henry III)*, p. 45 no. 185 (repeated at p. 97 no. 383) and pp. 238, 257 nos. 795, 895; *Staffordshire Plea Rolls* 7 part 1, p. 176.

25. *Select Cases from the Coroners' Rolls A.D. 1265–1413*, pp. 68–69.

26. *Select Cases from the Coroners' Rolls A.D. 1265–1413*, pp. 66–67.

27. *Select Cases from the Coroners' Rolls A.D. 1265–1413*, pp. 67–68.

28. *Select Cases from the Coroners' Rolls A.D. 1265–1413*, p. 68.

29. See, for example, *Select Cases from the Coroners' Rolls A.D. 1265–1413*, p. 68 (pennies, a sash, a purse, three knives); *Calendar of Coroners' Rolls of the City of London A.D. 1300–1378*, p. 124 (two abjurers' goods, average worth 10d., consisting of a tunic, a hood, a sword and two knives); *Somersetshire Pleas . . . (Close of 12th Century–41 Henry III)*, p. 321 no. 1244 (chattels, 12d.).

30. *London Eyre of 1244*, nos. 49, 93, 98, 117, 125, 127, 139–40, 151, 163; *London Eyre of 1276*, nos. 11, 20, 23, 28, 52, 65, 73, 81–82, 90, 97, 100, 106–10, 115, 123, 241, 262–63, 283, 316; Fuller, "Pleas of the Crown at Bristol," pp. 159, 163–65, 167–69, 171; *Calendar of Coroners' Rolls of the City of London A.D. 1300–1378*, pp. 84, 89–90; *Somersetshire Pleas . . . (Close of 12th Century–41 Henry III)*, pp. 46, 55, 228, 244, 255, 260, 270, 276, 295, 298, 306, nos. 91, 250, 747–48, 824, 884, 911, 960, 987, 1087, 1108, 1153; *Staffordshire Plea Rolls* 4, p. 73; *Staffordshire Plea Rolls* 6 part 1, p. 275; etc.

31. *Calendar of Inquisitions Miscellaneous*, 3, pp. 165–66 no. 440.

32. *Calendar of Inquisitions Miscellaneous*, 1, p. 18 no. 58.

33. *Calendar of Inquisitions Miscellaneous*, 1, p. 466 no. 1667.

34. *Calendar of Inquisitions Miscellaneous*, 1, p. 495 no. 1791.

35. *Curia Regis Rolls*, 11: 7–9 Henry III, p. 574 no. 2861.

36. *Fine Rolls, 1234–1242*, p. 127 no. 194.

37. *Calendar of Inquisitions Miscellaneous*, 1, 307 no. 1011.

38. See, for instance, *Curia Regis Rolls*, 12: 9–10 Henry III, p. 262 no. 1284 (one-half virgate).

39. *Calendar of Inquisitions Miscellaneous*, 1, 427 no. 1506.

40. *Calendar of Inquisitions Miscellaneous*, 2, p. 4 no. 16.

41. *Calendar of Inquisitions Miscellaneous*, 2, p. 27 no. 119.

42. *Calendar of Inquisitions Miscellaneous*, 1, pp. 455–56 no. 1623, and 2, pp. 8–9 no. 34.

43. *Calendar of Inquisitions Miscellaneous*, 1, p. 388 no. 1342.

44. *Calendar of Inquisitions Miscellaneous*, 1, pp. 466–67 no. 1668.

45. *Calendar of Inquisitions Miscellaneous*, 2, p. 288 no. 1176.

46. *Calendar of Inquisitions Miscellaneous*, 1, pp. 464, 476 nos. 1659 and 1709.

47. Shoemaker, *Sanctuary and Crime*, p. 125.

48. *Calendar of Inquisitions Miscellaneous*, 2, p. 39 no. 163.

49. *Fine Rolls, 1234–1242*, p. 232 no. 236.

50. *London Eyre of 1244*, no. 317.

51. *Staffordshire Plea Rolls* 4, p. 72.

52. *Fine Rolls, 1234–1242*, p. 413 no. 409.

53. *London Eyre of 1276*, no. 9.

54. For the two inquests, see *Calendar of Inquisitions Miscellaneous*, 1, pp. 485–86, 494 nos. 1754 and 1790.

55. *Calendar of Inquisitions Miscellaneous*, 3, p. 167 no. 446.

56. *Liberate Rolls, 1251–1260*, p. 75.

57. *Liberate Rolls, 1245–1251*, p. 182.

58. *Legal History: The Year Books* (online), Seipp number 1319.050ss.

59. *London Eyre of 1276*, no. 66.

60. *London Eyre of 1276*, no. 186.

61. *Calendar of Coroners' Rolls of the City of London A.D. 1300–1378*, p. 72.

62. *Staffordshire Plea Rolls* 6 part 1, p. 275; Shoemaker, *Sanctuary and Crime*, p. 137.

63. *Somersetshire Pleas . . . (Close of 12th Century–41 Henry III)*, p. 238 no. 795.

64. *Somersetshire Pleas . . . (Close of 12th Century–41 Henry III)*, p. 229 no. 755.

65. *Somersetshire Pleas . . . (Close of 12th Century–41 Henry III)*, p. 291 no. 1066.

66. See also cases provided in Fuller, "Pleas of the Crown at Bristol," pp. 160, 171, with homicides possessing no chattels and 3s. 4d.

67. *Somersetshire Pleas . . . (Close of 12th Century–41Henry III)*, p. 298 no. 1108.

68. *Somersetshire Pleas . . . (Close of 12th Century–41 Henry III)*, p. 267 no. 942 (datable to 1243 or before).

69. *London Eyre of 1244*, no. 149, and *London Eyre of 1276*, no. 92.

70. See, for example, *Somersetshire Pleas . . . (Close of 12th Century–41 Henry III)*, pp. 102, 105, 236, 248, 318 nos. 384–85, 785, 849, 1221; *Select Cases from the Coroners' Rolls A.D. 1265–1413*, p. 103; *Staffordshire Plea Rolls* 4, p. 72; Fuller, "Pleas of the Crown at Bristol," pp. 160, 165, 168–71, 173.

71. Examples, all dating from the long thirteenth century down to the mid-fourteenth century, may be found in: *Somersetshire Pleas . . . (Close 12th Century–41 Henry III)*, pp. 52, 270, 324 nos. 231, 958, 1264; *Staffordshire Plea Rolls* 7, part 1, p. 176; *London Eyre of 1276*, nos. 172, 262; *Calendar of Inquisitions Miscellaneous*, 3, pp. 274, 315 nos. 728 and 832.

72. *London Eyre of 1276*, no. 79 (abjuration in 1257–58 for theft of an ox and a horse); *Calendar of Inquisitions Miscellaneous*, 3, p. 109 no. 315 (abjuration in 1358 for theft; the miscreant, who may have been a fence for rustled cattle and stolen goods, had cows, young oxen, yearling calves, sheep, a horse, pigs, three brass pails, a plumb line, etc.).

73. *Curia Regis Rolls*, 13: *11–14 Henry III*, p. 107 no. 466; *Fine Rolls, 1224–1234*, p. 162 no. 302.

74. *Calendar of Coroners' Rolls of the City of London A.D. 1300–1378*, pp. 87–89. Another case might be that of Walter Albus (Blandus), but I will address his circumstances more fully in chapter 5, p. 115.

75. *Calendar of Inquisitions Miscellaneous*, 1, pp. 525, 556 nos. 1933, 2074, and 2, p. 24 no. 102; *Somersetshire Pleas . . . (Close 12th Century–41 Henry III)*, pp. 41, 52, 103, 106, 298 nos. 166, 231, 383–85, 1108; *Select Cases from the Coroners' Rolls A.D. 1265–1413*, p. 37; *London Eyre of 1276*, no. 73.

76. *Calendar of Inquisitions Miscellaneous*, 2, pp. 82, 172 nos. 328, 691; *Staffordshire Plea Rolls* 6 part 1, p. 271.

77. *Curia Regis Rolls, 6: 11–14 John*, p. 350; *Close Rolls, 1237–1242*, p. 122; *Close Rolls, 1259–1261*, p. 247; *Patent Rolls, 1292–1301*, p. 127; *Select Cases from the Coroners Rolls A.D. 1265–1413*, pp. 69–70; *Somersetshire Pleas . . . (Close 12th Century–41 Henry III)*, p. 247 no. 842. See also Shoemaker, *Sanctuary and Crime*, p. 124.

78. See Shoemaker, *Sanctuary and Crime*, pp. 125–26. It is also implied in a case from 1238, *Close Rolls, 1237–1242*, p. 122.

79. See the customs redacted in Normandy on 13 November 1205 and approved by the leading nobles: *Calendar of Documents Preserved in France*, vol. 1: *A.D. 918–1206*, pp. 476–78 no. 1318.

80. Shoemaker, *Sanctuary and Crime*, p. 129.

81. Shoemaker, *Sanctuary and Crime*, p. 133.

82. Six pence was declared insufficient in another case from 1241: Shoemaker, *Sanctuary and Crime*, p. 133.

83. *Calendar of Inquisitions Miscellaneous*, 1, 603 no. 2254. For the resolution of the case, see pp. 129–30 of the current work.

84. Brand, "Chief Justice and Felon," pp. 27–34.

85. Brand, "Chief Justice and Felon," p. 40.

86. Brand, "Chief Justice and Felon," pp. 40–45.

87. Brand, "Chief Justice and Felon," pp. 45–46. Cf. Prestwich, *Edward I*, p. 339.

88. Brand, "Chief Justice and Felon," p. 46.

89. Brand, "Chief Justice and Felon," p. 46.

90. Prestwich, *Edward I*, p. 339. See also Brand, "Chief Justice and Felon," p. 46.

91. In 1356 judges made reference to another puzzling intervention by Edward I which still fascinated them fifty years after his death: *Legal History: The Year Books* (online), Seipp number 1356.134ass.

92. Stewart, "Outlawry as an Instrument of Justice in the Thirteenth Century," p. 45.

93. *Curia Regis Rolls, 3: 5–7 John*, p. 145.

94. *London Eyre of 1276*, no. 28; the case is dated 1252–53.

95. *Close Rolls, 1251–1253*, p. 137.

96. *Calendar of Inquisitions Miscellaneous*, 1, p. 385 no. 1331. For further on this case, see pp. 130–31 of the current work.

97. *Curia Regis Rolls, 8: 3–4 Henry III*, p. 279; *Curia Regis Rolls, 9: 4–5 Henry III*, p. 309; *Patent Rolls, 1266–1272*, p. 15; *Select Cases from the Coroners' Rolls A.D. 1265–1413*, p. 103; *Calendar of Coroners' Rolls of the City of London A.D. 1300–1378*, pp. 130–31; *Somersetshire Pleas . . . (Close of 12th Century–41 Henry III)*, pp. 55, 236, 247, 296 nos. 250, 785, 842, 1094; *London*

Eyre of 1276, nos. 204, 263, 316; Fuller, "Pleas of the Crown at Bristol," pp. 162–63; *Pleas of the Crown for . . . Swineshead*, p. 141; *Oxford City Documents*, p. 189; *Calendar of Inquisitions Miscellaneous*, 3, pp. 51, 109 nos. 145 and 315; Frampton, *A Glance at the Hundred of Wrotham*, pp. 11–13, 18. See also Shoemaker, *Sanctuary and Crime*, p. 127.

98. *Somersetshire Pleas . . . (Close 12th Century–41 Henry III)*, p. 323 no. 1254. In general, see Shoemaker, *Sanctuary and Crime*, p. 127.

99. Fuller, "Pleas of the Crown at Bristol," p. 163.

100. Fuller, "Pleas of the Crown at Bristol," pp. 162, 168; *Pleas of the Crown for . . . Swineshead*, p. 141; *Oxford City Documents*, p. 189.

101. Fuller, "Pleas of the Crown at Bristol," p. 166.

102. See, for example, *Close Rolls, 1259–1261*, p. 342.

103. *Mémoires historiques sur l'arrondissement de Valenciennes*, p. 176.

104. Shoemaker, *Sanctuary and Crime*, p. 134.

105. *Fine Rolls, 1224–1234*, p. 468 no. 133.

106. *Curia Regis Rolls*, 11: *7–9 Henry III*, p. 574 no. 2861.

107. *Fine Rolls, 1234–1242*, p. 127 no. 194.

108. A few examples: arson, *Fine Rolls, 1234–1242*, pp. 154–55 nos. 339–41; counterfeiting, *London Eyre of 1276*, no. 11; and theft, pp. 47–48 of the current work.

109. A number of instances: *Curia Regis Rolls*, 4: *7–8 John*, p. 115; *Curia Regis Rolls*, 7: *15–16 John*, p. 241; *Curia Regis Rolls*, 9: *4–5 Henry III*, p. 309; *Curia Regis Rolls*: 14: *14–17 Henry III*, p. 92 no. 464; *Fine Rolls, 1234–1242*, p. 122 no. 161; *Liberate Rolls, 1251–1260*, p. 75; *London Eyre of 1244*, nos. 98, 125, 127, 151; *London Eyre of 1276*, nos. 9, 20, 23, 42, 52, 58, 66, 106, 110, 112, 115, 172, 186, 242, 262, 283; Fuller, "Pleas of the Crown at Bristol," pp. 159–60, 163, 165, 167–71, 173; Whitley, "Sanctuary in Devon," pp. 305 no. 1 and 6, 306 nos. 20, 22–30, 308 no. 19, and 312–13 nos. 17 and 24; *Somersetshire Pleas . . . (Close of 12th Century–41 Henry III)*, pp. 46, 104, 106, 228, 236, 243–45, 248, 255, 257, 259–60, 270, 276, 281, 306–07, 321, 323–24 nos. 91, 384–85, 747, 785, 819, 824, 827, 847, 849, 884, 895, 907, 911, 958, 987, 1008, 1153, 1158, 1244, 1255, 1264; *Staffordshire Plea Rolls* 4, p. 73; *Select Cases from the Coroners' Rolls A.D. 1265–1413*, pp. 36–37, 68–69, 75–76; *Calendar of Inquisitions Miscellaneous*, 3, pp. 165–66 no. 440; *Calendar of Coroners' Rolls of the City of London A.D. 1300–1378*, p. 7; Frampton, *A Glance at the Hundred of Wrotham*, pp. 19, 47–48; etc.

110. For the two abjurations referred to, see *Curia Regis Rolls*, 7: *15–16 John*, p. 241 (dated 1214) and *Somersetshire Pleas . . . (Close of 12th Century–41 Henry III)*, p. 239 no. 797 (dated 1243 or earlier).

111. See, for example, *Somersetshire Pleas . . . (Close of 12th Century–41 Henry III)*, p. 298 no. 1108; *London Eyre of 1276*, p. 267 no. 942; *London Eyre of 1244*, no. 149; *London Eyre of 1276*, nos. 79, 82, 92, 100, 123. I could continue this list until, to coin a phrase, the rustled cows come home.

112. *Somersetshire Pleas . . . (Close of 12th Century–41 Henry III)*, p. 270 no. 960; *London Eyre of 1276*, no. 79.

113. *London Eyre of 1276*, nos. 20, 65.

114. *London Eyre of 1276*, nos. 57, 73.

115. Hale, *Historia placitorum coronae*, 1, p. 549.

116. *Middle English Dictionary*, 3, p. 376. The problem, perhaps impossibility, of differentiating surnames and nicknames in the thirteenth century is addressed in Olson, *A Mute Gospel*, pp. 100–10.

117. *London Eyre of 1276*, no. 38.

118. Whitley, "Sanctuary in Devon," p. 305 no. 1.

119. *Select Cases from the Coroners' Rolls A.D. 1265–1413*, pp. 68–69.

120. *Calendar of Inquisitions Miscellaneous*, 1, pp. 171, 175, 291, 607 nos. 525, 551, 948, 2270; *Select Cases from the Coroners' Rolls A.D. 1265–1413*, pp. 38, 67–70; *Calendar of Coroners' Rolls of the City of London A.D. 1300–1378*, pp. 64, 84, 87–90, 124; *Somersetshire Pleas . . . (Close of 12th Century–41 Henry III)*, pp. 38, 41, 45, 52, 57, 97–98, 102–03, 105–06, 229, 238, 260, 291, 293, 295, 303–04, 318 nos. 148, 166, 185, 189, 231, 263, 298, 305, 383–85, 755, 795, 910, 1066, 1077, 1087, 1108, 1144, 1221; *London Eyre of 1244*, nos. 49, 93, 140, 163; *London Eyre of 1276*, nos. 90, 97, 241; Fuller, "Pleas of the Crown at Bristol," pp. 159–60, 163–64, 167, 171; Whitley, "Sanctuary in Devon," pp. 305 nos. 13–14, 307 nos. 3, 8, 18, 308–09 nos. 1–2, 309 no. 15, 310–11 nos. 11–120, 311–12 nos. 13–15, 312 nos. 17–18; *Pleas of the Crown for . . . Swineshead*, p. 141; *Staffordshire Plea Rolls 4*, p. 72; *Staffordshire Plea Rolls 6 part 1*, p. 271; *Curia Regis Rolls, 6: 11–14 John*, p. 256; *Curia Regis Rolls, 7: 15–16 John*, pp. 241, 244; *Curia Regis Rolls, 15: 17–21 Henry III*, p. 326 no. 1304; *Fine Rolls, 1216–1224*, pp. 14, 25, 35 nos. 46, 99, 137; *Fine Rolls, 1224–1234*, p. 535 no. 142; *Fine Rolls, 1234–1242*, p. 165 no. 402; *Liberate Rolls, 1226–1240*, p. 467; *Liberate Rolls, 1245–1251*, p. 182; *Close Rolls, 1259–1261*, p. 256; *Patent Rolls, 1292–1301*, p. 127; *Patent Rolls, 1317–1321*, p. 38; *Patent Rolls, 1321–1324*, p. 38; etc.

121. *Select Cases from the Coroners' Rolls A.D. 1265–1413*, pp. 67, 86–87; Fuller, "Pleas of the Crown at Bristol," pp. 163–64; Whitley, "Sanctuary in Devon," pp. 311–12 nos. 14, 17.

122. *Calendar of Inquisitions Miscellaneous*, 1, p. 556 no. 2074.

123. Whitley, "Sanctuary in Devon," p. 310 no. 15.

124. *Curia Regis Rolls, 10: 5–6 Henry III*, p. 293.

125. Whitley, "Sanctuary in Devon," pp. 311–12 no. 15. Summerson, "Attitudes to Capital Punishment," p. 27, also offers speculation on this case.

126. Whitley, "Sanctuary in Devon," p. 313.

127. *Eyre of Northamptonshire, 3–4 Edward III*, 1, p. 189 (summarized in *Legal History: The Year Books* [online], Seipp number 1330.364ss).

128. Fuller, "Pleas of the Crown at Bristol," p. 159.

129. *London Eyre of 1244*, no. 139.

130. *Somersetshire Pleas . . . (Close of 12th Century–41 Henry III)*, p. 228 no. 748.

131. *London Eyre of 1276*, no. 81.

132. *Calendar of Inquisitions Miscellaneous*, 2, pp. 288, 317 nos. 1176 and 1296.

133. *London Eyre of 1244*, no. 146.

134. *London Eyre of 1244*, no. 117.

135. *Somersetshire Pleas . . . (Close of 12th Century–41 Henry III)*, p. 240 no. 804.

136. *Close Rolls, 1259–1261*, p. 247.

137. *Close Rolls, 1264–1268*, p. 329.

138. *Close Rolls, 1259–1261*, p. 247.

139. Fuller, "Pleas of the Crown at Bristol," pp. 163–64.

140. Fuller, "Pleas of the Crown at Bristol," p. 169.

141. *Somersetshire Pleas . . . (Close of 12th Century–41 Henry III)*, p. 48 no. 205.

142. *Patent Rolls, 1266–1272*, pp. 271, 285.

143. Cf. Whitley, "Sanctuary in Devon," p. 306 nos. 22–30.

144. *Curia Regis Rolls: 7: 15–16 John*, p. 247. Sartore, *Outlawry, Governance, and Law*, pp. 142–43.

145. *Calendar of Inquisitions Miscellaneous*, 1, 173 no. 540.

146. *Close Rolls, 1237–1242*, pp. 522–23. Shoemaker, *Sanctuary and Crime*, p. 134, appears to be referring to the same case (if so, his citation is in error) and presumes the father was pardoned from sanctuary. He acknowledges, however, that the record does not say this (p. 225 n. 128).

147. In general, see Shoemaker, *Sanctuary and Crime*, pp. 124–25; Pollock and Maitland, *History of English Law*, vol. 2, p. 590; Trenholme, *Right of Sanctuary*, pp. 43–44; Réville, "L'Abjuratio regni," pp. 18, 27. For documents of practice—court cases and administrative records—see *Calendar of Inquisitions Miscellaneous*, 1, pp. 171, 173, 175, 339–40, 373, 381, 389, 409, 414, 427, 455–56, 463–64, 466–67, 473, 475–76, 480, 484, 486, 492, 494–95, 505, 525, 580 nos. 525, 536–37, 551, 1133, 1280, 1314, 1348, 1437, 1459, 1506, 1623, 1649, 1653, 1658–59, 1667–68, 1695, 1701, 1709, 1727, 1743, 1755, 1777, 1788, 1790–91, 1855, 1933, 2177; "Inquisitiones post mortem" [*Archaeologia cantiana*], p. 300; *Close Rolls, 1237–1242*, pp. 332, 392, 419; *Close Rolls, 1247–1251*, p. 259; *Fine Rolls, 1224–1234*, p. 535 no. 142; *Fine Rolls, 1234–1242*, p. 339, 413 nos. 218 and 409; *Liberate Rolls, 1226–1240*, p. 467. This last reference illustrates the way a case can be accessed through different administrative sources, since an entry dealing with the same property occurs in the *Close Rolls, 1237–1242*, p. 192.

148. See, for example, *Calendar of Inquisitions Miscellaneous*, 1, pp. 307, 495 nos. 1011 and 1793. For the interpretative legal history of "year, day, and waste; *annus, dies, et vastum*," see Giles Jacob's *The Law-Dictionary*, vol. 4, 468–70.

149. *Calendar of Inquisitions Miscellaneous*, 1, p. 495 no. 1793.

150. *Close Rolls, 1247–1251*, p. 139; *Petitions to the Crown from English Religious Houses*, p. 14 no. 18.

151. *Curia Regis Rolls: 8: 3–4 Henry III*, pp. 41–42.

152. *Munimenta gildhallae londoniensis . . . 1, Liber albus*, pp. 86–87.

153. *Close Rolls, 1253–1254*, p. 60; *Close Rolls, 1256–1259*, p. 356; *Close Rolls, 1259–1261*, pp. 296–97; *Close Rolls, 1264–1268*, pp. 161, 329; *Fine Rolls, 1234–1242*, p. 127 no. 194.

154. *Close Rolls, 1247–1251*, pp. 154–55, 159, 305; *Close Rolls, 1259–1261*, p. 432.

155. *Close Rolls, 1237–1242*, p. 169.

156. *Fine Rolls, 1216–1224*, p. 357 no. 137; *Fine Rolls, 1234–1242*, p. 413 no. 409.

157. *Close Rolls, 1261–1264*, p. 60.

158. *Close Rolls, 1261–1264*, p. 218.

159. *Calendar of Inquisitions Miscellaneous*, 2, p. 234 no. 942.

160. *Fine Rolls, 1234–1242*, p. 165 no. 402.

161. *Calendar of Inquisitions Miscellaneous*, 1, p. 173 no. 540.

162. *Calendar of Inquisitions Miscellaneous*, 1, p. 388 no. 1342.

163. See, for example, *Curia Regis Rolls*, 7: *15–16 John*, p. 244; *Curia Regis Rolls*, 10: *5–6 Henry III*, p. 293; *Curia Regis Rolls*, 11: *7–9 Henry III*, p. 574 no. 2861; and *Legal History: The Year Books* (online), Seipp numbers 1315.047ss, 1332.192, 1334.028, and 1355.189ass; UK, National Archives, SC 8/87/4323, online at http://discovery.nationalarchives.gov.uk/SearchUI/Details?uri=C9148865.

164. *Legal History: The Year Books* (online), Seipp number 1352.096ass.

165. *Legal History: The Year Books* (online), Seipp number 1334.029.

166. See pp. 54–55.

167. *Curia Regis Rolls*, 10: *5–6 Henry III*, p. 341.

168. *Curia Regis Rolls*, 12: *9–10 Henry III*, p. 153 no. 742.

169. Pollock and Maitland, *History of English Law*, 2, p. 436.

170. *Curia Regis Rolls*, 12: *9–10 Henry III*, p. 262 no. 1284.

171. *Curia Regis Rolls*, 12: *9–10 Henry III*, p. 506 no. 2535.

172. Hillen, *History of the Borough of King's Lynn*, 2, p. 848.

Notes to Chapter 3

THE JOURNEY BEGINS

1. Cox, *Sanctuaries and Sanctuary Seekers*, pp. 241–42.

2. Bracton, *De legibus*, 2, p. 382. If the abjuration was before justices, they would have been the officers mentioned.

3. *Coutumiers de Normandie*, 2, p. 63 (xxii, 7), "Hoc audient omnes assistentes quod tu de cetero in Normanniam non intrabis; sic Deus et sacrosancta te adjuvent."

4. Cf. Shoemaker, *Sanctuary and Crime*, p. 120, and the editorial remarks in the *Eyre of Kent 6 & 7 Edward II*, p. lxxiii, for variant versions of the oath.

5. Discussed in Bezemer, *What Jacques Saw*, p. 114, with the source transcribed at p. 118.

6. *Coutumiers de Normandie*. 2, p. 68 (xxii, 13). On the history and variety of cases in the legal system to which the burning of residences and other modes of destruction applied, including the Norman custom, see Gessler, "Notes sur le droit d'arsin ou d'abattis," pp. 293–312, especially p. 299; *Mémoires historiques sur l'arrondissement de Valenciennes*, 3, pp. 212–13; Grand, "Justice criminelle," p. 93; and Gomart, "De la peine du bannissement," pp. 449–50. Such rituals occurred throughout contemporary Europe: Zaremska, *Les bannis au moyen âge*,

pp. 82–84; Gonthier, *Le châtiment du crime*, pp. 178–80. More generally on the use of fire in all aspects of legal process, see Leguay, *Le feu*, pp. 354–67; some of the practices seem to me to evoke theological ideas of the nature of hellfire, which is the subject of Barbezat's "In a Corporeal Flame," pp. 1–20.

7. Cf. Friedland, *Seeing Justice Done*, pp. 98–100. See more generally on the discourse and rituals of banishment, Robert Jacob, "Bannissement," pp. 1039–67.

8. *Inquisitions post mortem*, 10, p. 286 no. 333.

9. *Inquisitions post mortem*, 10, p. 326 no. 398.

10. Jordan, "A Fresh Look at Medieval Sanctuary," pp. 24–25; Shoemaker, *Sanctuary and Crime*, pp. 120, 137; Cox, *Sanctuaries and Sanctuary Seekers*, pp. 24–25.

11. Examples of choice: *Curia Regis Rolls*, 14: *14–17 Henry III*, pp. 92, 253 nos. 464 and 1190; *Select Cases from the Coroners' Rolls A.D. 1265–1413*, p. 9; *Calendar of Coroners' Rolls of the City of London A.D. 1300–1378*, pp. 84, 87–90. Examples of assignment: *Somersetshire Pleas . . . (Close of 12th Century–41 Henry III)*, p. 240 no. 804; *Select Cases from the Coroners' Rolls A.D. 1265–1413*, pp. 38, 66–70, 75–76, 103; *Calendar of Coroners' Rolls of the City of London A.D. 1300–1378*, 64, 72, 124, 130–31.

12. Fuller, "Pleas of the Crown at Bristol," p. 168.

13. Fuller, "Pleas of the Crown at Bristol," p. 171.

14. Jordan, "Fresh Look at Medieval Sanctuary," p. 25.

15. See Vincent, "In the Shadow of the Castle Wall" (forthcoming).

16. On the 1226 order, see *Patent Rolls, 1225–1232*, p. 25. On the 1389 order (*Statutes of the Realm*, 2, p. 68 [13 Richard II c.20]), see Sweetinburgh, "Royal Patrons and Local Benefactors," p. 124. Timothy Jones, *Outlawry in Medieval Literature*, p. 174 n. 17, drawing on Ives, *A History of Penal Methods*, p. 100, could be read as suggesting that this was specifically linked to the crown's desire to concentrate the abjurers, but given the date, I think that it was intended for and probably had far greater relevance to other sorts of travelers, such as the pilgrims who are explicitly mentioned in the statute.

17. There follow a few examples. Bristol: *Select Cases from the Coroners' Rolls A.D. 1265–1413*, p. 68; *Calendar of Coroners' Rolls of the City of London A.D. 1300–1378*, p. 84. Portsmouth: *Curia Regis Rolls*, 14: *14–17 Henry III*, pp. 92, 253 nos. 464 and 1190; *Select Cases from the Coroners' Rolls A.D. 1265–1413*, pp. 67–68; *Calendar of Coroners' Rolls of the City of London A.D. 1300–1378*, pp. 130–31. Southampton: *Calendar of Coroners' Rolls of the City of London A.D. 1300–1378*, pp. 130–31. Harwich: *Calendar of Coroners' Rolls of the City of London A.D. 1300–1378*, p. 124. Bawdsey: *Select Cases from the Coroners' Rolls A.D. 1265–1413*, p. 103. See also Cox, *Sanctuaries and Sanctuary Seekers*, p. 26.

18. Trenholme, *Right of Sanctuary*, p. 38; and chapter 6, p. 141 of the current work.

19. *London Eyre of 1276*, no. 123 note.

20. *Select Cases from the Coroners' Rolls A.D. 1265–1413*, pp. 67–68 (Dover and Portsmouth); *Calendar of Coroners' Rolls of the City of London A.D. 1300–1378*, pp. 124 (Dover and Harwich) and 130–31 (Dover and Southampton).

21. Cox, *Sanctuaries and Sanctuary Seekers*, p. 31.

22. Bracton, *De legibus*, 1, p. 382.

23. *Coutumiers de Normandie*, 2, p. 64 (xxii, 8).

24. *Calendar of Coroners' Rolls of the City of London A.D. 1300–1378*, pp. 130–31. For another three-day assignment to Dover from London, see *Calendar of Coroners' Rolls of the City of London A.D. 1300–1378*, pp. 89–90.

25. *Calendar of Coroners' Rolls of the City of London A.D. 1300–1378*, pp. 130–31.

26. *Calendar of Coroners' Rolls of the City of London A.D. 1300–1378*, p. 124.

27. *Calendar of Coroners' Rolls of the City of London A.D. 1300–1378*, p. 84.

28. Hill, "The King's Messengers 1199–1377," p. 3.

29. Cox, *Sanctuaries and Sanctuary Seekers*, pp. 28–30.

30. Brand, "Chief Justice and Felon," p. 27.

31. Brand, "Chief Justice and Felon," p. 27.

32. *Calendar of Coroners' Rolls of the City of London A.D. 1300–1378*, pp. 87–89.

33. *Curia Regis Rolls*, 14: *14–17 Henry III*, p. 92 no. 464.

34. *Curia Regis Rolls*, 14: *14–17 Henry III*, p. 253 no. 1190.

35. *Select Cases from the Coroners' Rolls A.D. 1265–1413*, p. 103.

36. Trenholme, *Right of Sanctuary*, pp. 40, 54. See also Réville, "L'Abjuratio regni," p. 17.

37. His views are discussed at some length in Cox, *Sanctuaries and Sanctuary Seekers*, pp. 22–25.

38. Shoemaker, *Sanctuary and Crime*, p. 120; Cox, *Sanctuaries and Sanctuary Seekers*, p. 32; Trenholme, *Right of Sanctuary*, p. 24; Réville, "L'Abjuratio regni," p. 17. The immemorial connection between banishment and penance is discussed in Zaremska, *Les bannis au moyen âge*, pp. 43–64.

39. Jordan, "A Fresh Look at Medieval Sanctuary," p. 25.

40. *Bibliothèque historique . . . de la Picardie et de l'Artois*, p. 287.

41. Shoemaker, *Sanctuary and Crime*, pp. 120, 142; Lambert, "Evolution of Sanctuary," p. 119.

42. Bracton, *On the Laws*, vol. 2, p. 382; *Eyre of Kent 6 & 7 Edward II*, 1, p. lxx.

43. Bracton, *On the Laws*, vol. 2, p. 382. See also Brand, "Chief Justice and Felon," p. 27.

44. *Coutumiers de Normandie*, 2, p. 64 (xxii, 8).

45. Cf. Jordan, "A Fresh Look at Medieval Sanctuary," pp. 25–26.

46. *Curia Regis Rolls*, 9: *4–5 Henry III*, p. 309.

47. *Calendar of Liberate Rolls, 1226–1240*, p. 40.

48. See Jordan, "A Fresh Look at Medieval Sanctuary," p. 26.

49. *Bibliothèque historique . . . de la Picardie et de l'Artois*, p. 287; *Mémoires historiques sur l'arrondissement de Valenciennes*, 3, p. 182.

50. Vincent, "In the Shadow of the Castle Wall" (forthcoming), has some good words to say about the low rate of winter travel in the late twelfth century.

51. *Select Cases from the Coroners Rolls A.D. 1265–1413*, pp. 86–87.

52. *Calendar of Coroners Rolls of the City of London A.D. 1300–1378*, p. 72.

53. *Calendar of Inquisitions Miscellaneous*, 1, p. 607 no. 2270.

54. Shoemaker, *Sanctuary and Crime*, pp. 112–13. A somewhat similar case in which abjurers claimed they were dragged from the king's highway is referenced in Musson, *Public Order*, p. 202.

55. Pollock and Maitland, *The History of English Law*, vol. 2, p. 579.

56. Shoemaker, *Sanctuary and Crime*, pp. 112–13.

57. *Select Cases from the Coroners' Rolls A.D. 1265–1413*, p. 9.

58. *Staffordshire Plea Rolls* (Staffordshire Historical Collections 10), p. 42.

59. For example, in the mid-thirteenth century a royal *bailli*, Étienne Tâtesaveur, conducted an inquest to find out who gave refuge to Jacquet Tartre, who had been exiled for the murder of a royal sergeant: *Série J, Trésor des chartes, supplément: Inventaire. J1028 à J1034, J1034^B no. 62.

60. See, for example, *Somersetshire Pleas . . . (12th Century–41 Henry III)*, pp. 306–07, 321 nos. 1153, 1158, 1244.

61. *Select Cases from the Coroners' Rolls A.D. 1265–1413*, p. 37. Bolland, in the editorial preface of the *Eyre of Kent 6 & 7 Edward II*, p. lxx, did not conclude that William was a guard doing his job, but simply a villager who happened to witness the escape.

62. Fuller, "Pleas of the Crown at Bristol," p. 153.

63. *Select Cases from the Coroners' Rolls A.D. 1265–1413*, pp. 75–76.

64. Cox, *Sanctuaries and Sanctuary Seekers*, pp. 32, 244, 264, 275, 277, 305.

65. *Calendar of London Trailbaston Trials under Commissions of 1305 and 1306*, no. 275.

66. *Calendar of Fine Rolls, 1224–1234*, p. 509 nos. 362–63.

67. Contra Trenholme, *Right of Sanctuary*, p. 42.

68. Jordan, "Administering Expulsion," pp. 242–43. For the argument with regard to Dover Castle, see pp. 71–72 of the current work.

69. See, for example, *The Medieval Records of a London City Church*, pp. 26–55.

70. Andrew Brown, *Civic Ceremony and Religion*, p. 65; Craig Wright, "The Palm Sunday Procession," pp. 346 and 350–51.

71. *Documents sur la ville de Millau*, p. 16 no. 33.

72. Cox, *Sanctuaries and Sanctuary Seekers*, p. 33; R. F. Wright, "The High Seas and the Church," pp. 30–31.

73. Coulson, "Peaceable Power in English Castles," pp. 69–75.

74. Coulson, "Peaceable Power in English Castles," p. 69.

75. Clarke and others, *Sandwich*, p. 68.

76. See, for example, *Pipe Rolls, 1199–1200*, pp. 208–09; *Pipe Rolls, 1200–1201*, p. 284; *Pipe Rolls, 1207–1208*, p. 97; *Pipe Rolls, 1211–1212*, p. 12.

77. For a list of the Constables of the castle and Port of Dover from the earliest known down through the mid-fourteenth century, see Lyon, *History of the Town and Port of Dover*, vol. 2, pp. 192–230. In general on the institutional and

administrative history of Dover and the Cinque Ports, see Katherine Murray, *The Constitutional History of the Cinque Ports*.

78. The Pipe Rolls provide extensive evidence of the paying of guards; the entries typically read, "Et in liberationibus constitutes . . . portario et uigilibus [*or* uigili] de Doura [*or a variant*]." The wages paid were fixed at £6 20d. for regular guards. See, for example, the *Pipe Rolls* volumes for the following years: *1198–1199*, p. 59; *1199–1200*, p. 208; *1200–1201*, p. 283; etc. For less-standard references to guards, the number of which may have been augmented from time to time, see *Pipe Rolls, 1211–1212*, p. 12 ("custodes operis castri de Doure").

79. Graham, "An Interdict on Dover," p. 327.

80. See, for example, the records of disputes in the years 1282–1285, edited in Statham, *Dover Charters and Other Documents*, pp. 16–27, nos. VIII–XIII.

81. Flight, "Dover Castle," has details and references the sources on this matter. (I owe this reference to Professor Vincent.)

82. *Pipe Rolls, 1204–1205*, p. 112.

83. Food and supplies: *Pipe Rolls, 1198–1199*, p. 59; *Pipe Rolls, 1199–1200*, pp. 208–09; *Pipe Rolls, 1201–1202*, p. 211; *Pipe Rolls, 1202–1203*, p. 23; *Pipe Rolls, 1229–1230*, p. 111, etc. Military equipment and related expenses: *Pipe Rolls, 1199–1200*, pp. 208–09; *Pipe Rolls, 1205–1206*, p. 47; *Pipe Rolls, 1208–1209*, p. 10.

84. *Patent Rolls, 1216–1225*, p. 129.

85. In general, see *Close Rolls, 1247–1251*, p. 476; *Close Rolls, 1296–1302*, pp. 344–45. For an example of a common prisoner, a homicide, in custody, see *Close Rolls, 1296–1302*, p. 582; *Patent Rolls, 1301–1307*, p. 44. For the incarceration of a political prisoner—in this case the lady of the Isle of Harty (now joined with the Isle of Sheppey, Kent) who was the widow of John de Champagne, the king's enemy—see *Fine Rolls, 1319–1327*, p. 291.

86. During civil war: *Close Rolls, 1259–1261*, p. 496; *Close Rolls, 1261–1264*, p. 3. During foreign war: *Close Rolls, 1296–1302*, p. 76.

87. Nicholas Vincent, in a personal communication and with reference to the story of the Justiciar, William Longchamps, who disguised himself as a woman in order to take ship in Dover, argued vigorously against my view. I do not quite see why the story tells against my suggestion, but see Vincent, "In the Shadow of the Castle Wall."

88. See, in general, Sweetinburgh, "Kentish Towns," pp. 137–65, which provides a broad comparative context for Dover's urban culture.

89. A larger and less plausible estimate is 6,000–7,000. It is based on the number of households extant in the mid-sixteenth century, that is, after the town's recovery from the demographic impact of the plague cycle. It also takes into consideration a recent and, in my opinion, inflated estimate of the residents of Sandwich, which many scholars believe had a smaller population than Dover's in the Middle Ages. If the new estimate, 5,000, for Sandwich is correct, then the estimate for Dover would have to be adjusted upward by as much as 2,000. On all these matters I have drawn on Lyon, *The History of the Town and Port of Dover*, vol. 1, p. 25; Dyer's figures in the *Cambridge Urban History of Britain*, vol. 1, pp. 758–64; and Clarke and others, *Sandwich*, pp. 30, 56.

90. The customal, or book of rights and privileges, describes the lineaments of administration: Lyon, *The History of the Town and Port of Dover*, vol. 2, 267–86.

91. *Close Rolls, 1272–1279*, p. 470. Heebøll-Holm, *Ports, Piracy and Maritime War*, pp. 63–65.

92. Kentish hospitals, including those in Dover, are discussed extensively in Sweetinburgh, "The Hospitals of Medieval Kent," pp. 111–36.

93. Lyon, *The History of the Town and Port of Dover*, vol. 1, pp. 39–51.

94. Sweetinburgh, "Royal Patrons and Local Benefactors," pp. 112–13.

95. *Petitions to the Crown from English Religious Houses*, pp. 93–94 no. 75.

96. Jones, *Outlawry in Medieval Literature*, p. 174 n. 117; Ives, *A History of Penal Methods*, pp. 100–01. I do not agree with Cox that comrades of the abjurers could have readily transferred the money to them while still in Dover; cf. Cox, *Sanctuaries and Sanctuary Seekers*, p. 31.

97. Safford, "An Account of the Expenses of Eleanor," pp. 116, 123.

98. Cf. Vincent, "In the Shadow of the Castle Wall" (forthcoming).

99. See Sweetinburgh, "The Hospitals of Medieval Kent," pp. 123–24, which also situates Dover's recluses in the eremitic culture of Kent.

100. Jourjon, "Notice sur le port et la ville de Tréguier," pp. 236–37.

101. *Close Rolls, 1231–1234*, p. 105; *Close Rolls, 1254–1256*, p. 272; *Close Rolls, 1259–1261*, p. 222; *Close Rolls, 1261–1264*, p. 52; *Liberate Rolls, 1251–1260*, pp. 323–24, 446, 449; *Liberate Rolls, 1260–1267*, p. 188. See also Clay, *Hermits and Anchorites*, p. 78.

102. On the not unproblematic place-name evidence, see E. A. Jones, "Hidden Lives," pp. 28–29.

103. Licence, *Hermits and Recluses in English Society*, pp. 150–72; Farina, "Money, Books, and Prayers," pp. 171–85.

104. Safford, "An Account of the Expenses of Eleanor," pp. 116, 123.

105. On the church's role in the culture of Dover and of other urban centers in the region, see Sweetinburgh, "Kentish Towns," pp. 158–63.

106. Graham, "An Interdict on Dover," pp. 326–27; Sweetinburgh, "The Hospitals of Medieval Kent," p. 123.

107. Cf. Ives, *A History of Penal Methods*, p. 101.

108. Réville, "L'Abjuratio regni," p. 18, is typical.

109. For a first and very preliminary attempt at an overview of English inns, see Hare, "Inns, Innkeepers and the Society of Later Medieval England," pp. 477–97.

110. Statham, "Dover Chamberlains' Accounts," pp. 77, 83.

111. Summerson, "The Criminal Underworld," pp. 197–224.

112. On the stereotype and reality of Dover-based piracy, see Heebøll-Holm, *Ports, Piracy and Maritime War*, pp. 67–69.

113. On the saying, see Skeat, "Dr. Pegge's Alphabet of Kenticisms," p. 134.

114. *Parliament Rolls of Medieval England*, Edward II, SC 9/21.

115. Graham, "An Interdict on Dover," p. 327.

116. *Patent Rolls, 1292–1301*, p. 417.

117. Ives, *A History of Penal Methods*, p. 100 n. 12, and for a fuller discussion, Ruding, *Annals of the Coinage of Great Britain*, vol. 1, p. 211.

118. On the limbs, see Clarke and others, *Sandwich*, pp. 56, 61. See also Vincent, "In the Shadow of the Castle Wall" (forthcoming).

119. On the vexing questions surrounding Dover's, the other Cinque Ports', and their limbs' role in military affairs, see Rodger, "The Naval Service," pp. 636–51; Rose, "The Value of the Cinque Ports," pp. 41–43; Heebøll-Holm, *Ports, Piracy and Maritime War*, p. 67.

120. *Nonarum Inquisitiones*, pp. 394–95. For an example of wartime service in 1297 and its consequences for Dover shipmen, see *Close Rolls, 1297–1302*, pp. 110–11. More generally, see Rose, "The Value of the Cinque Ports," pp. 43–52.

121. Safford, "An Account of the Expenses of Eleanor," pp. 117–18, 126–27, 130–33, and 136. Further on the costs incident to Eleanor's marriage, especially the expenses, allegedly in arrears, of one of the diplomats overseeing it, see the petition, dated 1336, in *Petitions to the Crown from English Religious Houses*, pp. 12–13 no. 16.

122. Cf. Shoemaker, *Sanctuary and Crime*, p. 120.

123. Jordan, "A Fresh Look at Medieval Sanctuary," p. 26.

124. The classic articulation of the character of liminality is Victor Turner's essay "Betwixt and Between: The Liminal Period in *Rites de passage*," which first appeared in print in his *Forest of Symbols*, pp. 93–111, but has been reprinted numerous times. See also Turner and Turner, *Image and Pilgrimage in Christian Culture*.

125. Trenholme, *Right of Sanctuary*, p. 42.

126. Bracton, *On the Laws and Customs of England*, vol. 2, p. 382.

127. Parkin, "The Ancient Cinque Port of Sandwich," p. 199.

128. *Chronicles of the Reigns of Edward I. and Edward II.*, vol. 1, p. 307: "inter nautas de Doveria et Witsand, ita quod naves non transierunt nec passagium ibidem fuit longo tempore."

129. Chaplais, *English Diplomatic Practice*, pp. 220–21.

130. *Calendar of Coroners Rolls of the City of London A.D. 1300–1378*, pp. 72, 87–89, 130–31. For the same directive at Bristol and Southampton, consult pp. 84, 130–31 of this *Calendar*.

131. See the information compiled at the British Marine Life Study Society, online at http://www.glaucus.org.uk/Tides.htm.

132. *Calendar of Coroners' Rolls of the City of London A.D. 1300–1378*, pp. 87–89.

133. See p. 77.

134. *Eyre of Kent 6 & 7 Edward II*, p. lxxiii.

135. Cox, *Sanctuaries and Sanctuary Seekers*, p. 31.

136. Wright, "The High Seas and the Church," p. 31.

137. Clark and others, *Sandwich*, p. 31. See also Vincent, "In the Shadow of the Castle Wall" (forthcoming).

138. Rigg, *St. Anselm of Canterbury*, pp. 154–55.

139. For reference to *La Nicholas*, see *Patent Rolls, 1317–1321*, p. 122 (15 March 1318).

140. *Patent Rolls, 1321–1324*, pp. 375–76 (various documents dated 26 September 1323 and 24 March 1324).

141. Kowaleski, "The Shipmaster as Entrepreneur," pp. 165–82.

142. See Lambert and Ayton, "The Mariner in Fourteenth-Century England," pp. 153–76. Note that they offer almost nothing on Dover.

143. As a crewman: *Liberate Rolls, 1267–1272*, p. 41 no. 367. As a baron: *Close Rolls, 1272–1279*, p. 470.

144. *Parliament Rolls of Medieval England*, Edward II, SC 9/21.

145. See the names of Dover ships in *Close Rolls, 1253–1254*, p. 25, and *Close Rolls, 1323–1327*, pp. 609–12.

Notes to Chapter 4

LIFE AMONG STRANGERS

1. A number of very sophisticated websites tout Wissant's present-day and recent historical interest for tourists, and these are replete with excellent photographs of the town and its environs: see, for example, http://www.a-taste-of -france.com/wissant-france.html.

2. The best study of medieval Wissant remains Haigneré's long entry, "Wissant," in vol. 3, pp. 273–301, of the late nineteenth-century *Dictionnaire historique et archéologique du Pas-de-Calais*. See also his list of sources in *Dictionnaire topographique . . . arrondissement de Boulogne-sur-Mer*, pp. 346–49.

3. Sumption, *The Hundred Years' War*, vol. 1, p. 532; Grierson, "The Relations between England and Flanders," pp. 80–81; Holmes, *Ancient Britain*, p. 580. Hermansart, "Les anciennes communautés," p. 333, refers to its appellation as the *britannicus portus*.

4. *Comptes de la ville d'Ypres*, vol. 1, pp. 248–49 (for records of communication between Ypres and Wissant in 1307–08). More generally, see Haigneré, *Dictionnaire historique et archéologique du Pas-de-Calais*, vol. 3, p. 281.

5. *The True Chronicles of Jean le Bel*, pp. 32, 35, 37, 50.

6. *Close Rolls, 1256–1259*, p. 484. Hermansart, "Ambassade de Raoul de Brienne," pp. 165–68; Chaplais, *English Diplomatic Practice*, pp. 220–25.

7. See pp. 85–87.

8. Haigneré, *Dictionnaire historique et archéologique du Pas-de-Calais*, vol. 3, pp. 279–87.

9. *Close Rolls, 1242–1247*, p. 53.

10. *Liberate Rolls, 1260–1267*, p. 189: "Liberate to Stacius de Whitsaund 55 l. 12 s., and to John Mayor of Dover 41 l. 17 s. 8 d., both at the coming Easter Exchequer, for freight of ships provided for the king's consort A. queen of England on her last voyage to England from beyond seas."

11. *Close Rolls, 1254–1256*, p. 34. Further on the gift and the elephant's fate, see Cassidy and Clasby, "Matthew Paris and Henry III's Elephant," pp. 1–6.

12. Safford, "An Account of the Expenses of Eleanor," pp. 132, 136.

13. Hermansart, "Ambassade de Raoul de Brienne," pp. 165–68.

14. Leguay, *Pauvres et marginaux*, pp. 68–70. See also Gonthier, *Cris de haine et rites d'unité*, pp. 97–100.

15. Kapferer, *Fracas et murmures*, pp. 57, 69.

16. *Song of Roland*, lines 1428–29. There is some dispute as to whether Sens is meant. The *Chanson* uses *Seinz*, which has been variously interpreted as Sens, Saintes, and Xanten (p. 218).

17. *Inferno*, Canto 15, lines 4–6.

18. Holloway, *Twice-Told Tales*, pp. 229–30; Isba, *Gladstone and Dante*, pp. 122–23.

19. Holmes, *Ancient Britain*, p. 306; Guest, "Julius Caesar's Invasion of Britain," p. 222; Lewin, *The Invasion of Britain*, p. 15.

20. The author of the Latin chronicle that provides information on this regional usage used the vernacular word in retelling a fantastic story about a woman in the region who suffered excruciating stomach pains in 1291 and was said, though the author acknowledged that the report was hard to believe, to have vomited up fourteen big black living spiders, nine big black frogs, and two black hairy polecats (*furones, qui vulgo dicuntur wissantz*) with big white teeth, long black ears, and heads as big as goose eggs. Before she died and on the same day, she also threw up two greasy fat rats that seemed to be pregnant. Yes, hard to believe. *Die Kölner Weltchronik*, pp. 58–59, "Circa eadem tempora [1291] accidit quoddam singulare et mirabile, ymmo difficile audientibus ad credendum. In territorio namque Gandanensi comitatus Flandrensis in villa, que lingua ipsius patrie Velske [modern: Velzeke-Ruddershove] nominatur, quedam mulier dolore intestinorum sue ventris miserabiliter cruciata unica die per os suum evomuit XIIII araneas vivas, nigras et grossas, item IX ranas similiter nigras et grossas, item duos furones, qui vulgo dicuntur wissantz, nigros, pilosos cum magnis dentibus albis et auribus longis atque nigris, quorum capita fuerunt grossa ad modum ovorum anserinorum. Item evomuit eodem die duos rattos adeo pingues et grossos, quasi viderentur esse pregnantes. Tandem eadem mulier miserabiliter cruciata vitam morte solvit. Ad quod quidem spectaculum fama percurrente tota illa patria concurrebat."

21. Cousin, "Sur des fouilles archéologiques à Wissant," p. 210, "un village dont l'aspect est loin d'être agréable." Guilbert, *Histoire des villes de France*, vol. 2, p. 111, refers to a royal report from 1738 remarkably similar to Cousin's.

22. Kapferer, *Fracas et murmures*, pp. 83–84; Grierson, "The Relations between England and Flanders," p. 81.

23. *Récits d'un bourgeois de Valenciennes (XIV siècle)*, p. 235.

24. Sumption, *The Hundred Years' War*, vol. 1, p. 532; Hermansart, "Anciennes communautés," pp. 331 n. 1, 520.

25. Haigneré, *Dictionnaire historique et archéologique du Pas-de-Calais*, vol. 3, pp. 288–89.

26. "Caesar's Campaigns in Gaul," p. 412.

27. Haigneré, "Fermes de la ville de Wissant," p. 260; "Séance du 5 février 1903," p. 52.

28. C. P. Stacey, *Official History of the Canadian Army*, vol. 1, p. 352 (I owe this reference to Dr. Paul Miles).

29. The quotation is from "Wissant: A Forgotten Port," p. 304. On the capture of Calais, see Rose, *Calais*, pp. 7–22.

30. Haigneré, *Dictionnaire historique et archéologique du Pas-de-Calais*, vol. 3, pp. 285, 288; Rose, *Calais*, pp. 9, 23–24.

31. Grierson, "Relations between England and Flanders," p. 81.

32. "Caesar's Campaigns in Gaul," p. 412.

33. Grierson, "Relations between England and Flanders," p. 80.

34. On the iconic status of the herring in Wissant, see Kapferer, *Fracas et murmures*, pp. 93–119.

35. Cousin, "Sur des fouilles archéologiques à Wissant," p. 210, "ses rues pour la plupart ensablées, ses maisons sans étage, généralement couvertes en chaume, ses quelques petits bateaux de pêche qu'on traîne péniblement sur le plage jusqu'au pied des dunes, où ils sont retenus avec leurs ancres pour ne pas être emportés à la derive."

36. Kapferer, *Fracas et murmures*, pp. 81–89.

37. London, National Archives, *Ancient Petitions*, SC 8/10/478, p. 476 col. a, "par Whitsond pur peril de lunge mer."

38. London, National Archives, *Ancient Petitions*, SC 8/10/478; SC 8/10/484. *Parliament Rolls of Medieval England*, Edward I, Petition 3.

39. London, National Archives, *Ancient Petitions*, SC 8/10/478; SC 8/10/484.

40. Or, variously, Brykun, Britun, Briton. The *Old French-English Dictionary*, s.vv. "bricun" and "bricon," renders the epithet/last name as either "fool, scoundrel, rogue, rascal, poor wretch" or "snare, trap." See also Rothwell, "From Latin to Anglo-French and Middle English," p. 590.

41. *Liberate Rolls, 1267–1272*, p. 104 no. 907.

42. *Patent Rolls, 1258–1266*, p. 381.

43. *Patent Rolls, 1258–1266*, p. 210.

44. *Liberate Rolls, 1260–1267*, p. 95.

45. *Close Rolls, 1259–1261*, p. 397.

46. *Liberate Rolls, 1260–1267*, p. 73. The clerk who enrolled this was confused, copied Witsand as Sandwich, and compounded his error by calling Eustace the mayor. In the margin, the place name mistake is corrected.

47. "Restas des comptes des officiers du conté de Bouloigne" (1325–1326), p. 394; "Chest la revenue de la terre . . . tres haute, tres noble et pouissant Dame Marguerite d'Evreus" (1338), p. 316; and "Chest la revenue de la conté de Bouloigne" (1339–1340), pp. 349–50. Following Bernard, "L'état ancien du Boulonnais," p. 141, the *prévôt* of Wissant was sometimes also called a *bailli*, much as the royal *prévôt* of Paris was sometimes referred to as a *bailli* because of his high official status; Jordan, *Men at the Center*, pp. 69–70. In 1338–40 the *bailli* of Wissant was Jehan de Pernes. Around the same the time the viscount was Simon Lemon. See also *Dictionnaire topographique . . . arrondissement de Boulogne-sur-Mer*, pp. 259, 348.

48. Canterbury Cathedral Archives possesses a large number of charters and confirmations to this effect; abstracts for several dealing with Wissant may now be accessed through the UK's National Archives database at http://www.nationalarchives.gov.uk/a2a/results.aspx?tab=2&Page=1&ContainAllWords=wissant. Editions of several relevant ones will appear in *Norman Charters*, nos. 77–96, especially 94–96 (also discussed at pp. 98–108 [according to the pagination of the proofs]).

49. *Norman Charters*, p. 99 (tentative proofs pagination).

50. Jordan, *Louis IX*, pp. 46–47.

51. On the nature of the French communes, see Vermeesch, *Essai sur les origines et la signification de la commune dans le nord de France*, and Jordan, "Communal Administration in France," pp. 292–313. For an instance of the use of Wissant's seal, its adhesion as Wissant-sur-Mer (*Wissant supra Mare*) on 16 August 1303 to the French protest of Pope Boniface VIII's policies toward the French king, see *Documents relatifs aux États généraux*, p. 447. There is a useful description of the structure of Wissant's municipal government in the fourteenth century in Haigneré, *Dictionnaire historique et archéologique du Pas-de-Calais*, vol. 3, pp. 286–87, but he was unaware of the relevant thirteenth-century evidence that proves that these structures were well in place at that time.

52. Deseille, "Communication . . . de M. J. Lecat," p. 318.

53. See, for example, *Registre criminel de Sainte-Geneviève*, p. 348.

54. On the jurisdictional crazy-quilt of High Medieval Paris, see Lombard-Jourdain, "Fiefs et justices parisiens," pp. 301–88. (This draws in good part on the pioneering work of Louis Tanon, who edited the *Registre criminel de Sainte-Geneviève*.)

55. *Registre criminel de Sainte-Geneviève*, p. 357: "misimus ad ballivum bononiensem, prepositum et majorem et scabinos communie de Wissant."

56. For the entire case, see *Registre criminel de Sainte-Geneviève*, pp. 357–58.

57. *Patent Rolls, 1216–1225*, p. 129.

58. *Dictionnaire topographique du départment du Pas-de-Calais*, p. 405; Haigneré, *Dictionnaire historique et archéologique du Pas-de-Calais*, vol. 3, pp. 299–300.

59. For various opinions, see Héliot, "Anciennes églises gothiques du Boulonnais," p. 105; Dufossé, http://www.mincoin.com/php1/wissb.php (accessed 29 June 2012); "L'histoire et le patrimoine" http://membres.multimania.fr/histopale /wissant.htm (accessed 29 June 2012).

60. *Dictionnaire topographique du département du Pas-de-Calais*, p. 405; "Notes et commentaires," p. 378.

61. Haigneré, *Dictionnaire historique et archéologique du Pas-de-Calais*, vol. 3, p. 284; Grierson, "Relations between England and Flanders," pp. 80–81; "Notes et commentaires," p. 378.

62. Ives, *A History of Penal Methods*, p. 101.

63. Ultimately these claims go back to the hagiographical traditions captured by Jacobus de Voragine in the *Golden Legend* (pp. 21–27). See also Le Goff, *In Search of Sacred Time*, p. 44.

64. Ebon, *Saint Nicholas*, p. 60.

65. Deseille, "Les pèlerinages populaires du pays Boulonnais," p. 378.

66. *Red Book of the Exchequer*, vol. 2, pp. 670, 792–93; *History of the County of Bedford*, vol. 1, pp. 399–400; *Dictionnaire topographique du département du Pas-de-Calais*, p. 405; Haigneré, *Dictionnaire historique et archéologique du Pas-de-Calais*, vol. 3, p. 286; Mermet and Dufossé, *Saint-Inglevert*, pp. 24–25.

67. For the first suggestion, see *History of the County of Bedford*, vol. 1, p. 400 n. 2, and Mermet and Dufossé, *Saint-Inglevert*, p. 43; for the second, I am indebted to Nicholas Vincent.

68. Mermet and Dufossé, *Saint-Inglevert*, pp. 24–33. More generally on alien priories and the breakdown of the system under the pressures of proto-nationalism during the Hundred Years' War, see New, *History of the Alien Priories*. Cf. Heale, *The Dependent Priories of Medieval English Monasteries*.

69. Kapferer, "Boulogne devient une ville," p. 64; Sartore, *Outlawry, Governance, and Law*, p. 68.

70. Kapferer, "Boulogne devient une ville," p. 65.

71. Kapferer, "Boulogne devient une ville," pp. 75–77.

72. Cf. Parsons, "The Beginnings of English Administration in Ponthieu," pp. 371–403.

73. Cox, *Sanctuaries and Sanctuary Seekers*, p. 31. "It is . . . somewhat puzzling to wonder what became of these abjurors when they landed on foreign shores."

74. The collection of essays, *Exile in the Middle Ages*, treats other sorts of expatriates and thus, to some extent, provides a comparative perspective, but it is not helpful on abjurers per se.

75. For reference to the butchers of Wissant, see "Chest la revenue de la conté de Bouloigne" (1339–1340), p. 351.

76. For the use of taverns in this way, see Geremek, *Les marginaux parisiens*, p. 135, and for the general association of taverns and marginalized groups, see Le Person, "L'exclusion," p. 239.

77. Reyerson, "Medieval Hospitality," pp. 40–42.

78. On the taverns serving the University's nations, see Geremek, *Les marginaux parisiens*, p. 330 n. 51. On the nations themselves, see Kibre, *The Nations in the Medieval Universities*.

79. The quoted word is Leff's usage in *Paris and Oxford Universities*, p. 53.

80. Cf. Timothy Jones, *Outlawry in Medieval Literature*, p. 39.

81. Cousin, "Sur les fouilles archéologiques faites à Wissant," pp. 210–14. See also Haigneré, *Dictionnaire historique et archéologique du Pas-de-Calais*, vol. 3, pp. 273–78.

82. Cousin, "Sur des fouilles archéologiques faites à Wissant," p. 212: "j'en conclus qu'il y a eu là une cimetière d'une vaste étendue."

83. Haigneré, *Dictionnaire historique et archéologique du Pas-de-Calais*, vol. 3, p. 284.

84. There is a somewhat pious history of the Virgin's shrine in Boulogne: Montrond, *Notre-Dame de Boulogne-sur-Mer*. For the thirteenth-century renown of the shrine, see pp. 32–33, 35–37. The possible connection to the cemetery at Wissant is noted at p. 25. See also Kapferer, "Boulogne devient une ville," pp. 70, 80–81.

85. Demaitre, *Leprosy in Premodern Medicine*, pp. 247–48. For the similar situation in England, see Rawcliffe, "Curing Bodies and Healing Souls," p. 108, and on the intermeshing of ideas of physical and spiritual illness and the need for intervention in both spheres, see Rawcliffe, *Leprosy in Medieval England*, p. 64.

86. On the leprosarium of Wissant, see Haigneré, *Dictionnaire historique et archéologique du Pas-de-Calais*, vol. 3, p. 297. On hospices serving ideally, if not always in practice, as way stations for sick pilgrims, including lepers, see Prigent and Tichey, *Le moyen âge féodal*, p. 20. Such service appears to have been extended by hospices near the Virgin's shrine in Boulogne; see Montrond, *Notre-Dame de Boulogne-sur-Mer*, p. 40.

87. UK, National Archives, SC 8/324/E606, online at http://discovery .nationalarchives.gov.uk/SearchUI/Details?uri=C9682595.

88. Brand, "Chief Justice and Felon," p. 47, and pp. 121–22 of the current work.

89. Stell, "John [John de Balliol]."

90. Small, "Grain for the Countess," pp. 56–63.

91. Small, "Grain for the Countess," pp. 57–59, 61.

92. Geremek, *Marginaux parisiens*, p. 286.

93. Cf. Langdon, "Minimum Wages and Unemployment Rates," pp. 36–43; Van Bavel, *Manors and Markets*, pp. 302–03.

94. Olson, *A Mute Gospel*, p. 97.

95. Le Grand, "Les Maisons-Dieu et léproseries," pp. 84–90.

96. I know of no comprehensive study of migrant labor in medieval Europe or, for that matter, northern France and Flanders, but it was a common feature of the rural, and to some extent, urban landscape; cf. Bresc, "Justice et société," pp. 26–27, for instances in southeastern France, and Van Bavel, *Manors and Markets*, pp. 209, 302–03, for the later medieval Low Countries.

97. On these matters, see Bonne, "Étude sur le condition des étrangers en France," pp. 94–95.

98. Viollet, *Précis de l'histoire du droit français*, pp. 311–15.

99. Fuller, "Pleas of the Crown at Bristol," p. 167.

100. Geremek, *Marginaux parisiens*, pp. 238–73; James Murray, *Bruges, Cradle of Capitalism*, p. 343; Nowacka, "Persecution, Marginalization, or Tolerance," pp. 182–83.

101. Thus, *Grand coutumier de France*, p. 182 cap. XII. More generally, see Nowacka, "Persecution, Marginalization, or Tolerance," pp. 185–86 and in general on prostitution in Paris, pp. 181–96. See also Zaremska, *Les bannis au moyen âge*, pp. 78–80.

102. Janin, "Documents relatifs à la peine du bannissement," p. 420; *Recueil des monuments inédits du Tiers-État*, vol. 4, p.198; Zaremska, *Les bannis au moyen âge*, p. 80.

103. Zaremska, *Les bannis au moyen âge*, p. 80; Murray, *Bruges, Cradle of Capitalism*, p. 343; Dean, *Crime in Medieval Europe*, pp. 86–90.

104. For the examples of banishment for felony mentioned, see Janin, "Documents relatifs à la peine du bannissment," p. 420–21.

105. On the population, see James Murray, *Notarial Instruments in Flanders*, p. 81. On the number of brothels, see James Murray, *Bruges, Cradle of Capitalism*, p. 336.

106. Gonthier, 'Sanglant coupaul!', p. 72.

107. James Murray, *Bruges, Cradle of Capitalism*, p. 337.

108. Rouffy, "Les viguiers d'Aurillac au XIIIe siècle," p. 50.

109. James Murray, *Bruges, Cradle of Capitalism*, pp. 340–41.

110. *Registre criminel de Sainte-Geneviève*, p. 350. I am not certain why Nowacka conflates the case of one Alison Lenglesche (p. 348) with Margaret's; cf. Nowacka, "Persecution, Marginalization, or Tolerance," pp. 182–83.

111. Cox, *Sanctuaries and Sanctuary Seekers*, p. 32.

112. Zaremska, *Les bannis au moyen âge*, pp. 98, 161–71; Gonthier, *Cris de haine et rites d'unité*, pp. 177–78; Gonthier, *Le châtiment du crime*, pp. 139–40.

113. Dean, *Crime in Medieval Europe*, pp. 129–30.

114. Curveiller, "L'étranger à Dunkerque," pp. 26, 29–30; Moal, "Entre méfiance et accueil," pp. 39–40.

115. *Jurades de la ville d'Agen*, p. 21.

116. Verger, "L'Université [de Paris]," pp. 10–11.

117. *Compte général du receveur d'Artois pour 1303–1304*, p. 237 no. 3982. A comprehensive study of spies (*espies, espions, insidiatores, exploratores*; cf. Alban and Allmand, "Spies and Spying," p. 74) and "listeners" (*ecoutez*) both private and governmental remains to be written. (But see Alban and Allmand, "Spies and Spying," pp. 73–101, on the Hundred Years' War.) These terms/categories appear throughout fiscal records; see, for example, the abundant information for just two small Savoyard towns, Billiat and Pont-d'Ain: *Comptes de dépenses de la châtellenie de Billiat*, pp. 111,129, 143; *Comptes de dépenses de la châtellenie de Pont-d'Ain*, part 1, pp. 147, 154, 161; *Comptes de dépenses de la châtellenie de Pont-d'Ain*, part 2, pp. 11, 20, 30, 43.

118. Tison, "Ordonnances de police de Calais, au XIIIe siècle," p. 494.

119. Alban and Allmand, "Spies and Spying," p. 85. For the typical—even stereotypical—view of minimal policing, see Gonthier, *Le châtiment du crime*, pp. 64–71.

120. "Restas des comptes des officiers du conté de Bouloigne" (1325–1326)," p. 394; "Chest la revenue de la terre . . . tres haute, tres noble et pouissant Dame Marguerite d'Evreus" (1338), p. 316; "Chest la revenue de la conté de Bouloigne" (1339–1340), p. 350, 374–75. See also Haigneré, *Dictionnaire historique et archéologique du Pas-de-Calais*, vol. 3, p. 288; Safford, "An Account of the Expenses of Eleanor," pp. 130, 132.

121. Backhouse and de Hamel, *The Becket Leaves*, p. 32.

122. Cf. Timothy Jones, *Outlawry in Medieval Literature*, p. 40.

123. On the sources, in this case for Paris, see Geremek, *Les marginaux parisiens*, pp. 56–68. The *Grand coutumier de France* of the fourteenth century offers a comprehensive description of the varieties and limits of high justice in the kingdom: pp. 637–42 cap. VIII.

124. *Administrative Korrespondenz der französischen Könige um 1300*, pp. 322–23 no. 208 (see also p. 490 no. 464, which appears to refer to the same case).

125. *Compte général du receveur d'Artois pour 1303–1304*, p. 117 no. 1981.

126. Geremek, *Les marginaux parisiens*, p. 136; Gauvard, "Violence citadine et réseaux de solidarité," p. 1124.

127. Toureille, *Crime et châtiment au moyen âge*, p. 124.

128. Roux, *Paris*, pp. 45–47.

129. Geremek, *Les marginaux parisiens*, p. 79; further on neighborhood patterns, see p. 89.

130. On theories of the origin of the name of the *rue des Anglais*, see Bouniol, *Rues des Paris*, vol. 3, p. 133. On the location of Master William's residence, see *Registre criminel de Sainte-Geneviève*, p. 362.

131. Mason, *Mission of St. Augustine*, p. 94.

132. Geremek, *Les marginaux parisiens*, p. 140.

133. Geremek, *Les marginaux parisiens*, pp. 251–57; Beaurepaire, *Essai sur l'asile religieux*, p. 71.

134. For an example of the prohibition in the statutes of Charles II of Anjou, see Giraud, *Essai sur l'histoire de droit français*, vol. 2, p. 32. See also Geremek, *Les marginaux parisiens*, p. 158.

135. *Confessions et jugements de criminels au Parlement de Paris*, p. 115. This is considered in context on p. 106 of the current work.

136. See p. 106.

137. *Droit coutumier de Cambrai*, p. 11 no. xli.

138. On the exchange of lists, see Janin, "Documents relatifs à la peine du bannissment," pp. 419, 426; Gomart, "De la peine du bannissement," pp. 461–62; Hamel, "Bannis et bannissements à Saint-Quentin," p. 128. For published examples of the lists, see "Monition et proclamation des bannis de la ville de Saint-Quentin," pp. 259–60; "Lettre des prevost, jurés, et échevins de Valenciennes," pp. 260–61; and the "Lettre des maire et jurés de Laon," pp. 261–62.

139. Gonthier, *Délinquance*, p. 245. In chapter 5 I will address the question of the illicit and licit return of English abjurers to England. As in the English case this could only be achieved on the continent by the issuance of a formal pardon.

140. See chapter 1, p. 21.

141. Perrin's activities are discussed in Geremek, *Les marginaux parisiens*, pp. 134–35. On Philippot (Little Phil) Cavillon, see pp. 106-08 and 111 of the current work.

142. *Recueil des monuments inédits du Tiers-État*, vol. 8, p. 53.

143. The thirteenth-century feud between the *Harincs* (father and son, both named William) and the *Anglicus* family (the brothers Hannekin and William), which led to the latter's deaths, involved what appear to have been natives of Ghent ("Flandrisches Urkunden-Buch," p. 75 nos. 30–31), although the Anglicus clan could possibly have been of remote English origin.

144. *Registre criminel de la justice de Saint Martin des Champs*, pp. 37–38. If the hyphen is misplaced in the transcription "Jehan Poule-Cras," as Professor Vincent has suggested to me could be the case, then the proper translation of the name might be John-Paul the Fat rather than John Fat-Hen. In either case, it seems reasonable to conclude that he was a large man.

145. Zaremska, *Les bannis au moyen âge*, p. 77; Gonthier, *Cris de haine et rites d'unité*, pp. 203–06; Gonthier, *'Sanglant coupaul!'*, p. 72; Gauvard, "Violence citadine et réseaux de solidarité," p. 1125; Turning, *Municipal Officials*, p. 141.

146. Jourjon, "Notice sur le port et la ville de Tréguier," p. 237. Part of the chant supposedly sung on the saint's feast day was, "Sanctus Yvo erat Brito, / Advocatus et non latro, / Res miranda populo." The word *advocatus* evokes

Yves' defense of the poor, but the whole phrase also plays on the stereotype of lawyers, *advocati*, as thieves.

147. *Registre criminel de Saint-Germain-des-Prés*, p. 416.

148. *Registre criminel de la justice de Saint Martin des Champs*, pp. 40–43. Roux, *Paris*, pp. 38–39.

149. *Registre criminel de la justice de Saint Martin des Champs*, pp. 34–35.

150. *Registre criminel de la justice de Saint Martin des Champs*, p. 75.

151. *Registre criminel de la justice de Saint Martin des Champs*, p. 100.

152. *Registre criminel de la justice de Saint Martin des Champs*, p. 115.

153. See p. 103.

154. *Registre criminel de la justice de Saint Martin des Champs*, pp. 37–38.

155. *Comptes de la ville d'Ypres*, vol. 1, p. 397.

156. *HF*, XXIV, 455 no. 33. Michel, *L'administration royale dans la sénéchaussée*, p. 46.

157. *Actes normands de la Chambre des comptes sous Philippe de Valois*, p. 79.

158. *Confessions et jugements de criminels au Parlement de Paris*, pp. 114–22. A great deal of the information that fleshes out this case was assembled by the editors. See also Lanhers, "Crimes et criminels," pp. 336–37.

159. Grand, "Justice criminelle," p. 102; Rouffy, "Les viguiers d'Aurillac au XIIIe siècle," p. 50.

160. *Actes normands de la Chambre des comptes sous Philippe de Valois*, p. 272.

161. Cf. Bull, *The Miracles of Our Lady of Rocamadour*.

162. For example, Bull, *The Miracles of Our Lady of Rocamadour*, p. 186.

163. The choice of this notoriously derogatory word (Gonthier, *'Sanglant coupaul!'*, pp. 158–60) was, I presume, that of the interrogators.

164. *Confessions et jugements de criminels au Parlement de Paris*, p. 118 n. 2.

165. An excellent study of the *Châtelet*, including its personnel, procedures, and procedural lapses, is Glasson's "Le Châtelet de Paris," pp. 45–92.

166. *Comptes Henri de Taperel*, p. 57. For an evocative description of the lowest prison, see Jager, *Blood Royal*, p. 24.

167. *Comptes Henri de Taperel*, p. 57 (*en la fosse*). See also Ducoudray, *Origines du Parlement de Paris*, p. 895; Telliez, "Geôles, fosses, cachots," pp. 171–73. *Old French-English Dictionary*, p. 329 s.v. "fosse."

168. *Grand coutumier de France*, pp. 183–84 cap. XIII. See also Peters, "Prison before the Prison," p. 39.

169. L'Engle, "Justice in the Margins," p. 147.

170. Boutillier, *Somme rural*, p. 870.

Notes to Chapter 5

RETURNING HOME

1. A real *Philippus le Petyt*, felon, who helps inspire this make-believe, appears in the *Calendarium Inquisitionum post mortem sive escaetarum*, vol. 1, sub

anno 26 Edward I. He abjured from Herefordshire slightly before May 1298; *Calendar of Inquisitions Miscellaneous*, vol. 1, pp. 492 and 494 nos. 1777 and 1788.

2. *Legal History: The Year Books* (online), Seipp number 1328.031.

3. For example, *Legal History: The Year Books* (online), Seipp number 1406.104.

4. *London Eyre of 1276*, no. 38.

5. Hurnard, *The King's Pardon for Homicide before A.D. 1307*, p. 143.

6. For cases beyond those to be discussed, see Whitley, "Sanctuary in Devon," p. 303; *Rolls of the Justices in Eyre . . . 1221, 1222*, p. 375 no. 857; *Legal History: The Year Books* (online), Seipp number 1318.090ss. See also Hurnard, *The King's Pardon for Homicide before A.D. 1307*, pp. 89–92.

7. *Série J, Trésor des chartes, supplément: Inventaire. J1028 à J1034, J1034ᴮ* no. 52. This was rarely if ever the case in England, though informal concords may have preceded pardons; Hurnard, cf. *The King's Pardon for Homicide before A.D. 1307*, p. 21.

8. Zaremska, *Les bannis au moyen âge*, pp. 11–24, on forced pilgrimage, including the victim's family's prior approval in certain jurisdictions. See also Ducoudray, *Les Origines du Parlement de Paris*, p. 907; Kittell, "Reconciliation or Punishment," pp. 6–7.

9. *Somersetshire Pleas . . . (Close of 12th Century–41 Henry III)*, p. 45 no. 189. For other cases that make clear the transformation of status from abjurer to outlaw (*sicut de wavia* for a woman) as a consequence of illegal return, see *Somersetshire Pleas . . . (Close of 12th Century–41 Henry III)*, pp. 38 and 41 nos. 148 and 166.

10. Réville, "L'Abjuratio regni," p. 27.

11. *Select Cases from the Coroners' Rolls A.D. 1265–1413*, p. 80.

12. *Legal History: The Year Books* (online), Seipp numbers 1327.097 and 1327.130ass.

13. *Legal History: The Year Books* (online), Seipp number 1325.132.

14. Hamil, "The King's Approvers," p. 243.

15. *Legal History: The Year Books* (online), Seipp number 1337.154ass.

16. Cf. Toureille, *Crime et châtiment au moyen âge*, pp. 258–59.

17. Gomart, "De la peine du bannissement," p. 452; Small, "Profits of Justice," p. 160.

18. *Registre criminel de Sainte-Geneviève*, p. 360.

19. *Coutumes de Beauvaisis*, no. 1904; *Établissements de saint Louis*, vol. 1, p. 505 and vol. 3, p. 180. Gonthier, *Délinquance*, p. 245.

20. *Fors de Béarn*, pp. 66, 121 articles 178, 37.

21. *Coutume de Saint-Sever*, pp. 39, 84–85 no. 36. The law stipulated that thefts amounting to 30s. could be punished capitally. But if it reached this amount by a series of smaller thefts (the equivalent of minor shoplifting, one might say), the judges could mitigate the penalty. If a recidivist was convicted for a string of small thefts, the judges were forbidden from mitigating the penalty when the total value reached 6s. of the local money.

22. *Olim*, vol. 3, pp. 1498–99.

23. Zaremska, *Les bannis au moyen âge*, pp. 96–97; Schubert, *Räuber, Henker, arme Sünder*, pp. 100–01.

24. *Olim*, vol. 2, p. 704.

25. *Annales . . . de Colmar*, p. 186.

26. *Catalogue des manuscrits et documents . . . de la ville de Metz*, p. 127. (Was this perhaps tailored to a crime involving shipping?)

27. See two cases dating from 1301, one for the rape of a virgin, the other for an unspecified offense, narrated in the *Annales . . . de Colmar*, pp. 186 and 188, as well as the information on the punishment for blasphemy in Toulouse summarized in Turning, *Municipal Officials*, pp. 147–48; Turning, "The Right to Punish," p. 12. More generally, see Gonthier, *Le châtiment du crime*, pp. 160–61.

28. *Registre criminel de Saint-Maur-des-Fossés*, p. 322.

29. Many instances occur in the *Registre criminel de Saint-Maur des Fossés*, for example, pp. 322, 334, 338. See also Laingui and Lebigre, *Histoire du droit pénal*, vol. 1, pp. 116–17.

30. *Le Livre Roisin: coutumier lillois*, p. 112 no. 172; Summerson, "Attitudes to Capital Punishment," p. 124; *Très ancienne coutume de Bretagne*, p. 153 no. 112. For the penalty as prescribed and enforced in other jurisdictions, see *Mémoires historiques . . . Valenciennes*, vol. 3, pp. 185–86; *Compte général du receveur d'Artois pour 1303–1304*, p. 191 no. 3220; Lefils, *Histoire de Montreuil-sur-Mer*, p. 116; Fauqueux, *Beauvais*, pp. 38–39; Gonthier, *Le châtiment du crime*, pp. 168–69.

31. Le Foyer, *Exposé du droit pénal normand*, p. 231.

32. *Annales . . . de Colmar*, p. 186. Alternatively, the use of *turpiter* may be a way of challenging the appropriateness of the punishment.

33. Leguay, *Le feu*, pp. 359–61; Curveiller, *Dunkerque, ville et port*, p. 90; Gonthier, *Le châtiment du crime*, pp. 184–90. On costs, see Jordan, "Expenses Related to Corporal Punishment."

34. Cf. Zaremska, *Les bannis au moyen âge*, pp. 174–87.

35. Janin, "Documents relatifs à la peine du bannissement," p. 421; Gomart, "De la peine du bannissement," p. 452; Galabert, "L'état social à Saint-Antonin," p. 24. In the case of Saint-Antonin it is impossible, given the fragmentary nature of the municipal accounts before 1350, to determine how often such penalties were inflicted. That these accounts would have contained such details if they had survived is evident from the existing fragments which, for example, mention things like payments to men to remove and, implicitly, dispose of felons from gallows; *Comptes consulaires de Saint-Antonin*, vol. 1, p. 16. Presumably there would have been records of payments to those who carried out the punitive amputations. See also on the amputation of the foot in combination with a grain thief's branding and banishment in Aurillac in the Midi: Grand, "Justice criminelle," p. 95.

36. Friedland, *Seeing Justice Done*, pp. 57–60; this development persisted unevenly in time and space (pp. 89–100). For Foucault's take, see *Discipline and Punish*, pp. 3–103. See also Jordan, "Expenses Related to Corporal Punishment."

37. Janin, "Documents relatifs à la peine du bannissement," pp. 422, 426; Gomart, "De la peine du bannissement," pp. 452, 460–61. On the semantic field of *ribaud/ribaude*, see Gonthier, *'Sanglant coupaul!'*, pp. 148–49.

38. See chapter 2, p. 45.

39. See Gonthier, *Délinquance*, p. 245, for the evidence, not the explanation.

40. On English pardons, see Hurnard, *The King's Pardon for Homicide before A.D. 1307*, for the earlier part of the period covered in the present book. (Note that she limited her study to pardons for homicides, including those who abjured for homicide.) For the later part of the period covered in the present study, see Lacey, *The Royal Pardon*. Other jurisdictions, as remarked, offered similar opportunities. There is much fascinating information, much of it still unexcavated, in the UK National Archives: for example, on the Channel Islands. For some published records, see *Patent Rolls, 1292–1301*, p. 296; *Patent Rolls, 1313–1317*, pp. 16, 91, 275, 372, 375, 623; *Patent Rolls, 1317–1321*, pp. 38, 265, 330, 427, 534–35, 577–78. For Normandy and the ducal pardon, see Le Foyer, *Exposé du droit pénal normand au XIIIe siècle*, p. 243. For royal France and the comital pardon in the county of Clermont, see *Coutumes de Beauvaisis*, nos. 1536, 1731. For sub-comital pardons and their jurisdictional limitations in Clermont and mutatis mutandis elsewhere, see *Coutumes de Beauvaisis*, no. 1733. On municipal banishment in France and the question of whether the royal pardoning power could annul it, see Carbonnières, "Le privilège de bannissement," pp. 316–17. For pardons in continental jurisdictions more generally, see Zaremska, *Les bannis au moyen âge*, pp. 103–05. Exceptionally, Amiens selected one *bannitus* to return each year if he had not been exiled for murder, other homicides, sedition, or rape (*Recueil des monuments inédits du Tiers-État*, vol. 1, p. 114 no. 51); this was obviously in imitation of the alleged Roman custom in Judea, mentioned in the New Testament, to release one condemned man a year (notoriously, the release of Barabbas instead of Jesus in the only evidence we have of this custom).

41. Shoemaker, *Sanctuary and Crime*, p. 119; Stewart, "Outlawry as an Instrument of Justice in the Thirteenth Century," pp. 42–43; Brand, "Understanding Early Petitions," p. 103; Lacey, *The Royal Pardon*, p. 25. A pardon could also forgive an outlaw's crime: Hurnard, *The King's Pardon for Homicide before A.D. 1307*, pp. 32–33 (but cf. Lacey, p. 37 n. 42).

42. Sartore, *Outlawry, Governance, and Law*, p. 74.

43. See, for example, a case in 1278, where wives in France were permitted to stand surety for the pardons granted to their husbands, providing the latter agreed to answer the charges against them: Varin, *Archives . . . de Reims* [*Archives administratives*], vol. 1, pp. 958–59. See also pp. 126–27 of the current work.

44. But see now, Hurnard, *The King's Pardon for Homicide before A.D. 1307*, p. 180 n. 4 and p. 212.

45. *Fine Rolls, 1216–1224*, p. 14 no. 46 (with cross reference to the abjuration).

46. *Calendar of Inquisitions Miscellaneous*, vol. 2, p. 172 no. 691.

47. *Calendar of Inquisitions Miscellaneous*, vol. 2, p. 82 no. 328.

48. UK, National Archives, SC 8/319/E407, online at http://discovery.nationalarchives.gov.uk/SearchUI/Details?uri=C9529459.

49. *Patent Rolls, 1321–1324*, p. 38; *Calendar of Inquisitions Miscellaneous*, vol. 2, p. 172 no. 691.

50. *Legal History: The Year Books* (online), Seipp number 1285.005ss. Jacob, *The Law-Dictionary*, vol. 5, p. 32: "The effect of such Pardon by the King is to make the offender a new man . . . and not so much to restore his former, as to give him a new credit and capacity."

51. *Calendar of Inquisitions Miscellaneous*, vol. 2, p. 172 no. 691.

52. Lacey, *The Royal Pardon*, p. 76.

53. Cf. the king's relations with his abbot of Westminster, Richard de Ware, in the late 1270s; Jordan, *A Tale of Two Monasteries*, pp. 176–80.

54. Prestwich, *Plantagenet England*, p. 177.

55. Brand, "Chief Justice and Felon," p. 47.

56. Hurnard, *The King's Pardon for Homicide before A.D. 1307*, p. 32.

57. On crying outlaws' pardons, cf. Lacey, *The Royal Pardon*, pp. 53–54.

58. Hurnard, *The King's Pardon for Homicide before A.D. 1307*, p. 34.

59. Carbonnières, "Le privilège de bannissement," p. 315; Zaremska, *Les bannis au moyen âge*, p. 95; Gonthier, '*Sanglant coupaul!*', p. 41.

60. In such circumstances, according to Gonthier, *Délinquance*, p. 245, "dépaysement n'est jamais total."

61. See chapter 4, p. 102.

62. Hurnard, *The King's Pardon for Homicide before A.D. 1307*, p. 34.

63. See p. 69.

64. De Hamel, "Books and Society," p. 17.

65. Hurnard, *The King's Pardon for Homicide before A.D. 1307*, pp. 32, 217.

66. Hurnard, *The King's Pardon for Homicide before A.D. 1307*, p. 218.

67. Reconstructed from: *Close Rolls, 1242–1247*, p. 292; *Patent Rolls, 1232–1247*, pp. 328, 345, 367, 394, 419–20, 429, 486, 492, 496, 500; *Patent Rolls, 1247–1258*, pp. 3, 28, 186, 264, 275. See also Hurnard, *The King's Pardon for Homicide before A.D. 1307*, p. 217 n. 4.

68. Jordan, *A Tale of Two Monasteries*, p. 50, citing Maurice Powicke's assessment of Henry's state of mind in these days.

69. This is my best reconstruction of the laconic narrative of the case in *Patent Rolls, 1247–1258*, p. 388.

70. Hurnard, *The King's Pardon for Homicide before A.D. 1307*, p. 218 n. 2.

71. *Calendar of Inquisitions Miscellaneous*, vol. 1, p. 617 no. 2305.

72. Hurnard, *The King's Pardon for Homicide before A.D. 1307*, p. 218.

73. Hurnard, *The King's Pardon for Homicide before A.D. 1307*, p. 34.

74. Hurnard, *The King's Pardon for Homicide before A.D. 1307*, p. 34; Shoemaker, *Sanctuary and Crime*, p. 143.

75. See, for one of several examples, the case of Geoffrey of Northampton, 1235–36: *Fine Rolls, 1234–1242*, p. 122 no. 161 (with cross reference to the abjuration).

76. Cf. Zaremska, *Les bannis au moyen âge*, p. 155.

77. *Patent Rolls, 1258–1266*, p. 73, "Pardon to Richard de Ukynton of his abjuration of the realm, as it appears by inquisition made by the sheriff of Hereford before the coroners of that county, in full county that Warin le Chaluner of Ledebyry, of whose death he was indicted, is still alive, and the said Richard, in

his simplicity and fear, fled to the church of Ledebyry as guilty, and falsely admitting that he had killed the said Warin, abjured the realm, and the said Warin, by the procurement of the friends of the said Richard, afterwards returned to those parts, and before the coroners of the county acknowledged that he had fled into hiding because of his debts for the payment of which his goods did not suffice, and not maliciously in order that the said Richard might be charged with his death."

78. Further on Walter, see Stringer, "Some Documents Concerning a Berkshire Family," p. 25.

79. *Patent Rolls, 1266–1272*, p. 15.

80. *Fine Rolls, 1216–1224*, p. 25 no. 99, with cross-reference to the abjuration in the *Patent Rolls*.

81. For the thirteenth century, see Hurnard, *The King's Pardon for Homicide before A.D. 1307*, pp. 230–31. For the later period, see Lacey, *The Royal Pardon*, p. 47, with lists in her Appendix 4 of patrons who petitioned for pardons for other people.

82. Cf. Musson, "Queenship, Lordship and Petitioning," pp. 164–67, 168–72.

83. *Fine Rolls*, 1226–1240, pp. 154–55 nos. 339–41.

84. Lacey, *The Royal Pardon*, pp. 45–47; Musson, "Queenship, Lordship and Petitioning," pp. 157–64, 167–68; Sneddon, "Words and Realities," pp. 199–200.

85. For an example of the use of the language in wartime, see UK, National Archives, SC 8/9/441 (with references to supplementary records), online at http://discovery.nationalarchives.gov.uk/SearchUI/Details?uri=C9060567. On the more general point, see Scott, "The March Laws," p. 267. For exile in later Scottish law, see Morgan and Rushton, *Banishment*, pp. 29–42.

86. Hurnard, *The King's Pardon for Homicide before A.D. 1307*, pp. 232–33.

87. *Close Rolls, 1259–1261*, p. 372. For the complicated undoing of an abjuration in contested territory in one of the many Anglo-Scottish wars, see Brand, "Understanding Early Petitions," p. 103.

88. For clergy as patrons in the thirteenth century, see Hurnard, *The King's Pardon for Homicide before A.D. 1307*, p. 231.

89. Lacey, *The Royal Pardon*, Appendix 4.

90. See pp. 127–28.

91. *Calendar of Inquisitions Miscellaneous*, vol. 1, p. 603 no. 2254.

92. *Patent Rolls, 1292–1301*, p. 127.

93. Cf. Ormrod, "Murmur, Clamour and Noise," pp. 135–55; Harris, "Taking Your Chances," pp. 187–88. The quotation is from Sneddon, "Words and Realities," p. 202. The key study for France is Davis, *Fiction in the Archives*.

94. *Close Rolls, 1237–1242*, pp. 522–23.

95. *Close Rolls, 1259–1261*, p. 256. In general on Hugh's activity in the pardon market, see Hurnard, *The King's Pardon for Homicide before A.D. 1307*, p. 217.

96. *Patent Rolls, 1266–1272*, pp. 271, 285.

97. *Calendar of Inquisitions Miscellaneous*, vol. 1, p. 385 no. 1331; *Patent Rolls, 1281–1292*, p. 136.

98. UK, National Archives, SC 8/77/3820, online at http://discovery .nationalarchives.gov.uk/SearchUI/Details?uri=C9107594.

99. *Chronique et annales de Gilles le Muisit*, p. 97.

100. See, for example, *Petitions to the Crown from English Religious Houses*, pp. 110–11 no. 92.

101. Hurnard, *The King's Pardon for Homicide before A.D. 1307*, p. 158.

102. Brand, "Understanding Early Petitions," p. 103 (Edward I, Roll 12, item 556 [470]): "Ad peticionem Gregorii de Stradesheved', petentis quod cum indictatus fuisset per procuracionem Bartholomei Modipyt de minutis latrociniis, ut de aucis et una gallina, tempore quo fuit infra etatem .xij. annorum, et ipse fugam fecisset ad ecclesiam et deinde abjurasset regnum coram coronatore etc., et postmodum stetit in guerra regis in Vasconia etc., quod rex velit ei pacem suam concedere etc., ita responsum est: habeat breve de cancellaria coronatoribus quod faciant venire recordum abjuracionis coram rege."

103. *Patent Rolls, 1317–1321*, p. 123.

104. See the indices, s.v. "Pardons," in the *Patent Rolls, 1339–1340*; *Patent Rolls, 1340–1343*; and *Patent Rolls, 1343–1345*. See also Hurnard, *The King's Pardon for Homicide before A.D. 1307*, pp. 218–19, 311–21.

105. Lacey, *The Royal Pardon*, pp. 87, 100.

106. Lacey, *The Royal Pardon*, pp. 2, 85–175 (on military pardons per se, pp. 73, 100–06). For military pardons to those who would serve at sea, cf. Lambert and Ayton, "The Mariner in Fourteenth-Century England," p. 162.

107. Lacey, *The Royal Pardon*, pp. 105–06; Zaremska, *Les bannis au moyen âge*, pp. 105–07.

108. Hurnard, *The King's Pardon for Homicide before A.D. 1307*, pp. 273–97.

109. *London Eyre of 1244*, no. 221.

110. *Calendar of Inquisitions Miscellaneous*, vol. 1, p. 320 no. 1051.

111. For the variety of such punitive mutilations, prescribed and/or carried out: Schubert, *Räuber, Henker, arme Sünder*, pp. 79–80, 100, 124; Laingui and Lebigre, *Histoire du droit pénal*, vol. 1, p. 126; Ducoudray, *Origines du Parlement de Paris*, pp. 904–06; Jordan, *Men at the Center*, pp. 90–93; idem, *The Great Famine*, pp. 165–66; Cardevacque, "Le bourreau à Arras," p. 165; Théodore, "Executions des sentences criminelles à Lille," pp. 350–51; Leguay, *Vivres dans les villes bretonnes*, p. 463; Grand, "Justice criminelle," pp. 93–94; Rouffy, "Viguiers d'Aurillac au XIIIe siècle," p. 48; Lauzun, "Le Livre juratoire des consuls d'Agen," p. 391; *Comptes de dépenses de la châtellenie de Billiat*, p. 61; *Pleas before the King or His Justices, 1198–1212*, pp. 81–82 no. 739; Reynaud, "Statuts de la ville de Nice au XIIIe siècle," pp. 245, 247; Turing, *Municipal Officials*, pp. 147–48; Friedland, *Seeing Justice Done*, p. 100; Gonthier, *Le châtiment du crime*, pp. 141–42.

112. Hurnard, *The King's Pardon for Homicide before A.D. 1307*, pp. 55–59. Lacey cites the issuance of a letter of protection, which captures the function: *The Royal Pardon*, p. 71.

113. *Fine Rolls, 1216–1224,* p. 14 no. 46.
114. Cf. Hurnard, *The King's Pardon for Homicide before A.D. 1307,* p. 233.
115. Hurnard, *The King's Pardon for Homicide before A.D. 1307,* p. 32.
116. On these lists, see chapter 4, p. 102.
117. Hurnard, *The King's Pardon for Homicide before A.D. 1307,* p. 65.
118. Jacob, *New Law-Dictionary,* s.v. "Pardon."
119. Mazzinghi, *Sanctuaries,* p. 44.
120. Hurnard, *The King's Pardon for Homicide before A.D. 1307,* p. 66.
121. Hurnard, *The King's Pardon for Homicide before A.D. 1307,* pp. 304–05; Lacey, *The Royal Pardon,* pp. 51–52; Komornicka, "Contra signum nostrum," p. 214; Lanhers, "Crimes et criminels," pp. 327–29 (in part drawing on *Confessions et jugements de criminels,* pp. 156–58).
122. Hurnard, *The King's Pardon for Homicide before A.D. 1307,* p. 66. For a case detailing the suspicion, see *Close Rolls, 1251–1253,* pp. 504–05.
123. *Legal History: The Year Books* (online), Seipp number 1345.119rs.

Notes to Chapter 6

EPILOGUE: ATROPHY AND DISPLACEMENT

1. Naessens, "Judicial Authorities' Views of Women's Roles in Late Medieval Flanders," pp. 59 and 74.
2. The English justified expulsion of heretics through creative interpretation of the statute of 1401 against dissenters from Roman Catholicism (cf. *Legal History: The Year Books* [online], Seipp number 1495.017), which was later applied to Catholic adherents.
3. For a history of these developments down to the early fifteenth century, see New, *History of the Alien Priories in England to the Confiscation of Henry V.*
4. *Petitions to the Crown from English Religious Houses,* pp. 206–07 no. 161, petition dated 1330.
5. *Petitions to the Crown from English Religious Houses,* pp. 110–11 no. 92.
6. The most comprehensive study of the war is Sumption's *The Hundred Years' War:* the second and third volumes, especially, interweave high politics, battles, and the scourge of demobilized troops and so-called *routiers.* See also Grantham, "France," pp. 69–70; Geremek, *Les marginaux parisiens,* p. 138.
7. Alban and Allmand, "Spies and Spying," pp. 81–82.
8. *Actes normands de la Chambre des comptes sous Philippe de Valois,* p. 276.
9. Sumption, *The Hundred Years' War,* vol. 1, p. 447; Alban and Allmand, "Spies and Spying," pp. 80–87.
10. Ambühl, *Prisoners of War,* p. 85; Alban and Allmand, "Spies and Spying," pp. 75–80.
11. *Actes normands de la Chambre des comptes sous Philippe de Valois,* p. 277.
12. Ambühl, *Prisoners of War,* pp. 45–49.
13. For French spies and English apprehension about and measures against them, see Alban and Allmand, "Spies and Spying," pp. 87–100.

14. For the spies at work, see Sumption, *The Hundred Years' War*, vol. 1, pp. 159, 246–47, 254, 284–85, 346–413, 578.

15. Gauvard, *De grace especial*, vol. 1, p. 220 n. 126. *Old French-English Dictionary*, s.v. *boe*[1].

16. Gauvard, *De grace especial*, vol. 2, p. 744 n. 160.

17. *Legal History: The Year Books* (online), Seipp number 1346.051rs.

18. In chapter 3, reference was made on this point to Statham, "Dover Charters," pp. 16–27, nos. VIII–XIII.

19. Katherine Murray, *The Constitutional History of the Cinque Ports*, p. 155.

20. Grummitt, *The Calais Garrison*, p. 5.

21. Cf. Alban and Allmand, "Spies and Spying," pp. 82–83.

22. Abjuration to Calais has been little studied: Ives, *A History of Penal Methods*, p. 101. On French attitudes toward vagabondage in the period, see Geremek, *Les marginaux parisiens*, pp. 30–31. (He notes similar attitudes in Castile.) For England, too, see Bennett, "Compulsory Service," pp. 7–51.

23. So I surmise from a case noted in *Legal History: The Year Books* (online), Seipp number 1413.084abr.

24. UK, National Archives database, *Faversham Borough Custumal* (Kent History and Library Centre), Fa/LC c1400–1740, fols.15 r.–15 v. online at http://www.nationalarchives.gov.uk/a2a/records.aspx?cat=051-fa_2&cid=3–1&kw=dover%20abjure#3–1.

25. For a comprehensive survey of the individual sanctuaries, see Cox, *Sanctuaries and Sanctuary Seekers*, pp. 48–226. Trenholme, *The Right of Sanctuary*, pp. 47–60 mirrors much of Cox's work, but also provides a sketch of the inmates of chartered sanctuary (pp. 61–71). See also Daniel Thiery, *Polluting the Sacred*, p. 57.

26. For a rather strange treatment of chartered sanctuaries in comparison to the family and corporations as immune communities, see Wayne Logan, "Criminal Law Sanctuaries," pp. 321–91.

27. "THE King our Sovereign Lord considering that many of his Subjects heretofore, for their Offences and Merits, have been put to Execution of Death by the Laws of this Realm, and many other committing like Offences, for Tuition of their Lives have fled, and resorted to Churches, and other hallowed Places within this Realm, and there being, have abjured the Realm before the King's Coroners of the same; (2) divers of which Men (so abjuring) have been known to be very expert Mariners, and many other have been seen to be very able and apt Men for the Wars, and for Defence of this Realm, so that by the one mean and the other, the Strength and Power of this Realm is greatly diminished; (3) and divers of the said Persons which heretofore have abjured this Realm, being by Reason of their Abjurations in outward Realms and Countries, have not only procured many Men of the same to the Exercise and Practice of Archery, and have instructed them in the Feat and Knowledge thereof, to the great Increase and Fortifications of the same outward Realms, and Countries, but also the same abjured Persons have disclosed their Knowledges of the Commodities and Secrets of this Realm, to no little Damage and Prejudice of the same" (*Statutes made at* Westminster, Anno 22 Hen. VIII *and* Anno Dom. 1530, c. 14, online at Justis.com).

28. The 1536 statute alludes to the earlier abolition: "Where in the last Parliament begun and holden at *London* the third Day of *November* in the one and twentieth Year of the King's most gracious Reign, and from thence adjourned to *Westminster*, and there holden and continued by divers and sundry Prorogations, it was enacted, amongst other Things, That such Person and Persons which did flee or resort to any Parish Church, Cemitory or other like hallowed Place, for Tuition of his Life, by Occasion of any Murther, Robbery or other Felony by the same Person committed, and thereupon confessed any Murther, Felony or other Offence before a Coroner, for the which the same Person, by the Law of this Realm afore that Time used, should abjure and pass out of this Realm, shall be directed by the Coroner to take his Abjuration to any one Sanctuary being within this Realm, which the same Person would elect and choose, there to remain as a Sanctuary-man abjured during his natural Life" (*Statutes made at* Westminster, Anno 28 Hen. VIII, *and* Anno Dom. 1536, c. 1, online at Justis.com). See also Réville, "L'Abjuratio regni," p. 35; Zaremska, *Les bannis au moyen âge*, p. 75; and McGlynn's unpublished paper, "The Use and Abuse of Sanctuary in Henrician England."

29. Shoemaker, *Sanctuary and Crime in the Middle Ages*, pp. 162, 167.

30. Cox, *Sanctuaries and Sanctuary Seekers*, pp. 157, 165, 175.

31. "An Abjured Person shall be marked by the Coroner on his Thumb with a hot Iron; and if he refuse to take his Passage at the Time appointed by the Coroner, he shall lose the Benefit of Sanctuary" (*Statutes made at the Parliament begun at* London, *and continued afterwards by Prorogation and Adjournment to* Westminster, Anno 21 Hen . VIII *and* Anno Dom. 1529, c. 2, online at Justis.com). Bellamy, *Crime and Public Order*, p. 112; Trenholme, *The Right of Sanctuary*, p. 24.

32. *The Third Parliament, holden in the Fourth Year of the Reign of King* Hen. VII, Anno Dom. 1487 [1488], c. 13, online at Justis.com. Sharpe, *Judicial Punishment in England*, p. 23.

33. Trenholme, *Right of Sanctuary*, p. 29.

34. "The thumb is the most important single digit of the hand. Thumb loss, total or partial, is a disastrous injury to the manual worker. The loss of the thumb at the metacarpophalangeal joint [the second joint] decreases the effectiveness of the hand by 40%" (this according to the findings of the Committee on Medical Rating of Physical Impairment, cited in Kelly, "Subtotal Reconstruction of the Thumb," p. 582).

35. *OED*, s.v. "sinister" and "dexter.4"; *Middle English Dictionary*, s.v. "dexter."

36. "Un vocabulaire latin-français," p. 38. See also, for a visual manifestation of this proverbial sentiment, Caviness, "From the Self-Invention of the Whiteman," p. 3.

37. Corballis, "From Mouth to Hand"; see also, "Why Are More People Right-Handed?" (accessed online).

38. *Très ancienne coutume de Bretagne*, p. 443 no. 19.

39. Le Foyer, *Exposé du droit pénal normand au XIIIe siècle*, p. 243; Schubert, *Räuber, Henker, arme Sünder*, p. 100. Exceptionally, a sheep thief in

Languedoc ca. 1309–29 was condemned to lose his left hand; perhaps his right hand was already injured—see Dumas de Rauly, "Les pénalités anciennes," p. 227.

40. "[I]f after such Abjuration any Person so abjured came out of the same Sanctuary to the which he was assigned, and be taken without the same Sanctuary, not having the King's special Pardon or Licence so to do; that then every such Person abjured, and after Abjuration taken without Sanctuary whereunto he was assigned, should suffer like Pain of Death, and after such like Manner should be ordered, as he should have done and biden in case he had abjured this Realm for Murther or Felony, and after such Abjuration had returned again into this Realm, contrary to the Laws of this Land" (*Statutes made at* Westminster, Anno 28 Hen. VIII, *and* Anno Dom. 1536, c.1, online at Justis.com).

41. "All Sanctuaries and Places privileged, which have been used for Sanctuary, shall be utterly extinguished, except Parish Churches and their Church-yards, Cathedral Churches, Hospitals and Churches Collegiate, and all Churches dedicated, used as Parish Churches, and the Sanctuaries to either of them belonging, and *Wells* in the County of *Somerset, Westminster, Manchester, Northampton, Norwich, York, Derby* and *Lancaster*. (2) None of the said Places shall give Immunity or Defence to any Person which shall commit wilful Murder, Rape, Burglary, Robbery in the High-way or in any House, or in any Church or Chapel, or which shall burn wilfully any House, or Barn with Corn. (3) He that taketh Sanctuary in any Church, Church-yard, &c. may remain there forty Days, as hath been used, unless the Coroner repair to him to take his Abjuration; in which Case he shall abjure to any of the foresaid privileged Places, not being full of the Number appointed to them, *viz.* above twenty Persons, there to remain during Life. (4) If a privileged Person, daily called to appear before the Governor, shall make Default three Days, or if he commit any Felony, he shall lose the Benefit of Sanctuary. (5) A privileged Person abjuring to any of the aforesaid Places, shall be conducted from Constable to Constable directly, until he be brought to the Governor of the said privileged Place; and if that Place be full of his Number, then he shall be conducted to the next privileged Place, and so to the next, &c. until, &c." (*Statutes made at* Westminster, Anno 32 Hen. VIII. *and* Anno Dom. 1540, c. 12, online at Justis.com).

42. Cox, *Sanctuaries and Sanctuary Seekers*, pp. 74–77.

43. Haagen, *Imprisonment for Debt*, pp. 270–311. See also Réville, "L'Abjuratio regni," p. 41.

44. Continuance of Acts, etc., 1623, c. 23 s. VII, online at Justis.com.

45. William Jones, "Sanctuary, Exile, and Law," pp. 19–41.

46. *Legal History: The Year Books* (online), Seipp numbers 1406.104, 1418.001, 1439.006, 1456.009, and 1491.032; UK, National Archives, SC 8/302/15098, online at http://discovery.nationalarchives.gov.uk/SearchUI/Details?uri=C9518302; SC 8/181/9039, http://discovery.nationalarchives.gov.uk/SearchUI/Details?uri=C9294916; SC 8/183/9137, http://discovery.nationalarchives.gov.uk/SearchUI/Details?uri=C9295014. See also Cox, *Sanctuaries and Sanctuary Seekers*, pp. 319–33, and Réville, "L'Abjuratio regni," pp. 34–40, on the decay of sanctuary.

47. *Legal History: The Year Books* (online), Seipp numbers 1414.054.054abr, 1416.004abr, 1421.143abr, 1442.157abr, 1449.004, 1456.009, 1469.084, 1470.086ss, 1481.068, 1482.142ss, 1487.035, 1488.005, 1495.088, and 1526.012.

48. Bush, "You're Gonna Miss Me When I'm Gone," pp. 1225–85.

49. Morgan and Rushton, *Banishment*, p. 18.

50. Langbein, "The Historical Origins of the Sanction of Imprisonment," p. 39.

51. Cf. Emsley, "Albion's Felonious Attractions," pp. 67–86.

52. Sharpe, *Judicial Punishment in England*, pp. 30–31.

53. Cf. Shapiro, *Revolutionary Justice*.

54. Cf. Wahnich, *In Defence of the Terror*.

55. For a selected few studies of these systems, see Bamford, *Fighting Ships and Prisons*; idem, *Slaves for the Galleys*; Langbein, "The Historical Origins of the Sanction of Imprisonment," pp. 39–44, 53–58; Morgan and Rushton, *Banishment in the Early Atlantic World*, pp. 9–42 and 103–25; Toth, *Beyond Papillon*; Bender, *Angola under the Portuguese*, pp. 60–63; Kennan, *Siberia and the Exile System*. For further bibliography, see "History of Prisons," s.v. "Deportations/Penal Colonies/Galleys," online at http://www.falk-bretschneider.eu/biblio/biblio-5-1.htm. (I owe this bibliographical reference to Professor Guy Geltner.)

Bibliography

PRIMARY SOURCES

1235 Surrey Eyre. Edited by C.A.F. Meekings and David Crook. 2 vols. Surrey Record Society [Publications] 32. Guildford, UK: Surrey Record Society, 1979–83.

The 1258–9 Special Eyre of Surrey and Kent. Edited by Andrew Hershey. Surrey Record Society [Publications] 38. Woking, UK: Surrey Record Society, 2004.

1318. Cest le Compte Henry de Caperel, prevost de Paris. In *Collections des meilleurs dissertations, notices et traités particuliers relatifs à l'histoire de France* 19: 52–57. Edited by Constant Leber. Paris: G.-A. Dentu, 1838.

Actes du Parlement de Paris. Edited by Edgar Boutaric. 2 vols. Paris: Henri Plon, 1863–1867.

Actes et comptes de la commune de Provins de l'an 1271 à l'an 1330. Edited by Maurice Prou and Jules d'Auriac. Provins: Briard, 1933.

Actes normands de la Chambre des comptes sous Philippe de Valois (1328–1350). Edited by Léopold Delisle. Rouen: A. le Brument, 1871.

Administrative Korrespondenz der französischen Könige um 1300: Edition des 'Formelbuches' BNF ms. Lat. 4763, Verwaltung-Gerichtsbarkeit-Kanzlei. Edited by Hans-Günter Schmidt. Göttingen: Klaus Hess Verlag, 1997.

Annales et la Chronique des Dominicains de Colmar. Edited by Charles Gérard and Joseph Liblin. Colmar: Mme. Veuve Decker, 1854.

Archives de la ville de Lectoure: coûtumes, statuts, et records du XIIIme au XVIme siècle; documents inédits. Edited by P. Druilhet. Paris: H. Champion, 1885.

Bezemer, Kees. See below under "Secondary Sources."

Boutillier, Jean. *Somme rural, ou, Le grand coustumier général de practique civil et canon.* Paris: Barthélemy Macé, 1611.

Calendar of Chancery Warrants . . . A.D. 1244–1326. London: His Majesty's Stationery Office, 1927.

Calendar of Coroners' Rolls of the City of London A.D. 1300–1378. Edited by Reginald Sharpe. London: Richard Clay and Sons, 1913.

Calendar of Documents Preserved in France, Illustrative of the History of Great Britain and Ireland. Vol. I, A.D. 918–1206. London: Her Majesty's Stationery Office, 1899.

Calendar of Inquisitions Miscellaneous, 1219–1422. 7 vols. to date. London: His /Her Majesty's Stationery Office, 1916–.

Calendar of Inquisitions Post Mortem and Other Analogous Documents Preserved in the Public Record Office. 26 vols. to date. London: His/Her Majesty's Stationery Office, 1904–.

Calendar of London Trailbaston Trials under Commissions of 1305 and 1306. Edited by Ralph Pugh. London: Her Majesty's Stationery Office, 1975.

Calendarium Inquisitionum post mortem sive escaetarum, vol. I. London: G. Eyre and A. Strahan, 1806.

Catalogue des manuscrits et documents originaux relatifs de la ville de Metz et du pays messin. Metz: Lecouteux, 1850.

Charter Rolls. The Charter, Close, Curia Regis, Fine, Liberate, Patent, Pipe, Receipt (and Issue) Rolls have been published either with their name as the lead word or as *Calendars;* the notes in this book make clear, by referencing the years or reigns covered, which volumes are being cited. In their original appearance most, though by no means all, were published by Her or His Majesty's Stationery Office. Various companies have reprinted a number of them since.

"Chest la revenue de la conté de Bouloigne" (1339–1340). Edited by Ernest Deseille. *Mémoires de la Société académique de l'arrondissement de Boulogne-sur-Mer* 9 (1878–79): 327–78.

"Chest la revenue de la terre . . . tres haute, tres noble et pouissant Dame Marguerite d'Evreus" (1338). Edited by Ernest Deseille. *Mémoires de la Société académique de l'arrondissement de Boulogne-sur-Mer* 9 (1878–79): 303–26.

Chronicles of the Reigns of Edward I. and Edward II. Edited by William Stubbs. 2 vols. London: Longman, etc., 1883.

Close Rolls. See explanatory note at Charter Rolls, above.

"Un compte de menues dépenses de l'Hôtel du roi Philippe VI le Valois pour le premier semestre de l'année 1337." Edited by Robert Fawtier. Essay XVI in *Autour de la France capétienne: personnages et institutions,* edited by Jeanne Stone. London: Variorum Reprints, 1987.

Compte général du receveur d'Artois pour 1303–1304. Edited by Bernard Delmaire. Brussels: Académie Royale de Belgique / Koninklijke Academie van België, 1977.

Comptes consulaires de Saint-Antonin, vol. I. Edited by Georges Julien and others. Saint-Antonin: Société des amis du vieux Saint-Antonin, 2003.

Comptes de dépenses de la châtellenie de Billiat (Ain) aux XIVe siècle (1317–372) et la charte de franchises de la ville (1324). Paris: Association Les Amis du Château des Allymes et de René de Lucinge, 1997.

Comptes de dépenses de la châtellenie de Pont-d'Ain au début du XIVe siècle (1296–1328). Part 1. Paris: Association Les Amis du Château des Allymes et de René de Lucinge, 1992.

Comptes de dépenses de la châtellenie de Pont-d'Ain au début du XIVe siècle (1328–1340). Part 2. Paris: Association Les Amis du Château des Allymes et de René de Lucinge, 1992.

Comptes de la ville d'Ypres de 1267 à 1329. Edited by G. Des Marez and E. De Sagher. 2 vols. Brussels: Kiessling, P. Imbreghts, 1909–13.

Comptes Henri de Taperel. See *1318. Cest le Compte Henry de Caperel.*

Confessions et jugements de criminels au Parlement de Paris (1319–1350). Edited by Monique Langlois and Yvonne Lanhers. Paris: S.E.V.P.E.N., 1971.

The Court of the Justiciar of England (1258–60). Edited by Andrew Hershey. London: The Seldon Society (in preparation).

Coutume d'Agen. Edited by Henry Tropamer. Bordeaux: Y. Cadoret, 1911.

Coutume de Saint-Sever (1380–1480): édition et commentaire des textes gascon et latin. Edited by Michel Maréchal and Jacques Poumarède. Paris: Éditions du C.T.H.S., 1988.

Coutumes de Beauvaisis of Philippe de Beaumanoir. Translated by F.R.P. Akehurst. Philadelphia: University of Pennsylvania Press, 1992.

Coutumiers de Normandie. Edited by Ernest-Joseph Tardif. 2 vols. Rouen and Paris: A. Lestringant / A. Picard et Fils, 1896.

Curia Regis Rolls. See explanatory note at Charter Rolls, above.

Dante. *The Inferno.* Translated by Robert and Jean Hollander. New York: Doubleday, 2000.

Documents relatifs aux États généraux et assemblées reunis sous Philippe le Bel. Edited by Georges Picot. Paris: Imprimerie nationale, 1901.

Documents sur la ville de Millau. Edited by Jules Artières. *Archives historiques du Rouergue* 7. Millau: Imprimerie Artières et Maury. 1930.

Droit coutumier de Cambrai. Edited by E. Meijers and A. de Blécourt. Haarlem: H. D. Tjeen Willenk en Zoon, 1932.

Établissements de Rouen: études sur l'histoire des institutions municipales de Rouen, Falaise, Pont-Audemer, Verneuil, La Rochelle, Saintes, Oleron, Bayonne, Tours, Niort, Cognac, Saint-Jean d'Angély, Angoulême, Poitiers, etc. Edited by Arthur Giry. 2 vols. Paris: F. Vieweg, 1883–85.

Établissements de saint Louis. Edited by Paul Viollet. 4 vols. Paris: Renouard, 1881–86.

Eyre of Kent, 6 & 7 Edward II, A.D. 1313–1314, vol. I. Edited by Frederic Maitland and others. Selden Society, Year Book Series 5.

Fine Rolls. See explanatory note at Charter Rolls, above.

"Flandrisches Urkunden-Buch." In Leopold Warnkönig, *Flandrische Staats- und Rechtsgeschichte bis zum Jahr 1305,* vol. III, part 2. 3 vols. Wiesbaden: Dr. Martin Sändig, 1839–42.

Fors de Béarn, législation inédite du 11.me au 15.me siècle. Edited by A. Mazure and J. Hatoulet. Pau and Paris: É. Vignancour, Bellen-Mandar, and Joubert, [1840?].

Fuller, E. A., ed. "Pleas of the Crown at Bristol, 15 Edward I." *Bristol and Gloucestershire Archaeological Society* 22 (1899): 150–78.

Giraud, Charles, ed. *Essai sur l'histoire de droit français au moyen âge.* 2 vols. Paris: Videcoq, Père et Fils, 1846.

Grand coutumier de France. Edited by Édouard Laboulaye and Rodolphe Dareste. Paris: Auguste Durand et Pedone-Lauriel, 1868.

Henry III Fine Rolls Project. http://www.finerollshenry3.org.uk.

Henry de Bracton, *On the Laws and Customs of England [De legibus].* Edited by George Woodbine. Translated by Samuel Thorne. 4 vols. Cambridge, MA: Belknap Press, 1968–77.

Hermansart, Pagart d'. "Ambassade de Raoul de Brienne, comte d'Eux et Guînes, connêtable de France, en Angleterre (1330)." *Bulletin du Comité des travaux historiques et scientifiques: Section d'histoire et de philologie* (1896): 165–68.

Inquisitions Miscellaneous. See *Calendar of Inquisitions Miscellaneous.*

"Inquisitiones post mortem." *Archaeologia cantiana* 2 (1859): 279–336.

Inquisitions post mortem. See *Calendar of Inquisitions Post Mortem.*

Jacobus, de Voragine. *The Golden Legend: Readings on the Saints.* Translated by William Ryan. Princeton: Princeton University Press, 2012.

Janin, Eugène. "Documents relatifs à la peine du bannissment (treizième et quatorzième siècles)." *Bibliothèque de l'École des chartes* 3 (1846): 419–26.

Jurades de la ville d'Agen (1345–1355). Edited by Adolphe Magen. Auch: L. Cocharaux, 1894.

Justis.com. *Justis: The Law Online.*

Kent Hundred Rolls. Online at http://www.kentarchaeology.ac/khrp/khrpa.html

Die Kölner Weltchronik 1273/88–1376. Edited by Rolf Sprandel. Munich: Monumenta Germaniae Historica, 1991.

Kunera—Database for Late Medieval Badges and Ampullae. Online through http://www.kunera.nl.

Legal History: The Year Books, Medieval English Legal History: An Index and Paraphrase of Printed Year Book Reports, 1268–1535. Compiled by David Seipp. Online at http://www.bu.edu/law/seipp/.

"Lettre des maire et jurés de Laon aux maire et jurés de Saint-Quentin." Edited by Amédée Piette. *Bulletin de la Société académique de Laon* 5 (1856): 261–62.

"Lettre des prevost, jurés et échevins de Valenciennes aux maieur et jurés de Saint-Quentin." Edited by Maurice de Chauvenet. *Bulletin de la Société académique de Laon* 5 (1856): 260–61.

Liberate Rolls. See explanatory note at Charter Rolls, above.

Littérature latine et histoire du moyen âge. Edited by Léopold Delisle. Paris: Ernest Leroux, 1890.

Le livre Roisin: coutumier lillois de la fin du XIIIe siècle. Edited by Raymond Monier. Paris and Lille: Éditions Dornat-Montchrestien and Émile Raoust, 1932.

Lois, enquêtes et jugements des pairs du Castel de Lille. Edited by Raymond Monier. Lille: Émile Raoust, 1937.

London, National Archives, *Ancient Petitions*, SC 8. Online at http://www .nationalarchives.gov.uk/catalogue/.

London Eyre of 1244. Edited by Helen Chew and Martin Weinbaum. Online at http://www.british-history.ac.uk/report.aspx?compid=35947.

London Eyre of 1276. Edited by Martin Weinbaum. Online at http://www .british-history.ac.uk/report.aspx?compid=35999.

Medieval Popular Religion, 1000–1500: A Reader. 2nd ed. Edited by John Shinners. Toronto: Broadview Press, 2007.

The Medieval Records of a London City Church: St Mary at Hill, 1420–1559. Edited by Henry Littlehales. London: K. Paul, Trench, Trübner & Co., 1904–05.

"Monition et proclamation des bannis de la ville de Saint-Quentin, vers 1300 et quelque." Edited by Charles Desmazes. *Bulletin de la Société académique de Laon* 5 (1856): 259–60

Munimenta gildhalle londoniensis; Liber albus, Liber custumarum, et Liber Horn. vol. I, *Liber albus.* Edited by Henry Riley. London: Longman, Green, London and Roberts, 1859.

Nonarum Inquisitiones in Curia Scaccarii, temp. Regis Edwardi III. London: G. Eyre and A. Strahan, 1807.

Norman Charters from English Sources: Antiquaries, Archives and the Rediscovery of the Anglo-Norman Past. Edited by Nicholas Vincent. London: Pipe Roll Society, 2013.

Olim, ou, Registres des arrêts rendus par la Cour du roi. Edited by Arthur Beugnot. 3 vols. Paris: Imprimerie Royale, 1839–48.

Oxford City Documents, Financial and Judicial, 1258–1665. Edited by James Thorold Rogers. Oxford: Clarendon Press, 1891.

Paris, Matthew. *Chronica majora*. Edited by Henry Luard. 7 vols. London: Her Majesty's Stationery Office, 1872–83.

Parker, John, ed. *Lancashire Assize Rolls: 4 John–13 Edward I*. Online at http://www.british-history.ac.uk/report.aspx?compid=69818.

Parliament Rolls of Medieval England, 1275–1504. Edited by C. Given-Wilson, P. Brand, A. Curry, R. E. Horrox, G. Martin, W. M. Ormrod and J.R.S. Phillips. Leicester: Scholarly Digital Editions and the National Archives, 2005. Online, http://www.sd-editions.com/PROME/home.html.

Patent Rolls. See explanatory note at Charter Rolls, above.

Petitions to the Crown from English Religious Houses c. 1272–c. 1485. Edited by Gwilym Dodd and Alison McHardy. Woodbridge, UK: Boydell Press, 2010.

Picot, Georges, ed. *Documents relatives aux États Généraux sous Philippe le Bel*. Paris: Imprimerie nationale, 1901.

Pipe Rolls. See explanatory note at Charter Rolls, above.

Pleas before the King or His Justices, 1198–1212, vol. III: *Rolls or Fragments of Rolls from the Years 1199, 1201, and 1203–1206*. Edited by Doris Stenton. London: Bernard Quaritch, 1967.

Pleas of the Crown for the County of Gloucester. Edited by Frederic Maitland. London: Macmillan and Co., 1884.

Pleas of the Crown for the Hundred of Swineshead and the Township of Bristol, A.D. 1221. Edited by Edward Watson. Bristol: W. Croft Emmons, 1902.

Récits d'un bourgeois de Valenciennes (XIV siècle). Edited by Kervyn de Lettenhove. Louvain: P. et J. Lefever, 1877.

Recueil des monuments inédits du Tiers-État. Edited by Augustin Thierry, Félix Bourquelot and Charles Louandre. 4 vols. Paris: F. Didot, 1850–70.

Red Book of the Exchequer. 3 vols. Edited by Hubert Hall. London: Her Majesty's Stationery Office, 1896.

Registre criminel de la justice de Saint Martin des Champs à Paris au XIVe siècle. Edited by Louis Tanon. Paris: Leon Willem, 1877.

Registre criminel de Sainte-Geneviève. In *Histoire des justices des anciennes églises et communautés de Paris*, edited by Louis Tanon, 347–412. Paris: L. Larose et Forcel, 1883.

Registre criminel de Saint-Germain-des-Prés. In *Histoire des justices des anciennes églises et communautés de Paris*, edited by Louis Tanon, 413–54. Paris: L. Larose et Forcel, 1883.

Registre criminel de Saint-Maur-des-Fossés. In *Histoire des justices des anciennes églises et communautés de Paris*, edited by Louis Tanon, 321–46. Paris: L. Larose et Forcel, 1883.

Registre de l'officialité de l'abbaye de Cerisy. Edited by Gustave Dupont. Caen: F. Le Blanc-Hardel, 1880.

Registre de Saint-Denis. In *Histoire des justices des anciennes églises et communatés de Paris,* edited by Louis Tanon, 557–61. Paris: L. Larose et Forcel, 1883.

"Restas des comptes des officiers du conté de Bouloigne" (1325–1326). Edited by Ernest Deseille. *Mémoires de la Société académique de l'arrondissement de Boulogne-sur-Mer* 9 (1878–79): 393–94.

Rolls of Divers Accounts for the Early Years of the Reign of Henry III. Edited by Fred Cazel. London: Pipe Roll Society, 1982.

Rolls of the Justices in Eyre Being the Rolls and Assizes for Gloucestershire, Warwickshire and Staffordshire, 1221, 1222. Edited by Doris Stenton. London: Bernard Quaritch, 1940.

Safford, E. W. "An Account of the Expenses of Eleanor, Sister of Edward III, on the Occasion of Her Marriage to Reynald, Count of Guelders." *Archaeologia* 77 (1928): 111–40.

Select Cases from the Coroners' Rolls A.D. 1265–1413. Edited by Charles Gross. London: Bernard Quaritch, 1896.

Série J, Trésor des chartes, supplément: Inventaire. J1028 à J1034. Compiled by Henri de Curzon. Online at http://www.archivesnationales.culture.gouv.fr/chan/chan/fonds/EGF/SA/InvSAPDF/SA_index_J/J_suppl_pdf/J1028_1034.pdf.

Skeat, Walter. "Dr. Pegge's Alphabet of Kenticisms, and Collection of Proverbial Sayings Used in Kent." *Archaeologia cantiana* 9 (1874): 50–147.

Somersetshire Pleas (Civil and Criminal), from the Rolls of the Itinerant Justices (Close of 12th Century–41 Henry III). Edited by Charles Chadwyck-Healey. London: Privately Printed, 1897.

Song of Roland. Translated by Glyn Burgess. London: Penguin Books, 1990.

Staffordshire Plea Rolls (Staffordshire Historical Collections). Online at http://www.british-history.ac.uk/source.aspx?pubid=462 as well as subsequent URLs (463, 464, 465, etc.).

Statham, Samuel. "Dover Chamberlains' Accounts, 1365–67." *Archaeologia cantiana* 25 (1902): 75–87.

———. *Dover Charters and Other Documents in the Possession of the Corporation of Dover.* London: J. M. Dent, 1902.

Statutes of the Realm, 11 vols. N.p.: [for the House of Commons], 1810–28.

The Treatise (Le Tretiz) *of Walter of Bibbesworth.* Translated by Andrew Dalby. Totnes, UK: Prospect Books, 2012.

Trés ancienne coutume de Bretagne. Edited by Marcel Planiol. Rennes: J. Plihon and L. Hervé, 1896.

The True Chronicles of Jean le Bel, 1290–1360. Translated by Nigel Bryant. Woodbridge, UK: Boydell Press, 2011.

U[nited] K[ingdom]. National Archives, various online databases. (References in the notes to the present book always specify the data sets [e.g., Canterbury Cathedral Archives] and provide the link at the time of access.)

Varin, Pierre, ed. *Archives . . . de Reims* (including *Archives administratives* and *Archives legislatives*). Paris: Crapelet, C. Lahure, 1839–53.

Viollet, Paul, ed. "Registres judiciaires de quelques établissements religieux du Parisis au XIIIe et XIVe siècle." *Bibliothèque de l'École des chartes* 34 (1873): 317–42.

"Visites pastorales de maître Henri de Vezelai." Edited by Léopold Delisle. *Bibliothèque de l'École des chartes* 54 (1893): 457–66 and plate.

"Un vocabulaire latin-français du XIVe siècle, suivi d'un recueil d'anciens proverbes." Edited by Ulysse Robert. *Bibliothèque de l'École des chartes* 34 (1873): 33–46.

Whitley, H. Michell. "Sanctuary in Devon." *Report and Transactions of the Devonshire Association for the Advancement of Science, Literature, and Art* 45 (1913): 302–13.

SECONDARY SOURCES

Alban, J. R., and C. T. Allmand, "Spies and Spying in the Fourteenth Century." In *War, Literature and Politics in the Late Middle Ages*, edited by C. T. Allmand, 73–101. Liverpool: Liverpool University Press, 1976.

Ambühl, Rémy. *Prisoners of War in the Hundred Years War: Ransom Culture in the Late Middle Ages*. Cambridge: Cambridge University Press, 2013.

Backhouse, Janet, and Christopher de Hamel. *The Becket Leaves*. London: British Library, 1988.

Baldwin, John. *Masters, Princes and Merchants: The Social Views of Peter the Chanter and His Circle*. 2 vols. Princeton: Princeton University Press, 1970.

Bamford, Paul. *Fighting Ships and Prisons: Mediterranean Galleys of France in the Age of Louis XIV*. St. Paul: University of Minnesota Press, 1973.

———. *Slaves for the Galleys of France, 1665 to 1700*. St. Paul: University of Minnesota Press, 1965.

"Bannis de Douai et la franchise de la Saint-Pierre d'août." *Souvenirs de la Flandre wallonne* 1 (1861): 3–9.

Barbezat, Michael. "In a Corporeal Flame: The Materiality of Hellfire before the Resurrection in Six Latin Authors." *Viator* 44 (2013): 1–20.

Barmash, Pamela. *Homicide in the Biblical World*. Cambridge: Cambridge University Press, 2005.

Bartlett, Robert. *Trial by Fire and Water: The Medieval Judicial Ordeal*. Oxford: Clarendon Press, 1986.

Beaurepaire, Charles de. *Essai sur l'asile religieux dans l'Empire romain et la monarchie française*. Paris: Durand, 1854.

Bell, Adrian, Chris Brooks, and Tony Moore. "Credit Finance in Thirteenth-Century England: The Ricciardi of Lucca and Edward I, 1272–1294." *Thirteenth Century England* 13 (2009): 101–16.

Bellamy, J. G. "The Coterel Gang: An Anatomy of a Band of Fourteenth-Century Criminals." *English Historical Review* 79 (1964): 698–717.

———. *Crime and Public Order in England in the Later Middle Ages*. London: Routledge and Kegan Paul, 1973.

Bender, Gerald. *Angola under the Portuguese: The Myth and the Reality.* Berkeley and Los Angeles: University of California Press, 1978.

Bennett, Judith. "Compulsory Service in Late Medieval England." *Past & Present* 209 (November 2010): 7–51.

Bentham, Jeremy. *Théorie des peines et des récompenses*, vol. I. 3rd ed. Paris: Bossange frères, 1825–26.

Bernard, Louis. "L'état ancien du Boulonnais: rapport." *Bulletin de la Société académique de l'arrondissement de Boulogne-sur-Mer* 2 (1873–78): 135–47.

Bezemer, Kees. *What Jacques Saw: Thirteenth Century France through the Eyes of Jacques de Revigny, Professor of Law at Orleans.* Frankfurt am Main: Vittorio Klostermann, 1997.

Bibliothèque historique, monumentale, ecclésiastique et littéraire de la Picardie et de l'Artois. Amiens: Duval et Herment, 1844.

Bimbenet, Jean-Eugène. "Examen de l'étude de M. Frémont sur la suppression de la haute police de l'état." *Mémoires de la Société d'agriculture, sciences, belles-lettres et arts d'Orléans*, 4th series, 14 (1870): 5–22.

Bonne, Louis-Charles. "Étude sur la condition des étrangers en France depuis l'origine de la monarchie jusqu'à nos jours." *Mémoires de la Société des lettres, sciences et arts de Bar-le-Duc* 7 (1877): 69–98.

Bougard, Pierre. "La fortune et les comptes de Thierry de Hérisson." *Bibliothèque de l'École de chartes* 123 (1965): 126–78.

Bouniol, Bathild. *Les rues de Paris: biographies, portraits, récits, légendes.* 3 vols. Paris: Bray and Retaux, 1872.

Bourquelot, Félix. *Histoire de Provins.* 2 vols. Provins and Paris: Lebeau; Précieux; etc., 1839–40.

———. "Notice sur le manuscrit intitulé Cartulaire de la ville de Provins (XIIIe et XIVe siècles)." *Bibliothèque de l'École de chartes*, 4th series, 2 (1856): 194–241, 428–60.

Brand, Paul. "Chief Justice and Felon: The Career of Thomas Weyland." In *The Political Context of Law*, edited by Richard Eales and David Sullivan, 27–47. London and Ronceverte, WV: Hambledon Press, 1987.

———. "Understanding Early Petitions: An Analysis of the Content of Petitions to Parliament in the Reign of Edward I." In *Medieval Petitions: Grace and Grievance*, edited by W. Mark Ormrod, Gwilym Dodd, and Anthony Musson, 99–119. York: York Medieval Press, 2009.

Bresc, Henri. "Justice et société dans les domaines de l'évêque de Fréjus dans la première moitié du XIVe siècle.' In *La Provence et Fréjus sous la première maison d'Anjou (1246–1382)*, edited by Jean-Paul Boyer and Thierry Pécout, 19–35. Aix-en-Provence: Publications de l'Université de Provence, 2010.

Brochon, Étienne-Henry. *Essai sur l'histoire de la justice criminelle à Bordeaux pendant le moyen âge.* Bordeaux: Crugy, 1857.

Brown, Andrew. *Civic Ceremony and Religion in Medieval Bruges c. 1300–1520.* Cambridge: Cambridge University Press, 2011.

Brown, Peter. "Society and the Supernatural: A Medieval Change." In *Society and the Holy in Late Antiquity.* Berkeley: University of California Press, 1982.

Bull, Marcus. *The Miracles of Our Lady of Rocamadour: Analysis and Translation.* Woodbridge, UK: Boydell Press, 1999.

Bullough, Vern, and Bonnie Bullough. *Women and Prostitution: A Social History.* Buffalo: Prometheus Books, 1987.

Bureau of Justice Statistics. Online at http://www.bjs.gov/.

Bush, Jonathan. "'You're Gonna Miss Me When I'm Gone': Early Modern Common Law Discourse and the Case of the Jews." *Wisconsin Law Review* 5 (1993): 1225–85.

"Caesar's Campaigns in Gaul." *Westminster Review* 77 (1862): 399–417.

Cambridge Urban History of Britain, vol. I: *600–1540*. Edited by D. M. Palliser. Cambridge: Cambridge University Press, 2000.

Carbonnières, Louis de. "Le privilège de bannissement de la ville de Tournai devant la chambre criminelle du Parlement de Paris sous Charles VI: contribution au statute du privilège." In *L'exclusion au moyen âge*, edited by Nicole Gonthier, 315–43. Lyon: Université Jean Moulin, 2007.

Cardevacque, Adolphe. "Le bourreau à Arras." *Mémoires de la Académie des sciences, lettres et arts d'Arras*, 2nd Series, 24 (1893): 163–210.

Cassidy, Richard, and Michael Clasby. "Matthew Paris and Henry III's Elephant." http://www.finerollshenry3.org.uk/redist/pdf/fm-06-2012.pdf.

Caviness, Madeline. "From the Self-Invention of the Whiteman in the Thirteenth Century to *The Good, The Bad, and The Ugly*." *Different Visions: A Journal of New Perspectives on Medieval Art* 1 (Fall 2008): 1–33. Online at http://differentvisions.org/issue1PDFs/Caviness.pdf.

———. "Giving 'the Middle Ages' a Bad Name: Blood Punishments in the *Sachsenspiegel* and Town Lawbooks," *Studies in Iconography* 34 (2013): 175–235.

Central Law Journal 55 (1902).

Chaplais, Pierre. *English Diplomatic Practice in the Middle Ages.* London and New York: Hambledon and London, 2003.

Chronique et annales de Gilles le Muisit. Edited by Henri Lemaître. Paris: Renouard, 1906.

Clanchy, Michael. "Highway Robbery and Trial by Battle in the Hampshire Eyre of 1249." In *Medieval Legal Records, Edited in Memory of C.A.F. Meekings*, edited by R. Hunnisett and J. Post, pp. 25–61. London: Her Majesty's Stationery Office, 1978.

Clarke, Helen, and others. *Sandwich, the 'Completest Medieval Town in England': A Study of the Town and Port from Its Origins to 1600.* Oxford and Oakville: Oxbow Books, 2010.

Clay, Rotha. *Hermits and Anchorites of England.* London: Methuen, 1914.

Cohen, Esther. "Roads and Pilgrimage: A Study in Economic Interaction." *Studi medievali* 21 (1980): 321–41.

Corballis, Michael. "From Mouth to Hand: Gesture, Speech, and the Evolution of Right-Handedness." *Behavioral and Brain Sciences* 26 (2003): 199–208.

Coulet, Noël. "Inns and Taverns." In *Dictionary of the Middle Ages*, vol. VI, edited by Joseph Strayer, 468–77. New York: Charles Scribner's Sons, 1985.

Coulson, Charles. "Peaceable Power in English Castles." *Anglo-Norman Studies* 23 (2000): 69–95.

Cousin, Louis. "Sur des fouilles archéologiques faites à Wissant en 1855." *Mémoires de la Société dunkerquoise pour l'encouragement des sciences, des letters et des arts* (1856 [for 1855]): 210–14.

Cox, J. Charles. *Sanctuaries and Sanctuary Seekers of Mediaeval England*. London: George Allen and Sons, 1911.

Coy, Jason. *Strangers and Misfits: Banishment, Social Control, and Authority in Early Modern Germany*. Leiden: Brill, 2008.

Crook, David. "A Petition from the Prisoners in Nottingham Gaol, c. 1330." In *Medieval Petitions: Grace and Grievance*, edited by W. Mark Ormrod, Gwilym Dodd, and Anthony Musson, 206–21. York: York Medieval Press, 2009.

Curveiller, Stéphane. *Dunkerque, ville et port de Flandre à la fin du moyen âge: à travers les comptes de bailliage de 1358 à 1407*. [Villeneuve d'Ascq:] Presses Universitaires de Lille, 1989.

———. "L'étranger à Dunkerque à la fin du moyen âge à travers une source comptable (fin XIVe-début XVe siècle)." *Annales de Bretagne et des Pays de l'Ouest* 117 (2010): 25–38.

Cuttino, George. *English Diplomatic Administration, 1259–1339*, 2nd ed. Oxford: Clarendon Press, 1971.

Davis, Natalie. *Fiction in the Archives: Pardon Tales and Their Tellers in Sixteenth-Century France*. Stanford: Stanford University Press, 1987.

De Hamel, Christopher. "Books and Society." In *Books and Society*, vol. II: *1100–1400*, edited by Nigel Morgan and Rodney Thomson. Cambridge: Cambridge University Press, 2008.

Dean, Trevor. *Crime in Medieval Europe, 1200–1550*. Harlow, UK: Pearson Education, 2001.

Dehaisnes, C. "État général des registres de la Chambre des comptes de Lille relatifs à la Flandre." *Annales du Comité flamand de France* 11 (1870–72): 291–353.

Deller, William. "The Texture of Literacy in the Testimonies of Late-Medieval English Proof-of-Age Jurors, 1270 to 1430." *Journal of Medieval History* 38 (2012): 207–24.

Demaitre, Luke. *Leprosy in Premodern Medicine: A Malady of the Whole Body*. Baltimore: The Johns Hopkins University Press, 2007.

Deseille, Ernest. "Communication . . . de M. J. Lecat." *Bulletin de la Société académique de l'arrondissement de Boulogne-sur-Mer* 4 (1885–90): 318–19.

———. "Les pèlerinages populaires du pays Boulonnais." *Bulletin de la Société académique de l'arrondissement de Boulogne-sur-Mer* 3 (1879–84): 368–80.

Dictionnaire topographique de la France: arrondissement de Boulogne-sur-Mer. Edited by Daniel Haigneré. In *Mémoires de la Société académique de l'arrondissement de Boulogne-sur-Mer* 11 (1881).

Dictionnaire topographique du department du Pas-de-Calais. Compiled by August-Charles-Henri, Comte de Loisne. Paris: Imprimerie nationale, 1907.

Ducoudray, Gustave. *Les Origines du Parlement de Paris et la justice aux XIIIe et XIVe siècles*. Paris: Hachette, 1902.

Dufossé, Frank. "Wissant, le dernier port d'échouage de France." http://www
.mincoin.com/php1/wissb.php.

Dumas de Rauly, Charles. "Les pénalités anciennes." *Recueil de l'Académie des
sciences, belles-lettres et arts de Tarn-et-Garonne* 7 (1891): 225–44.

Dunn, Caroline. "Prosecuting Ravishment in Thirteenth Century England." Unpublished. Thirteenth Century England XIII Conference, Paris, September 10,
2009.

Dyer, Christopher. "Poverty and Its Relief in Late Medieval England." *Past &
Present* 216 (August 2012): 41–78.

Ebon, Martin. *Saint Nicholas: Life and Legend.* New York: Harper and Row,
1975.

Emsley, Clive. "Albion's Felonious Attractions: Reflections upon the History of
Crime in England. In *Crime History and Histories of Crime: Studies in the His-
toriography of Crime and Criminal Justice in Modern History,* edited by Clive
Emsley and Louis A. Knafla, 67–86. Westport, CT: Greenwood Press, 1996.

*Exhibition Catalog: Medieval English Pilgrim Badges from the Robert P. Palazzo
Collection.* Medieval Academy of America, 76th Annual Meeting, March 15–
17, 2001, Arizona State University, Tempe, AZ. Typescript, 18 pp.

Farina, Lara. "Money, Books, and Prayers: Anchoresses and Exchange in
Thirteenth-Century England." In *Women and Wealth in Late Medieval Europe,*
edited by Theresa Earenfight, 171–85. New York: Palgrave Macmillan, 2010.

Fauqueux, Charles. *Beauvais, son histoire.* Beauvais: Imprimerie Centrale Administrative, 1938.

Flight, Colin. "Dover Castle: Knight's Fees Owing Castle-Guard Service at Dover."
http://www.kentarchaeology.ac/digiarchive/ColinFlight/dover-intro.pdf.

Flower, C. T. *Introduction to the Curia Regis Rolls, 1199–1230 A.D.* London:
Bernard Quaritch, 1944.

Forrest, Ian. "The Transformation of Visitation in Thirteenth-Century England."
Past & Present 221 (November 2013): 3–38.

Foucault, Michel. *Discipline and Punish: The Birth of the Prison.* Translated by
Alan Sheridan. New York: Random House, 1995.

Frampton, T. S. *A Glance at the Hundred of Wrotham . . . in the Days of the Early
Edwards.* London and Maidstone: Simpkin and Marshall / Burgiss-Brown,
1881.

Friedland, Paul. *Seeing Justice Done: The Age of Spectacular Capital Punishment
in France.* Oxford: Oxford University Press, 2012.

Friedman, David. "Making Sense of English Law Enforcement in the 18th Century." Online at http://www.daviddfriedman.com/Academic/England_18thc
./England_18thc.html.

Gabriel, Astrik. *Garlandia: Studies in the History of the Mediaeval University.*
Notre Dame, IN: Mediaeval Institute, 1969.

Galabert, Firmin. "L'état social à Saint-Antonin aux XIIe et XIIIe siècles," *Bulletin archéologique, historique et artistique de la Société archéologique de Tarn-
et-Garonne* 61 (1933): 17–28.

Gaposchkin, Cecilia. "From Pilgrimage to Crusade: The Liturgy of Departure,
1095–1300." *Speculum* 88 (2013): 44–91.

Gauvard, Claude. *"De grace especial": Crime, état et société à la fin du moyen âge*. 2 vols. Paris: Publications de la Sorbonne, 1991.

———. "Justification and Theory of the Death Penalty at the *Parlement* of Paris in the Late Middle Ages." In *War, Government and Power in Late Medieval France*, edited by C. T. Allmand, 190–208. Liverpool: Liverpool University Press, 2000.

———. "Les oppositions à la peine de mort dans le royaume de France: théorie at pratique (XIIe-XVe siècle)." In *La pena de muerte en la sociedad medieval = Crio et crimen* 4 (2007): 134–66.

———. "Violence citadine et réseaux de solidarité: l'exemple français aux XIVe et Xve siècles." *Annales: Économies, Sociétés, Civilisations* 48 (1993): 1113–26.

Géraud, Hercule. "Mercadier. Les routiers au treizième siècle." *Bibliothèque de l'École de chartes*, 1st series, 3 (1841): 417–47.

———. "Les routiers au douzième siècle." *Bibliothèque de l'École des chartes*, 1st series, 3 (1841): 125–47.

Geremek, Bronislaw. *Les marginaux parisiens aux XIVe et XVe siècles*. Translated by Daniel Beauvois. Paris: Flammarion, 1976.

Gessler, Jean. "Notes sur le droit d'arsin ou d'abattis." In *Mélanges Paul Fournier*, 293–312. Paris: Recueil Sirey, 1929.

Glasson, Ernest. "Le Châtelet de Paris et les abus de sa procédure aux XIVe et Xve siècles, d'après des documents récemment publiés." *Séances et travaux de l'Académie des sciences morales et politiques (Institut de France): compte rendu* 140 (1893): 45–92.

Gomart, Charles. "De la peine du bannissement appliquée par les communes, aux XIIe et XIIIe siècles," *Archives historiques et littéraires du nord de la France et du midi de la Belgique*, 3rd series, 5 (1855): 449–64.

Gonthier, Nicole. *Le châtiment du crime au moyen âge, XIIe–XVIe siècles*. Rennes: Presses Universitaires de Rennes, 1998.

———. *Cris de haine et rites d'unité: la violence dans les villes, XIIIème–XVIème siècle*. Turnhout, Belgium: Brepols, 1992.

———. *Délinquance, justice et société dans le Lyonnais médiéval de la fin du XIIIe siècle au début du XVIe siècle*. Paris: Arguments, 1993.

———. *'Sanglant coupaul!', 'Orde ribaude!': les injures au moyen âge*. Rennes: Presses Universitaires de Rennes, 2007.

Graham, Rose. "An Interdict on Dover, 1298–1299." In *English Ecclesiastical Studies: Being Some Essays in Research in Medieval History*, 324–29. London: Society for Promoting Christian Knowledge, 1929.

Grand, Roger. "Justice criminelle: procédure et peines dans les villes aux XIIIe et XIVe siècles." *Bibliothèque de l'École de chartes* 102 (1941): 51–108.

Grantham, George. "France." In *Agrarian Change and Crisis, 1200–1500*, edited by Harry Kitsikopoulos, 57–92. New York: Routledge, 2012.

Grierson, Philip. "The Relations between England and Flanders before the Norman Conquest," *Transactions of the Royal Historical Society*, 4th series, 23 (1941): 71–112.

Groot, Roger. "The Early Thirteenth-Century Criminal Jury." In *Twelve Good Men and True: The Criminal Trial Jury in England, 1200–1800*, edited by J. S. Cockburn and Thomas Green, 3–35. Princeton: Princeton University Press, 1988.

———. "The Jury in Private Criminal Prosecutions before 1215." *American Journal of Legal History* 27 (1983): 113–41.

Grummitt, David. *The Calais Garrison: War and Military Service in England, 1436–1558.* Woodbridge, UK: Boydell Press, 2008.

Guest, Edwin. "Julius Caesar's Invasion of Britain." *Archaeological Journal* 21 (1864): 220–42.

Guilbert, Aristide. *Histoire des villes de France.* 6 vols. Paris: Furne, 1844–48.

Haagen, Paul. *Imprisonment for Debt in England and Wales.* Unpublished Ph.D. dissertation. Princeton University, 1986.

Haigneré, Daniel. *Dictionnaire historique et archéologique du Pas-de-Calais.* 3 vols. Arras: Sueur-Charrey, 1873–83.

———. "Les fermes de la ville de Wissant." *Mémoires de la Société académique de l'arrondissement de Boulogne-sur-Mer* 15 (1889): 26–73.

Haines, Charles. *Dover Priory: A History of the Priory of St Mary the Virgin and St Martin of the New Work.* Cambridge: The University Press, 1930.

Halba, Eve-Marie. "Le vocabulaire du bannissement aux XIIe et XIIIe siècles." In *L'exclusion au moyen âge,* edited by Nicole Gonthier, 347–72. Lyon: Université Jean Moulin, 2007.

Hale, Matthew. *Historia placitorum coronae.* 2 vols. London: F. Gyles and others, 1736.

Hamel, Sébastien. "Bannis et bannissements à Saint-Quentin aux derniers siècles du moyen âge." *Hypothèses* 1 (2002): 123–33.

Hamil, Frederick. "The King's Approvers: A Chapter in the History of English Criminal Law." *Speculum* 11 (1936): 238–58.

Hare, John. "Inns, Innkeepers and the Society of Later Medieval England." *Journal of Medieval History* 39 (2013): 477–97.

Harrington, Joel. *The Faithful Executioner: Life and Death, Honor and Shame in the Turbulent Sixteenth Century.* New York: Farrar, Straus and Giroux, 2013.

Harris, Simon. "Taking Your Chances: Petitioning in the Last Years of Edward II and the First Years of Edward III." In *Medieval Petitions: Grace and Grievance,* edited by W. Mark Ormrod, Gwilym Dodd, and Anthony Musson, 173–92. York: York Medieval Press, 2009.

Hay, Douglas, et al. *Albion's Fatal Tree: Crime and Society in Eighteenth-Century England.* 2nd ed. London and New York: Verso, 2011.

Heale, Martin. *The Dependent Priories of Medieval English Monasteries.* Woodbridge, UK: Boydell Press, 2004.

Heebøll-Holm, Thomas. *Ports, Piracy and Maritime War: Piracy in the English Channel and the Atlantic c.1280–c.1330.* Leiden: Brill, 2013.

Héliot, Pierre. "Les anciennes églises gothiques du Boulonnais." *Mémoires de la Société des antiquaires de Picardie* 47 (1937): 1–105.

Hermansart, Pagart d'. "Les anciennes communautés d'arts et métiers de Saint-Omer." *Mémoires de la Société des antiquaires de la Morinie* 16 (1876–79): 1–744.

Hicks, Michael, ed. *The Fifteenth-Century Inquisitions Post Mortem: A Companion.* Woodbridge, UK: Boydell and Brewer, 2012.

Hill, Mary. *The King's Messengers 1199–1377: A List of All Known Messengers, Mounted and Unmounted, Who Served John, Henry III, and the First Three Edwards.* Phoenix Mill, UK: Allan Sutton, 1994.

Hillen, Henry. *History of the Borough of King's Lynn*. 2 vols. Norwich: East of England Newspaper Company, 1907.

"Histoire et le patrimoine." http://membres.multimania.fr/histopale/wissant.htm.

The Historical Gazetteer of England's Place-Names. http://placenames.org.uk.

"History of Prisons—A Selected Bibliography." http://www.falk-bretschneider.eu/biblio/biblio-index.htm.

History of the County of Bedford. 3 vols. Westminster: A. Constable, 1904–12.

Hoffman, Joseph, Marcy Kahn, and Steven Fisher. "Plea Bargaining in the Shadow of Death." *Fordham Law Review* 69 (2001): 2313–92.

Holloway, Julia. *Twice-Told Tales: Brunetto Latino and Dante Alighieri*. New York and elsewhere: Peter Lang, 1993.

Holmes, Thomas. *Ancient Britain and the Invasions of Julius Caesar*. Oxford: Clarendon Press, 1907.

Hostettler, John. *The Criminal Jury Old and New: Jury Power from Early Times to the Present Day*. Winchester, UK: Waterside Press, 2004.

Hunt, Edwin, and James Murray. *A History of Business in Medieval Europe*. Cambridge: Cambridge University Press, 1999.

Hurnard, Naomi. *The King's Pardon for Homicide before A.D. 1307*. Oxford: Clarendon Press, 1969.

Hyams, Paul. *Rancor and Reconciliation in Medieval England*. Ithaca, NY, and London: Cornell University Press, 2003.

———. "Trial by Ordeal: The Key to Proof in the Early Common Law." In *On the Laws and Customs of England: Essays in Honor of Samuel E. Thorne*, edited by Morris Arnold and others, 90–126. Chapel Hill: University of North Carolina Press, 1981.

Iglesias-Rábade, Luis. "The Multi-Lingual Pulpit in England 1100–1500," *Neophilologus* 80 (1996): 479–92.

Ireland, Richard. "The Presumption of Guilt in the History of English Criminal Procedure." *Journal of Legal History* 7 (1986): 243–55.

———. "Theory and Practice within the Medieval English Prison." *American Journal of Legal History* 31 (1987): 56–67.

Isba, Anne. *Gladstone and Dante: Victorian Statesman, Medieval Poet*. Woodbridge, UK: Boydell Press, 2006.

Ives, George. *A History of Penal Methods: Criminals, Witches, Lunatics*. New York: Frederick A. Stokes, 1914.

Jacob, Giles. *The Law-Dictionary: Explaining the Rise, Progress, and Present State of the English Law* . . . 6 vols. Corrected and augmented by T. E. Tomlins. American edition (2nd English edition). Philadelphia and New York: P. Byrne / I. Riley, 1811.

———. *A New Law-Dictionary: Containing, Interpretation and Definition of Words and Terms used in the Law* . . . London: E. and R. Nutt and R. Gosling, 1729.

Jacob, Robert. "Bannissement et rite de la langue tirée au moyen âge: du lien des lois et de sa rupture." *Annales: Histoire, Sciences Sociales* 55 (2000): 1039–79.

Jager, Eric. *Blood Royal: A True Tale of Crime and Detection in Medieval Paris*. New York and elsewhere: Little, Brown, 2014.

Jenks, Susanne. "Die 'Assize of Clarendon' von 1166." *Tijdschrift voor Rechtsgeschiedenis* 63 (1995): 27–43.

Jones, C. P. "*Stigma*: Tattooing and Branding in Graeco-Roman Antiquity." *Journal of Roman Studies* 77 (1987): 139–55.

Jones, E. A. "Hidden Lives: Methodological Reflections on a New Database of the Hermits and Anchorites of Medieval England." *Medieval Prosopography: History and Collective Biography* 28 (2013): 17–34.

Jones, Mark, and Peter Johnstone. *History of Criminal Justice*. 5th ed. Waltham, MA: Elsevier / Anderson Publishing, 2012.

Jones, Timothy. *Outlawry in Medieval Literature*. NY: Palgrave Macmillan, 2010.

Jones, William. "Sanctuary, Exile, and Law: The Fugitive and Public Authority in Medieval England and Modern America." In *Essays on English Law and the American Experience*, edited by William Jones, Craig Klafter, and others, 19–41. Arlington, TX: Texas A&M Press, 1994.

Jordan, William. "Administering Expulsion in 1306." *Jewish Studies Quarterly* 15 (2008): 241–50.

———. "Communal Administration in France, 1257–1270: Problems Discovered and Solutions Imposed," *Revue Belge de philologie et d'histoire* 59 (1981): 292–313.

———. "Expenses Related to Corporal Punishment in France." Forthcoming.

———. *The French Monarchy and the Jews from Philip Augustus to the Last Capetians*. Philadelphia: University of Pennsylvania Press, 1989.

———. "A Fresh Look at Medieval Sanctuary." In *Law and the Illicit in Medieval Europe*, edited by Ruth Karras, Joel Kaye, and E. Ann Matter, 17–32. Philadelphia: University of Pennsylvania Press, 2008.

———. *The Great Famine: Northern Europe in the Early Fourteenth Century*. Princeton: Princeton University Press, 1996.

———. *Louis IX and the Challenge of the Crusade: A Study in Rulership*. Princeton: Princeton University Press, 1979.

———. *Men at the Center: Redemptive Governance under Louis IX*. Budapest: Central European University Press, 2012.

———. *A Tale of Two Monasteries: Westminster and Saint-Denis in the Thirteenth Century*. Princeton: Princeton University Press, 2009.

Jourjon, Charles. "Notice sur le port et la ville de Tréguier." *Bulletin et mémoires, Société d'émulation des Côtes-du-Nord* 15 (1878): 235–52.

Jusserand, Jean-Jules. *Les Anglais au moyen âge: la vie nomade et les routes d'Angleterre au XIVe siècle*. Paris: Hachette, 1884.

Kaeuper, Richard. *Bankers to the Crown: The Riccardi of Lucca and Edward I*. Princeton: Princeton University Press, 1973.

Kapferer, Anne-Dominique. "1339–1505: entre les guerre et les trêves." In *Histoire de Boulogne-sur-Mer*, edited by Alain Lottin, 91–106. Boulogne: Editions Le Téméraire, 1998.

———. "Boulogne devient une ville (1113–1339)." In *Histoire de Boulogne-sur-Mer*, edited by Alain Lottin, 59–90. Boulogne: Editions Le Téméraire, 1998.

———. *Fracas et murmures: le bruit de l'eau dans un moyen-âge picard et boulonnais*. Amiens: Trois Cailloux, 1991.

Karras, Ruth. *Common Women: Prostitution and Sexuality in Medieval England.* New York: Oxford University Press, 1996.

Keen, Maurice Hugh. *The Outlaws of Medieval Legend.* London: Routledge and K. Paul, 1961.

Kelly, Alexander, Jr. "Subtotal Reconstruction of the Thumb: Tubed-Pedicle Flaps with Tactile Restoration." *AMA Archives of Surgery* 78 (1959): 582–85.

Kennan, George. *Siberia and the Exile System.* 2 vols. New York: Century, 1891.

Kibre, Pearl. *The Nations in the Medieval Universities.* Cambridge, MA: Medieval Academy of America, 1948.

King, James. "The Mysterious Case of the 'Mad' Rector of Bletchingdon: The Treatment of Mentally Ill Clergy in Late Thirteenth-Century England." In *Madness in Medieval Law and Custom,* edited by Wendy Turner, 57–80. Leiden: Brill, 2010.

Kitsikopoulos, Harry. "England." In *Agrarian Change and Crisis, 1200–1500,* edited by Harry Kitsikopoulos, 23–56. New York: Routledge, 2012.

Kittell, Ellen. "Reconciliation or Punishment: Women, Community, and Malefaction in the Medieval County of Flanders." In *The Texture of Society: Medieval Women in the Southern Low Countries,* edited by Ellen Kittell and Mary Suydam, 3–30. New York: Palgrave Macmillan, 2004.

Koldeweij, Jos. "Notes on the Historiography and Iconography of Pilgrim Souvenirs and Secular Badges." In *From Minor to Major: The Minor Arts in Medieval Art History,* edited by Colum Hourihane, 194–216. University Park, PA: Index of Christian Art, Department of Art and Archaeology, in association with Penn State University Press, 2012.

Komornicka, Jolanta. "Contra signum nostrum: The Symbolism of *Lèse-majesté* under Philip VI Valois." In *Crime and Punishment in the Middle Ages and the Early Modern Age: Mental-Historical Investigations of Basic Human Problems and Social Responses,* edited by Albrecht Classen and Connie Scarborough, 189–224. Berlin and Boston: Walter de Gruyter, 2012.

Kowaleski, Maryanne. "The Shipmaster as Entrepreneur in Medieval England." In *Commercial Activity, Markets and Entrepreneurs in the Middle Ages: Essays in Honour of Richard Britnell,* edited by Ben Dodds and Christian Liddy, 165–82. Woodbridge, UK: Boydell Press, 2011.

Labarge, Margaret. *Medieval Travellers: The Rich and the Restless.* London: H. Hamilton, 1982.

Lacey, Helen. *The Royal Pardon: Access to Mercy in Fourteenth-Century England.* Woodbridge, UK: Boydell Press, 2009.

Laingui, André, and Arlette Lebigre, *Histoire du droit pénal.* 2 vols. Paris: Cujas, [1979].

Lambert, Craig, and Andrew Layton. "The Mariner in Fourteenth-Century England." *Fourteenth Century England* 7 (2012): 153–76.

Lambert, T. B. "The Evolution of Sanctuary in Medieval England." In *Legalism: Anthropology and History,* edited by Paul Dresch and Hannah Skoda, 115–44. Oxford; Oxford University Press, 2012.

Langbein, John. "The Historical Origins of the Sanction of Imprisonment for Serious Crime." *Journal of Legal Studies* 5 (1976): 35–60.

———. *Torture and the Law of Proof: Europe and England in the Ancien Régime.* Chicago: University of Chicago Press, 2006.

Langdon, John. "Minimum Wages and Unemployment Rates in Medieval England: The Case of Old Woodstock, Oxfordshire, 1256–1357." In *Commercial Activity, Markets and Entrepreneurs in the Middle Ages: Essays in Honour of Richard Britnell*, edited by Ben Dodds and Christian D. Liddy, 25–44. Woodbridge, UK, and Rochester, NY: Boydell Press, 2011.

Lanhers, Yvonne. "Crimes et criminels au XIVe siècle." *Revue historique* 240 (1968): 325–38.

Lauzun, Ph. "Le Livre juratoire des consuls d'Agen." *Revue de l'Agenais* 37 (1910): 385–94.

Le Foyer, Jean. *Exposé du droit pénal normand au XIIIe siècle.* Paris: Recueil Sirey, 1931.

Le Goff, Jacques. *In Search of Sacred Time: Jacobus de Voragine and the Golden Legend.* Translated by Lydia Cochrane. Princeton: Princeton University Press, 2014.

Le Grand, Léon. "Les Maisons-Dieu et les léproseries du diocèse de Paris au milieu du XIVe siècle." *Mémoires de la Société de l'hiistoire de Paris et de l'Ile–de–France* 25 (1898): 47–178.

Le Person, Marie. "L'exclusion, source d'inspiration de la littérature arrageoise du XIIIe siècle." In *L'exclusion au moyen âge*, edited by Nicole Gonthier, 239–57. Lyon: Université Jean Moulin, 2007.

Leff, Gordon. *Paris and Oxford Universities in the Thirteenth and Fourteenth Centuries: An Institutional and Intellectual History.* New York and elsewhere: John Wiley and Sons, 1968.

Lefils, Florentin. *Histoire de Montreuil-rue-Mer et son château.* Paris: Office d'Édition du Livre d'Histoire, 1995. First published 1860.

Leguay, Jean-Pierre. *Le feu au moyen âge.* Rennes: Presses Universitaires de Rennes, 2008.

———. *Pauvres et marginaux au moyen âge.* Paris: Éditions Jean-Paul Gisserot, 2009.

———. *Vivre dans les villes bretonnes au moyen âge.* Rennes: Presses Universitaires de Rennes, 2009.

L'Engle, Susan. "Justice in the Margins: Punishment in Medieval Toulouse." *Viator* 33 (2002): 133–65.

Lewin, Thomas. *The Invasion of Britain by Julius Caesar.* London: Longman, Green, Longman, and Roberts, 1859.

Licence, Tom. *Hermits and Recluses in English Society, 950–1200.* Oxford: Oxford University Press, 2011.

Lloyd, Terence. *The English Wool Trade in the Middle Ages.* Cambridge: Cambridge University Press, 1977.

Lodge, R. A. "Language Attitudes and Linguistic Norms in France and England in the Thirteenth Century." *Thirteenth Century England* 4 (1992): 73–83.

Logan, F. Donald. *A History of the Church in the Middle Ages.* London: Routledge, 2002.

Logan, Wayne. "Criminal Law Sanctuaries." *Harvard Civil Rights-Civil Liberties Law Review* 38 (2003): 321–91.

Lombard-Jourdain, Anne. "Fiefs et justices parisiens au quartier des Halles." *Bibliothèque de l'École de chartes* 134 (1976): 301–88.

Lyon, John. *The History of the Town and Port of Dover and of Dover Castle, with a Short Account of the Cinque Ports.* 2 vols. Dover: Printed for the author by Ledger and Shaw, 1813–14.

MacLehose, William. *"A Tender Age": Cultural Anxieties over the Child in the Twelfth and Thirteenth Centuries.* New York: Columbia University Press, 2008.

Mandery, Evan. *Capital Punishment: A Balanced Examination.* Sudbury, MA: Jones and Bartlett, 2005.

Mason, Arthur. *The Mission of St. Augustine to England according to the Original Documents, Being a Handbook for the Thirteenth Centenary.* Cambridge: Cambridge University Press, 1897.

Masschaele, James. *Jury, State, and Society in Medieval England.* New York: Palgrave Macmillan, 2008.

Matthew, Donald. *The English and the Community of Europe in the Thirteenth Century.* Reading: University of Reading, 1997.

Mazzinghi, Thomas de. *Sanctuaries.* Stafford, UK: Halden and Son, 1887.

McCune, Pat. "Justice, Mercy, and Late Medieval Governance." *Michigan Law Review* 89 (1991): 1661–78.

McGlynn, Margaret. "The Use and Abuse of Sanctuary in Henrician England." Unpublished.

Mellinkoff, Ruth. "Cain and the Jews." *Journal of Jewish Art* 6 (1979): 16–38.

———. *The Mark of Cain.* Berkeley, Los Angeles, and London: University of California Press, 1981.

———. *Outcasts: Signs of Otherness in Northern European Art of the Late Middle Ages.* 2 vols. Berkeley, Los Angeles, and Oxford: University of California Press, 1993.

Mémoires historiques sur l'arrondissement de Valenciennes, vol. III. Valenciennes: Société d'agriculture, sciences et arts, 1873.

Mermet, Théophile, and Franck Dufossé. *Saint-Inglevert: promenade à travers les âges.* Bazinghen: Éditions A.M.A., 2006.

Michel, Robert. *L'administration royale dans la sénéchaussée de Beaucaire au temps de saint Louis.* Paris: A. Picard et fils, 1910.

Middle English Dictionary. Edited by Hans Kurath and others. 20 vols. to date. Ann Arbor: University of Michigan Press, 1952–2001.

Moal, Laurence. "Entre méfiance et accueil: à l'égard de l'étranger sur les côtes bretonnes à la fin du moyen âge." *Annales de Bretagne et des Pays de l'Ouest* 117 (2010): 39–60.

Monteil, Amans-Alexis. *Traité de matériaux manuscrits de divers genres d'histoire.* 2 vols. New edition. Paris: Imprimerie de E. Duverger, 1836.

Montrond, Maxime de. *Notre-Dame de Boulogne: son pèlerinage et ses fêtes.* 4th ed. Lille: J. Lefort, 1887.

Morel, Barbara. "De l'exclusion à la redemption: le comdamné dans l'iconographie judiciaire à la fin du moyen âge." In *L'exclusion au moyen âge*, edited by Nicole Gonthier, 259–72 and plates. Lyon: Université Jean Moulin, 2007.

Morgan, Gwenda, and Peter Rushton. *Banishment in the Early Atlantic World: Convicts, Rebels and Slaves*. London and elsewhere: Bloomsbury Academic, 2013.

Mundill, Robin. *England's Jewish Solution: Experiment and Expulsion, 1262–1290*. Cambridge: Cambridge University Press, 1998.

Murphy, Margaret. "'The Key of the County': Saggart and the Manorial Economy of the Dublin March *c*. 1200–1540." In *The March in the Islands of the Medieval West*, edited by Jenifer Ní Ghrádaigh and Emmett O'Byrne, 53–78. Leiden and Boston: Brill, 2012.

Murray, James. *Bruges, Cradle of Capitalism, 1280–1390*. Cambridge: Cambridge University Press, 2005.

———. *Notarial Instruments in Flanders between 1280 and 1452*. Brussels: Académie royale de Belgique / Koninklijke Academie van België, 1995.

Murray, Katherine. *The Constitutional History of the Cinque Ports*. Manchester: Manchester University Press, 1935.

Musson, Anthony. *Public Order and Law Enforcement: The Local Administration of Criminal Justice, 1294–1350*. Woodbridge, UK: Boydell, 1996.

———. "Queenship, Lordship and Petitioning in Late Medieval England." In *Medieval Petitions: Grace and Grievance*, edited by W. Mark Ormrod, Gwilym Dodd, and Anthony Musson, 156–72. York: York Medieval Press, 2009.

Naessens, Mariann. "Judicial Authorities' Views of Women's Roles in Late Medieval Flanders." In *The Texture of Society: Medieval Women in the Southern Low Countries*, edited by Ellen Kittel and Mary Suydam, 51–77. New York: Palgrave Macmillan, 2004.

Napran, Laura, and Elisabeth Van Houts, eds. *Exile in the Middle Ages: Selected Proceedings from the International Medieval Congress, University of Leeds, 8–11 July 2002*. Turnhout, Belgium: Brepols, 2004.

Neilson, George. *Trial by Combat*. Glasgow: William Hodge and Company, 1890.

New, Chester. *History of the Alien Priories in England to the Confiscation of Henry V*. Chicago: Privately printed, 1916.

New Cambridge Medieval History, vol. 5: *c. 1198-c. 1300*. Edited by David Abulafia. Cambridge: Cambridge University Press, 1999.

"Notes et commentaires." *Bulletin de la Société académique de l'arrondissement de Boulogne-sur-Mer* 1 (1864–72): 376–81.

Nowacka, Keiko. "Persecution, Marginalization, or Tolerance: Prostitutes in Thirteenth-Century Parisian Society." In *Difference and Identity in Francia and Medieval France*, edited by Meredith Cohen and Justine Firnhaber-Barker, 175–96. Farnham, UK, and Burlington, VT: Ashgate, 2010.

OED. See *Oxford English Dictionary*.

Official History of the Canadian Army in the Second World War. 3 vols. to date. Ottawa: E. Cloutier, 1955–.

Old French-English Dictionary. Compiled by Alan Hindley and others. Cambridge: Cambridge University Press, 2000.

Olson, Sherri. *A Mute Gospel: The People and Culture of the Medieval English Common Fields*. Toronto: Pontifical Institute of Mediaeval Studies, 2009.

Ormrod, W. Mark. "Murmur, Clamour and Noise: Voicing Complaint and Remedy in Petitions to the English Crown, *c.* 1300–*c.* 1460." In *Medieval Petitions: Grace and Grievance*, edited by W. Mark Ormrod, Gwilym Dodd, and Anthony Musson, 135–55. York: York Medieval Press, 2009.

Otis[-Cour], Leah. *Prostitution in Medieval Society: The History of an Urban Institution in Languedoc*. Chicago: University of Chicago Press, 1985.

O'Tool, Mark. "The *Povres Avugles* of the Hôpital des Quinze-Vingts: Disability and Community in Medieval Paris." In *Difference and Identity in Francia and Medieval France*, edited by Meredith Cohen and Justine Firnhaber-Baker, 157–73. Farnham, UK, and Burlington, VT: Ashgate, 2010.

Oxford English Dictionary. Online edition. http://www.oed.com.

Pagart d'Hermansart, Émile. *Histoire du bailliage de Saint-Omer, 1193 à 1790*, vol. I. Saint-Omer: H. d'Omont, 1898.

"Papal Elections." See S.L.E. "Papal Elections."

Parkin, E. W. "The Ancient Cinque Port of Sandwich." *Archaeologia cantiana* 100 (1984): 189–216.

Parsons, John. "The Beginnings of English Administration in Ponthieu: An Unnoticed Document of 1280." *Medieval Studies* 50 (1988): 371–403.

Peters, Edward. "Prison before the Prison: The Ancient and Medieval Worlds." In *The Oxford History of the Prison*, edited by Norval Morris and David Rothman, 3–47. Oxford: Oxford University Press, 1995.

Pollock, Frederick, and Frederic Maitland. *The History of English Law before the Time of Edward I*. 2 vols. 2nd ed. Cambridge: Cambridge University Press, 1898.

Porteau-Bitker, Annike. "Criminalité et délinquance féminines dans le droit pénal des XIIIe et XIVe siècles." *Revue historique de droit français et étranger* 58 (1980): 13–56.

Power, Daniel. "*Terra regis Anglie et terra Normannorum sibi invicem adversantur*: Les héritages anglo-normands entre 1204 et 1244." In *La Normandie et l'Angleterre au moyen âge*, edited by Pierre Boutet and Véronique Gazeau, 189–209. Caen: Centre de recherches archéologiques médiévales, 2003.

Prestwich, Michael. *Edward I*. Berkeley and Los Angeles: University of California Press, 1988.

———. *Plantagenet England, 1225–1360*. Oxford: Oxford University Press, 2005.

Prigent, Daniel, and François Tichey. *Le moyen âge féodal*. Paris: Épigones, 1987.

Pugh, Ralph. "Early Registers of English Outlaws." *American Journal of Legal History* 27 (1983): 319–29.

Rabben, Linda. *Give Refuge to the Stranger: The Past, Present, and Future of Sanctuary*. Walnut Creek, CA: Left Coast Press, 2011.

Rashdall, Hastings. *The Universities of Europe in the Middle Ages*. Eds. F. M. Powicke and A. B. Emden. 3 vols. Oxford: Oxford University Press, 1936.

Rawcliffe, Carol. "Curing Bodies and Healing Souls: Pilgrimage and the Sick in Medieval East Anglia." In *Pilgrimage: The English Experience from Becket to*

Bunyan, edited by Colin Morris and Peter Roberts, 108–40. Cambridge: Cambridge University Press, 2002.

———. *Leprosy in Medieval England*. Woodbridge, UK: Boydell Press, 2006.

Raynaud, Edmond. "Statuts de la ville de au XIII siècle." *Annales de la Société des lettres, sciences et arts des Alpes-Maritimes* 19 (1905): 233–53.

Réville, André. "'L'*Abjuratio regni*': Histoire d'une institution anglaise." *Revue historique* 50 (1892): 1–42.

Reyerson, Kathryn. "Medieval Hospitality: Innkeepers and the Infrastructure of Trade in Montpellier during the Middle Ages." *Proceedings of the Western Society for French History* 24 (1997): 38–51.

Rigg, J. M. *St. Anselm of Canterbury: A Chapter in the History of Religion*. London: Methuen, 1896.

Rodger, N.A.M. "The Naval Service of the Cinque Ports." *English Historical Review* 111 (1996): 636–51.

Röhrkasten, Jens. *Die englischen Kronzeugen, 1130–1330*. Berlin: Duncker und Humblot, 1990.

———. "Some Problems of the Evidence of Fourteenth Century Approvers," *Journal of Legal History* 5 (1984): 14–22.

Rose, Susan. *Calais: An English Town in France, 1347–1558*. Woodbridge, UK: Boydell Press, 2008.

———. "The Value of the Cinque Ports to the Crown, 1200–1500." In *Roles of the Sea in Medieval England*, edited by Richard Gorski, 41–57. Woodbridge, UK: Boydell Press, 2012.

Rossiaud, Jacques. *Medieval Prostitution*. Translated by Lydia G. Cochrane. New York: Basil Blackwell, 1988.

Roth, Mitchel. *Crime and Punishment: A History of the Criminal Justice System*. 2nd ed. Belmont, CA: Wadsworth, 2010.

Rothwell, William. "From Latin to Anglo-French and Middle English: The Role of the Multilingual Gloss." *Modern Language Review* 88 (1993): 581–99.

Rouffy, Pierre. "Les viguiers d'Aurillac au XIIIe siècle: juges et bourreaux." *Mémoires de l'Académie des sciences, belles-lettres et arts de Clermont-Ferrand* 46 (1873): 47–50.

Rouse, Richard, and Mary Rouse. "Expenses of a Mid Thirteenth-Century Paris Scholar: Gerard of Abbeville." In *Intellectual Life in the Middle Ages: Essays Presented to Margaret Gibson*, edited by Lesley Smith and Benedicta Ward, 207–26. London and Rio Grande, OH: Hambledon Press, 1992.

Roux, Simone. *Paris in the Middle Ages*. Translated by Jo Ann McNamara. Philadelphi: University of Pennsylvania Press, 2009.

Ruding, Rogers. *Annals of the Coinage of Great Britain and Its Dependencies from the Earliest Period of Authentic History to the Reign of Victoria*. 3 vols. 3rd ed. London: J. Hearne, 1840.

Ryan, John. "Less than Unanimous Jury Verdicts in Criminal Trials." *Journal of Criminal Law, Criminology and Police Science* 58 (1967): 211–17.

Sartore, Melissa. *Outlawry, Governance, and Law in Medieval England*. New York and elsewhere: Peter Lang, 2013.

Schubert, Ernst. *Räuber, Henker, arme Sünder: Verbrechen und Strafe im Mittelalter*. Darmstadt, Germany: Wissentschaftliche Buchgesellschaft, 2007.

Scott, William. "The March Laws: For Use or Ornament?" In *The March in the Islands of the Medieval West*, edited by Jenifer Ní Ghrádaigh and Emmett O'Byrne, 261–85. Leiden and Boston: Brill, 2012.

Schwinges, Rainer. "Student Education, Student Life." In *A History of the University in Europe*, vol. I, edited by Walter Rüegg and Hilde de Ridder-Symoens, 195–243. 2 vols. Cambridge: Cambridge University Press, 1992.

"Séance du 5 février." *Bulletin de la Commission départementale des monuments historiques du Pas-de-Calais* 3 (1903): 51–54.

Seward, Desmond. *The Hundred Years War: The English in France 1337–1453*. New York: Penguin, 1999.

Shapiro, Barry. *Revolutionary Justice in Paris 1789–1790*. Cambridge: Cambridge University Press, 1993.

Sharpe, J. A. *Judicial Punishment in England*. London and Boston: Faber and Faber, 1990.

Shoemaker, Karl. *Sanctuary and Crime in the Middle Ages, 400–1500*. New York: Fordham University Press, 2011.

Sigal, Pierre-André. *Les marcheurs de Dieu: pèlerinages et pèlerins au Moyen Âge*. Paris: A. Colin, 1974.

S.L.E. "Papal Elections." *American Ecclesiastical Review* 5 (1891): 415–36.

Slivinski, Al, and Nathan Sussman. "Taxation Mechanisms and Growth, in Medieval Paris." http://economics.uwo.ca/faculty/slivinski/researchpapers/ParispaperAugust10.pdf.

Small, Carola. "Grain for the Countess: The 'Hidden' Costs of Cereal Production in Fourteenth-Century Artois." *Proceedings of the Annual Meeting of the Western Society for French History* 17 (1990): 56–63.

———. "Profits of Justice in Early Fourteenth-Century Artois: The 'Exploits' of the Baillis." *Journal of Medieval History* 16 (1990): 151–64.

Sneddon, Shelagh. "Words and Realities: The Language and Dating of Petitions, 1326-7." In *Medieval Petitions: Grace and Grievance*, edited by W. Mark Ormrod, Gwilym Dodd, and Anthony Musson, 193–205. York: York Medieval Press, 2009.

Sokol, B. J., and Mary Sokol. *Shakespeare's Legal Language: A Dictionary*. London and New York: Continuum, 2004.

Statham, Samuel. *History of the Castle, Town, and Port of Dover*. London: Longmans, Green and Co.: 1899.

Stell, G. P. "John [John de Balliol] (*c.*1248x50–1314), King of Scots," in the *Oxford Dictionary of National Biography* Online at http://www.oxforddnb.com.

Stewart, Susan. "Outlawry as an Instrument of Justice in the Thirteenth Century." In *Outlaws in Medieval and Early Modern England: Crime, Government and Society, 1066–1600*, edited by John Appleby and Paul Dutton, 37–54. Farnham, UK: Ashgate, 2009.

Stones, E.L.G. "The Folvilles of Ashby-Folville, Leicestershire, and their Associates in Crime, 1326–1347." *Transactions of the Royal Historical Society*, 5th series, 7 (1957): 117–36.

Stringer, K. J. "Some Documents Concerning a Berkshire Family and Monk Sherborne Priory, Hampshire." *Berkshire Archaeological Journal* 63 (1967–68): 23–35.

Summerson, Henry. "Attitudes to Capital Punishment in England, 1200–1350." *Thirteenth Century England* 8 (2001): 123–33.

———. "The Criminal Underworld of Medieval England." *Journal of Legal History* 17 (1996): 197–224.

———. "The Early Development of the Peine Forte et Dure." In *Law, Litigants and the Legal Profession*, edited by Eric Ives and A. H. Manchester, 116–25. Royal Historical Society Studies in History 36. London: Royal Historical Society, 1983.

———. "Peacekeepers and Lawbreakers in Medieval Northumberland *c.* 1200–*c.* 1500." In *Liberties and Identities in the Medieval British Isles*, edited by Michael Prestwich, 56–76. Woodbridge, UK: Boydell Press, 2008.

Sumption, Jonathan. *The Hundred Years' War.* 3 vols. to date. Philadelphia: University of Pennsylvania Press, 1991–.

———. *Pilgrimage: An Image of Mediaeval Religion.* London: Faber and Faber, 1975.

Sweetinburgh, Sheila. "The Hospitals of Medieval Kent." In *Later Medieval Kent, 1220–1540*, edited by Sheila Sweetinburgh, 111–36. Woodbridge, UK: Boydell Press, 2010.

———. "Kentish Towns: Urban Culture and the Church in the Later Middle Ages." In *Later Medieval Kent, 1220–1540*, edited by Sheila Sweetinburgh, 137–65. Woodbridge, UK: Boydell Press, 2010.

———. "Royal Patrons and Local Benefactors: The Experience of the Hospitals of St Mary at Ospringe and Dover in the Thirteenth Century." In *Religious and Laity in Western Europe: Interaction, Negotiation, and Power*, edited by Emilia Jamroziak and Janet Burton, 111–29. Turnhout, Belgium: Brepols, 2006.

Taylor, Scott. "*Judicium Dei, vulgaris popularisque sensus*: Survival of Customary Justice and Resistance to Its Displacement by the 'New' *Ordines iudiciorum* as Evidenced by Francophonic Literature of the High Middle Ages." In *Crime and Punishment in the Middle Ages and the Early Modern Age: Mental-Historical Investigations of Basic Human Problems and Social Responses*, edited by Albrecht Classen and Connie Scarborough, 109–29. Berlin and Boston: Walter de Gruyter, 2012.

Telliez, Romain. "Geôles, fosses, cachots . . . lieux carcéreaux et conditions matérielles de l'imprisonnement en France à la fin du moyen âge." In *Enfermements: le cloître et la prison (Ve–XVIIIe siècle),* edited by Isabelle Heullant-Donat and Julie Claustre, 169–82. Paris: Publications de la Sorbonne, 2011.

Théodore, Émile. "Les executions des sentences criminelles à Lille avant la Révolution." *Mémoires de la Société centrale d'agriculture, sciences et arts du département du Nord*, 4th series, 2 (1923–25): 333–55.

Théry, Julien. "*Atrocitas/Enormitas*: Esquisse pour une histoire de la catégorie d'énormité' ou 'crime énorme' du Moyen Âge à l'époque moderne." *Clio@Themis. Revue électronique d'histoire du droit* 4 (March 2011). Online: http://www.cliothemis.com/Clio-Themis-numero-4.

Thiery, Daniel. *Polluting the Sacred: Violence, Faith and the 'Civilizing' of Parishioners in Late Medieval England*. Leiden and Boston: Brill, 2009.

Tison, G. "Ordonnances de police de Calais, au XIIIe siècle," *Bulletin de la Commission départementale des monuments historiques du Pas-de-Calais* 4 (1914–25): 493–95.

Titow, Jan. *English Rural Society, 1200–1350*. London: George Allen and Unwin, 1969.

Toth, Stephen. *Beyond Papillon: The French Overseas Penal Colonies, 1854–1952*. Lincoln, NE, and London: University of Nebraska Press, 2006.

Toureille, Valérie. *Crime et châtiment au moyen âge, Ve–XVe siècle*. Paris: Seuil, 2013.

———. "Larrons incorrigibles et voleur fameux. La récidive en matière de vol ou *la consuetudo* à la fin du moyen âge." In *Le criminel endurci: récidive et recidivists du moyen âge au XXe siècle*, edited by Françoise Briegel and Michel Porret, 43–54. Geneva: Droz, 2006.

Treharne, R. F. *The Baronial Plan of Reform, 1258–1263*. Manchester: Manchester University Press, 1971.

Trenholme, Norman. *The Right of Sanctuary in England: A Study in Institutional History*. Columbia, MO: University of Missouri, 1903.

Trotter, D. A. "Not as Eccentric as It Looks: Anglo-French and French French." *Forum for Modern Language Studies* 39 (2003): 427–38.

———. "(Socio)linguistic Realities of Cross-Channel Communication in the Thirteenth Century." *Thirteenth Century England* 13 (2009): 117–31.

Turner, Victor. *The Forest of Symbols: Aspects of Ndembu Ritual*. Ithaca, NY: Cornell University Press, 1967.

———, and Edith Turner. *Image and Pilgrimage in Christian Culture: Anthropological Perspectives*. New York: Columbia University Press, 1978.

Turner, Wendy. "Town and Country: A Comparison of the Treatment of the Mentally Disabled in Late Medieval English Common Law and Chartered Boroughs." In *Madness in Medieval Law and Custom*, edited by Wendy Turner, 17–38. Leiden: Brill, 2010.

Turning, Patricia. *Municipal Officials, Their Public, and the Negotiation of Justice in Medieval Languedoc: Fear Not the Madness of the Raging Mob*. Leiden and Boston: Brill, 2013.

———. "The Right to Punish: Jurisdictional Disputes Between Royal and Municipal Officials in Medieval Toulouse." *French History* 24 (2010): 1–19.

Tyerman, Christopher. *England and the Crusades, 1095–1588*. Chicago and London: University of Chicago Press, 1988.

Van Bavel, Bas. *Manors and Markets: Economy and Society in the Low Countries, 500–1600*. Oxford: Oxford University Press, 2010.

Van Houts, Elisabeth. "L'exil dans l'espace anglo-normand." In *La Normandie et l'Angleterre au moyen âge*, edited by Pierre Boutet and Véronique Gazeau, 117–27. Caen: Centre de Recherches Archéologiques et Historiques Médiévales, 2003.

Verger, Jacques. "L'Université [de Paris] ne represente elle pas tout le royaulme de France, voir tout le monde?" In *Relations, échanges, transferts en Occident au* cours des derniers siècles du moyen âge: homage à Werner Paravicini, edited by Bernard Guenée and Jean-Marie Moeglin, 9–23. Paris: Académie des Inscriptions et Belles-Lettres, 2010.

Vermeesch, Albert. Essai sur les origines et la signification de la commune dans le nord de France. Heule, Belgium: UGA, 1966.

Villegas-Aristizábal, Lucas. "Anglo-Norman Intervention in the Conquest and Settlement of Tortosa, 1148–1180." Crusades 8 (2009): 63–129.

Vincent, Nicholas. "In the Shadow of the Castle Wall: King Henry II and Dover, 1154–1179." Forthcoming.

———. "The Pilgrimages of the Angevin Kings, 1154–1272." In Pilgrimage: The English Experience from Becket to Bunyan, edited by Colin Morris and Peter Roberts, 12–45. Cambridge: Cambridge University Press, 2002.

Viollet, Paul. Précis de l'histoire du droit français. Paris: Larose et Forcel, 1886.

Wahnich, Sophie. In Defence of the Terror: Liberty or Death in the French Revolution. Translated by David Fernbach. London: Verso, 2012.

Warnkönig, Leopold. Flandrische Staats- und Rechtsgeschichte bis zum Jahr 1305. 3 vols. Wiesbaden: Dr. Martin Sändig, 1839–42.

———. Histoire consitutionelle et administrative de la ville de Bruges. Translated by A.-E. Gheldorf. Brussels: Verbeyst, 1856.

Watt, J. A. "The Papacy." In New Cambridge Medieval History, vol. 5, edited by David Abulafia, 107–63. Cambridge: Cambridge University Press, 2008.

Whitman, James. The Origins of Reasonable Doubt: Theological Roots of the Criminal Trial. New Haven, CT: Yale University Press, 2008.

"Why Are More People Right-Handed?" Scientific American, November 1, 2001. Online http://www.scientificamerican.com/article.cfm?id=why-are-more-people-right.

Willard, J. F., ed. The English Government at Work, 1327–1336. Vol. 3: Local Administration and Justice. Cambridge, MA: Mediaeval Academy of America, 1950.

Williams, David H. The Cistercians in the Early Middle Ages: Written to Commemorate the Nine Hundredth Anniversary of Foundation of the Order at Cîteaux in 1098. Leominster: Gracewing, 1998.

"Wissant: A Forgotten Port." Saturday Review 100 (1905): 303–04.

Woolgar, C. M. The Senses in Late Medieval England. New Haven, CT: Yale University Press, 2006.

Wright, Craig. "The Palm Sunday Procession in Medieval Chartres." In The Divine Office in the Latin Middle Ages: Methodology and Source Studies, Regional Developments, Hagiography, edited by Margot Fassler and Rebecca Baltzer, 344–71. Oxford: Oxford University Press, 2000.

Wright, R. F. "The High Seas and the Church in the Middle Ages." Parts I and II. Mariner's Mirror 53 (1967): 3–32 and 115–35.

Zaremska, Hanna. Les bannis au moyen âge. Translated by Thérèse Douchy. Paris: Aubier, 1996.

Index

GPSR Authorized Representative: Easy Access System Europe - Mustamäe tee
50, 10621 Tallinn, Estonia, gpsr.requests@easproject.com